Shakespeare's Ocean

UNDER THE SIGN OF NATURE:
EXPLORATIONS IN ECOCRITICISM

Editors
Michael P. Branch, SueEllen Campbell, John Tallmadge

Series Consultants
Lawrence Buell, John Elder, Scott Slovic

Series Advisory Board
Michael P. Cohen, Richard Kerridge, Gretchen Legler, Ian Marshall,
Dan Peck, Jennifer Price, Kent Ryden, Rebecca Solnit,
Anne Whiston Spirn, Hertha D. Sweet Wong

Shakespeare's Ocean

AN ECOCRITICAL EXPLORATION

Dan Brayton

University of Virginia Press *Charlottesville and London*

University of Virginia Press
© 2012 by the Rector and Visitors of the University of Virginia
All rights reserved
Printed in the United States of America on acid-free paper

First published 2012
First paperback edition published 2018
ISBN 978-0-8139-4124-0 (paper)

1 3 5 7 9 8 6 4 2

The Library of Congress has cataloged the hardcover edition as follows:
LIBRARY OF CONGRESS CATALOGING-IN-PUBLICATION DATA
Brayton, Daniel.
Shakespeare's ocean : an ecocritical exploration / Dan Brayton.
p.   cm. — (Under the sign of nature)
Includes bibliographical references and index.
ISBN 978-0-8139-3226-2 (cloth : acid-free paper)
ISBN 978-0-8139-3227-9 (e-book)
1. Shakespeare, William, 1564–1616—Knowledge—Natural history.
2. Sea in literature. 3. Ecocriticism. I. Title.
PR3039.B73 2012
822.3'3—dc23
2011035953

*For
Antonia J. Losano,
shipmate and
soulmate*

CONTENTS

List of Figures — ix
Preface — xi
Acknowledgments — xiii

Introduction: Shakespeare and the Global Ocean — 1
1. Backs to the Sea? The Terrestrial Bias — 15
2. Consider the Crab — 43
3. Shakespeare's Benthic Imagination — 62
4. Tidal Bodies — 86
5. Royal Fish: Shakespeare's Princely Whales — 107
6. Shakespeare among the Fishmongers — 136
7. Prospero's Maps — 166
   Coda: Toward a Terraqueous Ecocriticism — 196

Notes — 203
Bibliography — 227
Index — 245

FIGURES

1. Frontispiece of *The Mariners Mirrour*, 1588 — 3
2. Edward Wright, *Hydrographiae Descriptio*, 1599 — 83
3. Fool's Cap, 1590 — 84
4. Joachim Camerarius, Emblem XII — 124
5. Joachim Camerarius, Emblem VII — 125
6. Joachim Camerarius, Emblem V — 128
7. Johan Wierix, *Three Beached Whales*, 1577 — 129
8. Willem van der Gouwen, *Beached Whale*, 1598 — 130
9. Jan Saenredam, Beached Whale near Beverwijk, 1601 — 131
10. Pieter van der Heyden, after Pieter Brueghel the Elder, *Big Fish Eat Little Fish*, 1557 — 161
11. Giuseppe Arcimboldo, *Water*, 1566 — 163
12. Wind Rose, seventeenth century — 183
13. Sea chart, 1532, and 400 years later — 184
14. Ptolemaic world map, sixteenth century — 186
15. Martin Waldseemüller, World Map, 1508 — 188
16. Albrecht Dürer, Terrestrial Map (The Eastern Hemisphere), 1515 — 190

PREFACE

Beyond all things is the ocean.
SENECA

This book was born of nostalgia for a childhood spent on the water. Nostalgia—pain felt for a vanishing past—is born of the desire to speak with the dead, as Stephen Greenblatt reminds us in the opening pages of *Shakespearean Negotiations*. The dead with whom I have yearned to speak are the mariners from all corners of this globe whose knowledge of the ways of the sea has been lost with them. Born in one historic Massachusetts fishing town and raised in another, I often wonder if I was the last child, not in the woods, but on the water (to borrow a phrase from the journalist Richard Louv). The sea's bounty, like time itself, seemed to stretch infinitely from the rocky shores of my childhood. The first saltwater fish I pulled up, using a hand line of tarred hemp tied to a black iron hook baited with a clam, was a cod—iconic of the cold New England waters. A few summers later my father, grandfather, and I loaded an ancient wooden skiff with flounder and the occasional unwanted skate. We threw the skates back and took the flounder home, cleaned and fried them in batter, and ate every one. Today, the groundfish of the Northwest Atlantic (cod, flounder) that I grew up fishing, once so astonishingly abundant as to be the subject of legend (and the basis of many fortunes), are alarmingly depleted (even skate are nearly fished out), the entire marine ecosystem nearly destroyed by human means.

At the start of the twenty-first century we are just beginning to conceive of the ocean's finitude. In 1992—the year I graduated from college—commercial fishing on the Grand Banks of Newfoundland was shut down by the

Canadian government. Long the richest fishery in the history of the world, the Banks were fished out. As Charles Clover notes in *The End of the Line*, "The Newfoundland cod collapse was the nightmare that shook the world out of its complacent assumption that the sea's resources were renewable and being managed in an enlightened manner" (111). The nightmare goes on. The 2010 Gulf oil spill destroyed entire ecosystems as well as endangering and impoverishing the lives of countless people. At it happened, the spill coincided with the spawning of the drastically overfished Atlantic bluefin tuna, which—as did the American bison in the nineteenth century—hovers on the verge of extinction because of unchecked human appetite. It is eminently apparent that we can no longer deny the human role in the history of the global ocean.

While my graduate training was in early modern English literature, owing to unforeseen contingencies I have had the opportunity for the past decade to acquire what sailors call "sea time." In addition to spending much of my free time sailing on salt water I have worked on sailing research vessels in the company of marine scientists, marine policy experts, professional mariners, and students from numerous colleges and universities. On voyages in the Atlantic, the Pacific, and the Gulf of Mexico I have witnessed many of the results of the human tendency to treat the ocean as an inexhaustible larder. I have listened as a salmon farmer in Oregon described shooting the skulls off sea lions that occasionally marauded among his fish; I have met watermen in Louisiana who shoot alligators for fun; I have seen firsthand tons of bycatch (commercially undesirable fish) thrown off a trawler to rot or be eaten by scavenging gulls. Once I spent the night at the wharf in Papeete, the harbor at Tahiti, watching in horror as dozens of kill boats used steel cranes to offload the frozen carcasses of large marine predators—swordfish, marlin, tuna of many varieties, wahoo—onto an immense factory processor without ceasing, day and night. It seemed they had taken every last big fish they could find in the Pacific. These experiences, and many others like them, lie behind my efforts to locate in literature a representation of human life that defines humanity as part and parcel of the marine environment, not just its plunderer. My hope here is to shed light on how William Shakespeare offers a counterexample to the culture of plunder we now take for granted, for he imagined the ocean not as a void, waste space, adversary, or vast fish cooler but as an integral part of our being.

ACKNOWLEDGMENTS

This book would have never have been written without the support of many colleagues and friends. John Elder has long been my hero and staunch supporter. Timothy Billings is an intellectual pioneer and comrade-in-arms. David Price brought me to the Green Mountains in the first place and encouraged my nautical obsessions. I could not imagine a more generous colleague than Jay Parini. I continually rely on the wisdom and humanity of Brett Millier and the friendly support of Marion Wells, Ian Barrow, Kathy Morse, Yumna Siddiqi, Becky Gould, Cates Baldridge, Jim Berg, and Anna Harlan. I am forever grateful to Alison Byerly, the paragon of provosts, for her herculean efforts on my behalf, to Susan Campbell for her genuine commitment to supporting junior faculty, to Barbara Correll, for her stellar advising, and to Middlebury College for its generous leave policy. I would like to thank David Kramer for his intellectual support over the past decade-and-a-half. Several chapters would not have been possible without access to materials at the Folger Shakespeare Library and the Thomas Fisher Rare Book Library of the University of Toronto; I am grateful to the librarians at both of these fine institutions.

 Writing a book is a solitary endeavor, but finishing it for publication is not. The sharp eye and sharper wit of David Steinhardt shaped and strengthened my writing; his input was crucial at nearly every stage. On several occasions Wayne Losano rapidly and thoroughly culled my wordy prose. Megan Battey's work on acquiring images and permissions was simply

Acknowledgments

heroic, for which I am sincerely grateful. Thanks, too, to Jane Chaplin for sharing her skills. I am grateful to Steve Mentz for his pathbreaking work in blue cultural studies, and to Lynne Bruckner for being a wonderful collaborator on *Ecocritical Shakespeare*. I am also thankful to the staff at the University of Virginia Press, particularly Angie Hogan, Boyd Zenner, Morgan Myers, and Ellen Satrom, and to John Tallmadge and Rob Watson for their wonderful feedback. Beth Ina's assistance was invaluable in finishing the manuscript.

Interdisciplinary work depends on collaboration, and I have been fortunate to work with two excellent off-campus maritime studies programs: the Williams-Mystic Program in American Studies at Mystic Seaport (CT), and Sea Education Association, of Woods Hole (MA). Jim Carlton, Director of Williams-Mystic, changed the course of my career when he offered me a job in 2004, as did the rest of our Mystic crew: Rich King, Lisa Gilbert, Katy Hall, Peter Sorensen, Nicole Dobroski, Matt and Emily Geeza, Glenn Gordinier, and Josiah Gardner. Glenn, along with Eric Roorda, the National Endowment for the Humanities, and the Munson Institute, helped set this project in motion in their wonderful NEH Summer Institute. To my Sea Semester friends, Paul Joyce, Mary Malloy, John Odin Jensen, Kara Lavender Law, and Captains Steve Tarrant, Sean Bercaw, Beth Doxsie, and Elliot Rappaport, I am grateful for many a fine voyage.

Some debts are immeasurable. My mother, Joan G. Brayton, enchanted my world by reading aloud and sharing her love of language, music, and silliness. My father, Daniel E. Brayton, never ceases to impart his boundless enthusiasm for learning and the sea. My sister, Hope E. Brayton, teaches me to be receptive to the unexpected, and my children, Nico and Nell, astonish and delight me with their exuberance and love for all things living. A visit with them to Flat Rock Beach, Quissett Harbor, or Kingsland Bay rekindles my motivation to write. First and last, I could not navigate the voyage of this life without the companionship of Antonia J. Losano, who puts the wind in my sails and shines her light across the water. In ways uncountable she made this book possible. I dedicate it to her with all my heart.

Parts of the introduction and of several chapters in this work have appeared previously in print; see "Shakespeare and the Global Ocean," in *Ecocritical*

Acknowledgments

Shakespeare, edited by Lynne Dickson Bruckner and Daniel Brayton, 173–190 (Farnham, UK: Ashgate, 2011); "Sounding the Deep: *Shakespeare and the Sea* Revisited," *Forum for Modern Language Studies* 46, no. 2 (2010): 189–206; and "Royal Fish: Shakespeare's Princely Whales," in *The Indistinct Human in Renaissance Literature*, edited by Jean Feerick and Vin Nardazzi, 47–65 (New York: Palgrave, 2012).

Shakespeare's Ocean

Introduction

Shakespeare and the Global Ocean

> Which is the best of Shakespeare's plays? I mean in what mood
> and with what accompaniment do you like the sea best?
>
> JOHN KEATS, *Letter to Jane Reynolds, 1817*

This book explores the historical, textual, and material relationship between William Shakespeare and the global ocean. In yoking the name of a poet widely considered the paragon of literary achievement to a phrase employed by marine scientists to describe the vast body of salt water covering our planet, I wish to foreground the maritime dimension of the early modern imaginary and symbolic relationship to the biophysical environment. The phrase "global ocean" (or "world ocean") is standard in the marine sciences (oceanography, marine ecology, marine biology), signifying the interconnected biotic and physical properties of the great body of salt water that covers approximately 70 percent of the Earth's surface (I use *global* to gesture to the Globe, the open-air theater where Shakespeare worked after 1599).[1] If the present global environmental crisis is the product of past ways of seeing, discursive formations, and ideologies, then surely our present predicament of clinging (or, in Shakespeare's terms, "cleaving") to an overheated and increasingly overloaded planet leads us to rethink the literary and cultural history of the seas.[2]

The physical geography and social history of England inevitably put a maritime stamp on the works of its most celebrated poet. The British Isles have an immensely long coastline in proportion to their area; it is physically impossible to be much more than fifty miles from the sea anywhere in England. London at the end of the sixteenth century and the start of the seventeenth was the early modern center of English shipping, "the centre of maritime and mercantile England . . . and the Thames was the preeminent maritime superhighway," as Julie Sanders points out in her discussion of the "liquid landscapes" of Caroline England.[3] The sea was not only locally and literally present in late Renaissance English life, it was also culturally and economically of increasing centrality to the nation-state. Within two decades of Shakespeare's death, "at least half the King's subjects derived their living directly or indirectly from the sea."[4] Moreover, as Steve Mentz observes, "The expansion in maritime travel that began with the Portuguese exploration of the Canaries, Madeira, and the Azores in the fifteenth century, and in England a century later with the voyages of Raleigh, Drake, Cavendish, and others, generated a surge of interest in the maritime world, including (in England) the massive compilations of Hakluyt and Purchas."[5] Attendant on this expansion of trade, interest, and representation was a conceptual shift about the significance of an ocean whose vast size and potential were beginning to become apparent to statesmen, navigators, and literary artists. A glance at the frontispiece from *The Mariners Mirrour*, a compendium of essential technical information for navigators assembled by the Dutch mariner Lukas van Waghenaer as the *Spieghel der Zeevaerdt* in 1584 and first "Englished" by Anthony Ashley in the highly significant year 1588 (when the English defeated Spain's Mighty Armada, thereby establishing England's primacy as a sea power), reveals some of the complexity of this engagement with the global ocean (figure 1). The composition of this image suggests the metaphor of the sea as a stage, with mariners as actors in a *naumachia*, or nautical drama, and a group of cartographers assembled around a blank globe as playwrights of a sort.[6]

The vastness of the global ocean was perhaps the major conceptual "discovery" of early modern European navigators and cartographers, and representing it preoccupied not merely intellectuals with technical skills but artists as well. Painters illustrated human life as a sea voyage on canvas, and intellectuals of several stripes were actively engaged in rethinking the ocean's relationship to civilization.[7] The interconnections between these vast bodies of salt water—currents, prevailing winds, capes past which all become the Great Southern Ocean—were some of the most important discoveries of the era. As the historian J. H. Parry accurately claimed, "All the seas of the world are one."[8] Alfred Crosby, similarly, argued for the significance of the conceptual mastery of the winds by fifteenth-century Portuguese *marinheiros*, sailors who learned the best routes across oceans not by sailing rhumb

Introduction

FIGURE 1. Frontispiece of *The Mariner's Mirror* by Lucas Jansz Waghenaer, 1588. (© National Maritime Museum, Greenwich, London)

lines (straight courses) but by seeking the best winds, leading them to develop the *Volta do Mar*, the "turn to sea."⁹ The literature of the late Renaissance, produced at the moment when the conceptual implications of what Immanuel Wallerstein terms "the modern world-system" fired the imaginations of writers and artists, thus offers a rich arena for expanding the parameters of what constitutes the biophysical environment in literary scholarship.¹⁰

Coming to terms with the vastness of a blue planet had enormous implications for thinking about humanity's place in the cosmos, and Shakespeare's writings reflect this conceptual challenge. The marine environment —not just the surface of the global ocean but the invisible life (and death) contained in its depths—is a major feature of his writings, and a reconsideration of its significance in the plays and poems can deepen our understanding of the playwright's environmental imagination. One of the few writers to have imagined a profound relationship between humanity and the ocean, Shakespeare thought globally about the material and biophysical circumstances of human life. He did so in large part as a result of the transformation of the sixteenth-century *imago mundi* to include a vast new body of salt water that offered an immense and protean reservoir for reflecting on human life. Astride the border of the natural and the supernatural, Shakespeare's ocean is both "rich and strange," baffling for its immensity and mutability, yet boundless in its potential to renew art and life.[11] Shakespeare continually depicts human life as a process implicated in what he called "Neptune's empire" (*Hamlet*, 1.1. 106.12).[12]

We have much to learn from a poet who saw human life as something intimately linked to the sea. Rereading Shakespeare from a "thalassalogical" perspective (Gr. *thalassa*, the sea) can offer fresh insights about both environmental history and the environmental present.[13] It will become clear that by "Shakespeare" I mean not just a historical personage possessed of unparalleled poetic ability but also a cultural "text that continues to be decoded and *produced* in new ways."[14] Scholars in recent years have contested the national and international provenance of that text in productive ways; the present volume aims to do so by foregrounding the ways in which that text represents the marine environment.[15]

Ecocritical scholarship strives to represent the human impact on the biophysical environment, yet even the most encompassing efforts to expand the parameters of ecocriticism have neglected the central significance of the ocean and marine life in the Shakespeare corpus. In redressing this neglect the following chapters explore Shakespeare's articulation of the human in terms of a marine environment to which we belong and for which we are to some extent responsible. Each chapter takes a different approach to developing a simple argument: that in his vividly imagined depictions of the marine environment—beaches, the seafloor, reefs, islands—as spaces in which humans partially belong, Shakespeare imagines a profound ontological rela-

Introduction

tionship between humanity and the sea that is not merely metaphorical but material. His ocean is deeply yet obscurely involved in human existence, contributing to the stuff of the human body, changing the course of individual and familial lives, providing a reservoir of metaphorical material from which to forge meaning, and frequently taking or transforming characters' lives. Hence, my readings excavate the idea of a strange kinship between humanity and the ocean—an idea that destabilizes the notion of an entirely terrestrial human ontology and of the biblical cosmology of "the deep." The ocean as Shakespeare imagined it is the source of powerful and distinctive aesthetic effects, vividly demonstrating what Coleridge called the poet's "esemplastic imagination," his ability to assemble an imaginary totality.[16]

In rereading Shakespeare's works through the lens of marine environmental history, then, I hope to offer both a model *of* environmental writing and a model *for* environmental criticism.[17] Global climate change reminds us of the possibility that famine, like the grain shortages in Shakespeare's day, remains a constant presence in civilization. The anthropogenic devastation of the Earth also demonstrates quite vividly the stakes of ignoring the human history of the sea: in the words of Bruno Latour, "The concern for the environment begins at the moment when there is no more environment, no zone of reality in which we could casually rid ourselves of the consequence of human political, industrial, and economic life."[18] The realization that the sea *has* a human history (shared by visionary poets and marine scientists) occurs at the moment when it is historically possible that the sea as we have known and imagined it for millennia—vast, copious, and mysterious—will *be* history, in the colloquial sense.

Literary study compels us to imagine alternatives to an increasingly unsustainable hic et nunc and that artists possessed of great insight can glimpse truths about natural phenomena that foreshadow the insights of ecology, at times outstripping the capacity of science to make these truths fully apparent. In furthering this line of thought I join other scholars who have demonstrated the genuinely ecological insights of poets.[19] Anachronistic as it may seem to approach Shakespeare through the lens of a scientifically based marine environmental history, doing so may teach us to appreciate anew the richness of the poet's imagination as well as to live more mindfully in a profoundly aquatic world. Thus, I frame my readings of Shakespeare's richly nuanced poetics of the marine environment in terms of a strategic presentism. Once a derogatory term deployed by historians to describe those incapable of granting the past its alterity—of understanding it as "another country"—and thereby granting it an integrity separate from present concerns, presentism has come to signify something quite different in current ecocritical theory. Ursula K. Heise's argument for presentism as a viable approach for ecocritical scholarship has challenged ecocritics and historicists alike. Heise argues for a "triple allegiance" to "the scientific study of nature, the scholarly analysis of cultural representations, and the political struggle for more sustainable ways of inhabiting the natural world."[20] As North American colleges and universities clamor to jump on the bandwagon of "sustainability," not merely in infrastructural initiatives such as composting and recycling but also in their curricula, it is well worth remembering that Shakespeare, who gestures frequently to environmental disasters, meteorological anomalies, grain shortages, starvation, floods, and the effects of humanity on the physical environment, was deeply concerned with the sustainability of human culture—agriculture, land management, the politics of land tenure, and even maritime law—as well.

While it would be folly to posit a twenty-first-century scientific awareness of marine science on Shakespeare (let alone the portfolio of topics pertaining to the anthropogenic transformation of marine ecosystems by resource extraction, pollution, and climate change), his writings nevertheless persistently entertain the idea of a deep mutuality between humanity and the marine environment. That mutuality is historically mediated. Thus, at the same time that I take a presentist approach, I also find the work of marine environmental historians and the methods and insights of historicist scholarship indispensible for decoding early modern literary and visual texts. Reading for what Stephen Greenblatt famously termed "a poetics of culture" offers unmatched conceptual leverage on early modern literature, enriching our understanding of the discourse of nature in the English Renaissance.[21] Galvanized by cultural materialism as well, I examine the materiality of (cultural) texts and the textuality of matter by attending to the specificity of early modern *things* such as dried salt cod and pickled herring (see chapter 5) that link human and marine life in Shakespeare's imagination.[22]

I intend this book, then, as both an ecocritical reading of Shakespeare's maritime imagination and a Shakespearean reading of ecocriticism.[23] For the poet from Stratford paid a great deal more attention to the ocean—to the human implications of its newly discovered global scale and to its influence on human lives—than have ecocritics. Literature scholars suffer from a

Introduction

collective case of "ocean deficit disorder" (to modify Louv again).[24] A field that defines itself by a neologism (*ecocriticism*), based on another neologism (*ecology*), ecocriticism is a pursuit in which scholarship and environmental advocacy (albeit of a general kind) are inextricably intertwined.[25] Ecocritics argue that literary scholarship can no longer be content to relegate nature, place, and the nonhuman to the setting or background against which the "real" drama of plot and character unfold, but they have yet to pay any attention to either marine ecology or the literature of the sea (Anglophone or otherwise), let alone glimpse the far-reaching implications of a global ocean transformed over the centuries by human beings. A scholarship that models itself on the holistic discipline of ecology can only ignore the global ocean at the cost of severely limiting the scope of its inquiry. The Earth's surface is, after all, nearly three-quarters water, all but about 4 percent of that salt water.

The life sciences teach us that animals—even terrestrial bipeds—inhabit bodies constituted by approximately the same percentage of water as Earth itself, and as biologists often remind us, human beings evolved from marine organisms. Thus, the sea is deeply part of human ontology; we share a strange and ancient kinship with marine animals. The human animal is, evolutionarily and somatically speaking, a creature *of* water, even if we do tend to live on land, sharing the mammalian traits not just with other landlubberly species but also with the whales (*cetacea*), seals (*phocae*), and manatees and dugongs (*sirenia*). The stuff of which we are made, thus, is linked to forces such as the tides and retains the traces of a marine ancestry, "dwelling as we do," writes Kimberly Patton, "in salty amniotic fluid for nine months while our temporary fetal gill slits recapitulate phylogeny."[26] Patton describes our aquatic ontogeny succinctly: "Fish until we emerge, we can extract oxygen from air easily only at birth after a full-term pregnancy." In the words of Deborah Cramer, who has written extensively on the marine environment, "We are of the sea, and the sea is of us."[27] Similarly, in a recent discussion of the importance of "oceanic studies," Patricia Yeager muses, "How liquid are we? While human bodies seem substantial and geocentric and while many creation myths insist that our fundament is clay or earth, we are mostly made out of water: not geo- but aquacentric."[28] Such insights into the relationship between human and marine life are born of scientific awareness and are neither obvious nor intuitive; indeed, the foundational stories of Western culture, as I argue in chapter 1, have tended to deny or suppress humanity's aquatic (or aquacentric) ontology. The scholarly discourse of ecocriticism has followed suit, defining its field of inquiry in terms of the land and thereby neglecting the waters that have always lain beyond its shores—as well as our biological links to them.

While Patton and Cramer deploy a normative "we" in the discursive mode of science writing, in both instances the pronoun denotes the subject of liberal humanism, for which the normative "we" presumably denotes all human beings. In a posthumanist age what is meant by "our being" is anything but uncontested; moreover, a tension about "our" nature exists even within what little humanities scholarship exists concerning the marine environment. The environmental ethicist Clark Wolf claims that "most of us cannot regularly 'see' or 'feel' marine ecosystems," evoking the subject of humanism in insisting on the terrestrial ontology of humans.[29] By "us," presumably, Wolf means the majority of human beings, yet the claim more accurately describes humanities scholars than oceanographers or lobster fishermen, who regularly interact with marine ecosystems. One goal of this book is to challenge the normativity of that "us" by demonstrating the contingency, indeed the culturally constructed nature, of the sea's strangeness. At the same time, I approach Shakespeare's writings as a model of engagement with the ocean that looks very much like a proto-human ecology.

Shakespeare had no knowledge of embryonic development or biochemistry, but he presciently shared Cramer's and Patton's insights about a profound ontological connection between human life and the global ocean: just as we are part of this watery world, the ocean is part of our being. The salinity of human blood, sweat, and tears is the same as that of seawater, a chemical link between humanity and the ocean that Shakespeare points out poetically: "Were our tears wanting to this funeral, / These tidings would call forth their flowing tides" (*I Henry VI*, 1.1.87). These lines evoke a somatic linkage between human life and the marine environment. The poet could not have known of the chemical and biological dimensions of human ontology, nor could he have known much about the vast submarine world to which "we" (human beings) have only had much empirical access since the mid-nineteenth century, yet the newly discovered global ocean was nevertheless for him an essential feature of human life.

Shakespeare employs the term *ocean* thirty-five times, referring to an "angered ocean" (*Antony and Cleopatra*), an "ambitious ocean" (*Julius Caesar*), a "hungry ocean" (Sonnet 64), a "salt-waved ocean" (*The Rape of Lucrece*), a "wild ocean" (*Two Gentlemen of Verona*), a "wild and wasteful ocean"

Introduction

(*Henry V*), "Neptune's Ocean" (*Macbeth*), and "our ocean" (*King John*). Shakespeare also refers to *the sea* (far more often than he uses the word *ocean*), employing other synonyms as well, each laden with its own connotations and overtones. In *King Lear* it is "the roaring sea" and "the vexed sea," while in *Othello* the saltwater realm is "the enchafèd flood."[30] The final Chorus of *Henry V* refers to "the deep-mouthed sea," personifying the waters by giving them a voice (5.0, 1.11). These examples evince a plasticity of meaning that may well have been the basis for the ocean's appeal to an artist of Ovidian imagination, drawn to transformation, mutability, and the mind's capacity to shape the world. Imagining the trajectory of human life meant, for him, shaping poetry in which the human relationship to salt water is essential.

If the humanistic appeal, which retraces an aquatic animal phylogeny in human ontogeny (the prevalence of salt water on the globe and in our own chemical and biological constitution) seems weak cause for posthumanist ecocritics to turn to the sea, then the presentist perspective is more compelling—and more urgent. Human activity has demonstrably caused ecological regime shifts—and collapse—in marine ecosystems from the Caribbean to the Gulf of Maine, from the California Coast to the Baltic. Only recently have scholars begun to realize the dramatic impact of resource extraction—fishing, whaling, sealing, oil drilling (and spilling)—on the marine biosphere. Humans have drastically overfished keystone species (including tuna, turtles, and marine mammals) at an ever-increasing pace, removing vast numbers of predators and grazers that regulate marine ecosystems, destabilizing those environments by rendering them more susceptible to contagion and boom/bust fluctuations in population.[31] What happens on land alters the chemical and biological composition of seawater, just as encroaching waters can radically alter coastlines and human lives.[32] As Bill McKibben points out in *The End of Nature*, the data supporting early models of anthropogenic climate change were provided by two oceanographers working on carbon sequestration in surface mixing. In the twenty-first century even the pH balance of seawater is changing as carbon emissions increase the acidity of seawater.[33]

More spectacular evidence of the human impact on the global ocean is the so-called Eastern Garbage Patch, a vast area (larger than Texas) in the Pacific Ocean in which the North Pacific Subtropical Gyre deposits floating objects, containing millions of tons of plastic garbage—a mass of nonbiodegradable waste that exceeds the total quantity of surface biomass (marine life) in the same region. The Garbage Patch (and others like it) has attracted a good deal of popular attention in recent years. Charles Moore was one of the first to note this phenomenon while on a yacht race across the eastern Pacific in the 1990s and in the past decade has done much to raise public awareness about it.[34] The oceanographer Curtis Ebbesmeyer actually predicted the existence of such regions of waste flotsam even before they began to be observed and has written about them extensively.[35] In the summer of 2007, I sailed through the North Pacific Subtropical Convergence Zone on a month-long voyage under sail aboard the *SSV Robert C. Seamans*, owned and operated by Sea Education Association (based in Woods Hole, MA), from Honolulu to San Francisco, observing at first hand hundreds of discarded plastic oil drums, beer coolers, mooring balls, fishing nets, net floats, and myriad other objects on the surface of the vast ocean.[36] Each day at noon and midnight scientists and students scooped samples of plastics (often too small to be seen by the naked eye) from the surface in a fine-mesh net. There was not a day in over four weeks when the surface was free of microplastics (small pieces ranging from the size of a marble to chips barely visible to the naked eye), with our counts ranging from seven to nearly three hundred items each day of the voyage.[37] While the phenomenology of the Garbage Patch is debated (is it best imagined as a raft of junk twice the size of Texas or as an immense watery vacant lot with occasional litter?), to sail through it for days on end is to experience personally what Bill McKibben means by "the end of nature" (if by "nature" we mean that which is not made by human beings)—or what Latour means when he theorizes a historical conjuncture at which "there is no more environment," or at least none that remains free of "the consequence of human political, economic, and industrial life."[38] Marine scientists and mariners have seen the proof of McKibben's and Latour's arguments: the beaches of islands in the world's most remote archipelagoes are littered with plastic debris and the corpses of pelagic seabirds, which ingest plastic items as they feed.

Increasingly overfished, massively polluted, rising in temperature and acidity, with "dead zones" and regions where aerosolized toxic algal blooms can kill small animals in the surf, the global ocean no longer belongs to a measureless alterity that we could never fully fathom or exploit. These are only some of the consequences of six centuries of human exploitation of an entity long thought to be timeless, threatening, ineffable, and infinitely

Introduction

copious. If the modern marine sciences have demonstrated that none of these assumptions is remotely true, they also teach us with growing credibility that the sea's finitude concerns us all.[39] While it hardly seems likely that a sophisticated commentary on the human relationship to the ocean would be hidden in such plain view, Shakespeare's writings adumbrate our condition, a situation in which the fate of humanity appears reflected in the ocean (and vice versa) in peculiar and instructive ways. The present condition of the global ocean argues beseechingly for a conceptual holism that is both presentist and historicist in scope; it also enjoins us to look long and hard at historical habits of thinking about the sea as an entity standing apart from the biophysical environment.

The devastated condition of marine ecosystems registers the results of humanity's self-ascribed (or theologically appointed) dominion over living things as well as a tendency to ignore the possibility, let alone the necessity, of stewardship on a global scale.[40] Ineluctably tied to the land by ecological processes which have only recently been discerned and by meteorological processes that have long been taken seriously, the sea can only be divorced from the traditional "environment" (land, nature, and all that is green) by defining the waters in terms of an alterity that removes them from that part of nature to which we feel we belong. As Kimberly Patton observes in her study of the spiritually cathartic role of the sea in several religious traditions, "Most human beings do not really grasp that anything we might do to the oceans might harm them," in part because of the nearly universal religio-cultural status of the ocean as a given, uncreated feature of the planet (or the Creation).[41] This is spectacularly true of ecocritics, most of whom pay no attention to the global or world ocean at all, perhaps because it has never crossed their minds to consider the sea as a contingent and, at least partially, culturally constructed entity.[42]

Reading Shakespeare through the conceptual lens of the nascent discipline of marine environmental history opens up new vistas on the human relationship to the global ocean, for Shakespeare's nuanced model of what constitutes the biophysical environment gives us something more useful for conceptualizing a terraqueous world than the writings of the Romantic poets and American nature writers, which have been the primary interest of mainstream ecocriticism. This approach also opens the way to recuperating the work of previous scholars of Shakespeare's ocean, such as Alexander Falconer and L. C. Knights. Natural history, theology, and literary tradition shaped the poet's extraordinary talent for empirical observation. Shakespeare frequently implies that the best access to the wild deep is through art and that art itself is always a form of dissimulation and misrepresentation (consider Ariel's song). As Jonathan Raban puts it, "Shakespeare's sea—the silver sea; the triumphant sea; the hungry sea; the sea of glory; the boundless sea; the multitudinous seas incarnadined by Macbeth's bloody hands—has a quality of brilliant irrealism."[43] This "irrealism," which we might also describe as an effort to imagine the plasticity and fungibility of aquatic phenomena and an unseen marine environment, is a representational challenge that the poet returned to again and again in his career.

Astute readers have long acknowledged Shakespeare's love of the sea. As Keats asked (see the epigraph), in what mood, and with what accompaniment, do we like the sea best? In another idiom Walter Cohen observes: "Nearly all Shakespearean drama includes a political or military conflict, most often between sovereign states and thus with imperial aspirations at stake. In the majority of the works, that conflict has a maritime dimension; and the sea (including its fish and storms), ships, voyaging, and sailing have a role in several other plays as well—literally, metaphorically, or both."[44] While Cohen acknowledges the significance of the maritime world throughout the corpus, he leaves it at that—a gesture, nothing more. Yet Shakespeare's career-long preoccupation with marine phenomena—whales, wrecks, pirates, and the wonders of the seafloor—attest to his interest in the marine environment. Auden saw in Shakespeare's ocean a protoromantic vision of "the deep" as a dangerous, fascinating, and ultimately sublime object, yet his overblown characterization of "the enchafèd flood" derives from Romantic proponents of the cult of the sublime. More compelling is what G. Wilson Knight wrote about Shakespeare's maritime bent at roughly the same time.[45] Knight convincingly demonstrates the ubiquity of the sea in Shakespeare's works, arguing that it stands for a primordial chaos against which art itself functions as a bulwark. Shortly thereafter, in the postwar period, Alexander Falconer's *Shakespeare and the Sea* (1964), the result of its author's experiences in the Royal Navy, offered an authoritative account of the Bard's knowledge of maritime terms. Falconer reminds us that "Shakespeare lived through a long-drawn-out naval war which lasted for eighteen years"; understandably, his "interest in the navy and in the sea held him throughout his life."[46] England's arrival on the international stage as a major sea power took place in the

Introduction

lifetime of the poet; this arrival was a central preoccupation of national political discourse.

Most current scholarship fails to note the sophistication of Shakespeare's maritime imagination, the extraordinary degree to which human lives are connected with the sea, or the remarkable specificity of his descriptions of marine phenomena that are assumed to be beyond the ken of a playwright from Warwickshire. Only one recent monograph has been published on the Shakespeare's maritime imagination, Steve Mentz's delightfully concise and readable *At the Bottom of Shakespeare's Ocean*.[47] This all-too-brief study offers close readings of nautical topoi in Shakespeare and in the writings of Melville, Charles Olson, and Eduard Glissant, for whom the sea held a similar fascination.[48] Mentz unpacks key passages that attest to Shakespeare's maritime interests and in doing so builds a case for a "blue cultural studies." This formulation contests the hegemony of all that is "green" in current ecocriticism and calls for a more aquatic and interdisciplinary environmental scholarship.[49] Yet his emphasis on the supernatural and lethal nature of the sea in Shakespeare's imagination paints only a partial picture. For in addition to being deadly and frightening, the ocean in Shakespeare's writings is also redemptive, fecund, and emancipatory; it is wild and savage but also magically protean and strangely familiar. "All my fortunes are at sea," exclaims Antonio in *The Merchant of Venice* (1.1.177). If we consider that Antonio's argosies, thought to be lost, return safely to port, or that in *The Tempest* the ocean is the condition of possibility for a redemptive rearrangement of the political and social order, we are invited to imagine an ocean that is at least as providential as it is destructive. My emphasis, then, is less squarely on the sea as the site of a threatening alterity and more squarely on its plasticity of meaning.

The chapters that follow are nonetheless intended as a contribution to "blue" early modern cultural studies. I examine natural history and theology, emblem literature, paintings, and prose pamphlets about the sea.[50] What unites them is the exploration of a marine environmental imagination in which the sea is at the forefront of the human experience of the natural world. Each chapter develops a different focal point: the strange creatures of the shore, the tide that threatens to overwhelm human bodies, the riches that lie at the bottom of the sea, the possibility of human kinship with marine animals, and similar topics. Without attempting to be exhaustive in my account of Shakespeare's maritime imagination, I discuss numerous scenes, metaphors, terms, and ideas about the ocean that span the playwright's career.

Chapter 1, "Backs to the Sea? The Terrestrial Bias," is a critique of ecocritical scholarship. I argue that the use of "the land" as a conceptual foundation for ecocritical scholarship perpetuates a cosmogony that defines the ocean as a void. Chapter 2, "Consider the Crab," examines how Shakespeare both exploited and resisted the Western tendency to define oceanic space in terms of radical alterity. In chapter 3, "Shakespeare's Benthic Imagination," I explore the metaphor of human life as a sea voyage and the language of sounding and fathoming, both of which signify the measurement of depth (Gr. *benthos*), as a metaphor for knowledge and the self. In chapter 4, "Tidal Bodies," I trace Shakespeare's career-long preoccupation with the tides and his interest in a somatic connection between human and marine life. In chapter 5, "Royal Fish: Shakespeare's Princely Whales," I map the genealogy of the idea of human kinship with whales and dolphins from classical and biblical culture to early modern natural history, Dutch art, sermons, and Shakespearean drama. Chapter 6, "Shakespeare among the Fishmongers," explores the material and symbolic status of fish in scenes in *Twelfth Night, Romeo and Juliet, Hamlet,* and *The Tempest,* arguing that the playwright frequently collapses the relationship between the fish market and the marriage market to evoke the transience of the material body. Chapter 7, "Prospero's Maps," explores representations of the winds in early modern painting, cartography, and *The Tempest,* arguing that Shakespeare's frequent personification of the winds engages with the history of navigation. I end with a coda in which I reflect on the book's two-pronged scholarly commitment, to Shakespeare studies and to ecocriticism.

1

Backs to the Sea?

THE TERRESTRIAL BIAS

> How inappropriate to call this planet "Earth" when clearly it is "Ocean."
> ARTHUR C. CLARKE

These are the best and the worst of times for ecocritics, propelled as we are by a growing sense of professional legitimacy in the face of a looming sense of environmental catastrophe. New signs of ecological overload, collapse, and the wrong kinds of regime shifts appear almost daily to remind us that the Earth's biosphere is in crisis and that this crisis is the result of human activity. The oil that was hemorrhaging into the Gulf of Mexico as I completed the manuscript of this book wreaked, in a matter of months, irreparable harm to the once-rich marine ecosystems of the region and to formerly thriving fishing and beach communities, demonstrating yet again how much humanity desperately needs to rethink its energy use, development patterns, food systems, and methods of waste disposal. While the present study was begun long before the explosion on the Deepwater Horizon oil rig that killed eleven oil workers and countless sea turtles, fish, seabirds, and shorebirds, that event brought renewed attention to the general crisis of the marine environment. Even as the very problem that motivates many of us, the unsustainable human "footprint" on the natural world, broadens and deepens around the globe, our work becomes more relevant.

As the overheated global ocean produces major cyclonic storms with increasing frequency (witness Hurricanes Katrina and Rita), vividly demonstrating the stakes of expanding the human footprint on this planet, the new millennium has produced a perfect storm of environmental literary scholarship, with a growing body of anthologies, overviews, and critical studies all aimed at expanding, critiquing, and diversifying ecocriticism, which in the twenty-first century constitutes not so much a subfield as a metafield of literary scholarship, a commitment not limited to traditional historical periods and genres.[1] Its practitioners nearly always aim at two audiences, those in our particular subfields of literary study (such as Shakespeare, Victorian literature, or the novel) and those who identify themselves primarily as ecocritics.[2] Two developments have converged to align the perspectives of significant sections of the fields (meta- and sub-) of ecocriticism. First, growing public awareness about the causes and effects of global climate change—and the attendant "debate" over the "theory" of global warming in the international media—imparts an increasing tone of urgency to the work of scholars seeking a greater engagement with social justice (as environmental justice), environmental ethics, and activism than the academy has hitherto tended to support.[3] Scholars interested in rethinking, historicizing, and theorizing contemporary notions of what constitutes nature and the environment are producing a burgeoning body of ecocritical scholarship. This confluence of forces has produced widespread interest in ecopoetics and ecopolitics throughout academia, particularly in the Anglophone academy. As a result, ecocritical scholarship is increasingly impelled beyond its traditional boundaries, American Nature Writing and British Romanticism, to fresh fields and pastures new—a centrifugal movement that I wholeheartedly endorse. Yet this expansion has yet to take ecocriticism to sea.

I see nothing wrong with a love of the land (which I share), but its deep encoding in the terminology and conceptual categories that define ecocritical inquiry profoundly limits our object of study and keeps us from reaching beneath the surface of what the poet Mary Oliver describes as the "green and black cobbled coat" of the sea.[4] Viewed from afar this planet is mostly blue, yet the extent of its oceanic blues is hidden beneath a land-loving mentality that can be difficult to displace. By acknowledging the rich literary presence of the ocean in Anglophone literature (particularly in the works of a celebrated writer whom many of us imagine we have read carefully) and incorporating the interdisciplinary potential of the marine sciences, ecocriticism can expand its scope and reclaim bygone models for conceptualizing the human relationship to the biophysical environment, which may well be more helpful than the prevalent post-Romantic ones we now espouse.

Part of what makes the term *ecocriticism* meaningful is the metonymic chain of related signifiers that articulate the commitments, achievements, and scholarly horizons of its practitioners, terms such as *ecology, environment, green,* and *the land*. Every subfield (and metafield) of literary scholarship produces its own terminology. Keywords and phrases tend to multiply with the expansion of the subfield (or metafield); working within the discipline begins with making basic distinctions. Consider how productive have been some of the distinctions made in literary study: those between metaphor and metonymy, imperialism and orientalism, georgic and pastoral, sex and gender, epic and romance. Some of these distinctions pertain to different subfields; others pertain to all of literary study and begin to appear self-evident after years of use. Like any other scholarly idiolect, ecocriticism employs a host of key terms and phrases that might seem from afar to overlap but which, on close inspection, mark crucial distinctions.[5] Similes abound, such as "environmental criticism, literary-environmental studies, literary ecology, literary environmentalism, [and] green cultural studies."[6] Lawrence Buell has claimed that this approach (however labeled), "implies a . . . methodological holism" that is, as Sharon O'Dair and others have argued, largely chimerical.[7] As ecocriticism has grown more theoretically and methodologically self-conscious, scholars have begun to critique the undertheorized conceptual categories that form a kind of terminological substratum that undergirds, and undermines, the work of ecocritics.

The term *nature*, for example, offers slippery conceptual footing, as Dana Phillips argues in his rather brutal critique of ecocritical terminology and methodology. For Phillips, ecocritics are not genuinely interdisciplinary but hampered by an endemic tendency to employ scientific concepts merely as metaphors:

> The infamous gaps between the arts and the sciences . . . are apt to be papered over rhetorically. All too often, little or no effort is made to confront these gaps directly and to bridge them argumentatively, where that is plausible (sometimes, of course, the gaps are simply unbridgeable, and the disciplines may have little, if anything, to say to one another). The inevitable result is that basic errors of fact and interpretation, especially of the latter, are perpetuated under the banner of interdisciplinarity.[8]

I am much less skeptical of the claims and procedures of scholars who draw ideas and inspiration from ecology than is Phillips (I am also less confident than he in his own ability to adjudicate what he considers "errors of fact and interpretation"). Nonetheless, this chapter attempts to bridge one of the "gaps" he posits—that between literary scholarship and the marine sciences. This gap is created, as I shall demonstrate, in the discursive production of what I shall call *the terrestrial bias*, a tendency to locate the subject of ecocritical inquiry in a green and landlocked space.

It is not the term *nature* that I find troubling, although, as Timothy Morton has recently argued, it is often employed with imprecision by well-meaning yet scientifically hazy literature professors.[9] The term is too pervasive and useful to be expunged from the critical vocabulary and too contested to drop from view. Yet of all the terms that help us to do the kind of conceptual anchoring on which scholarship can be built, the idea of the land—generally used as a transhistorical, universal ground of meaning—strikes me as the most pervasive and worthy of scrutiny. Unlike *nature* and *ecology*, both of which have been subjected to rigorous theoretical scrutiny, *the land* remains largely unexamined in ecocritical discourse, and its ubiquity in current scholarship both delimits and limits the scope of our work. Even as it expands centrifugally across the subfields, ecocritical scholarship is held inward by a centripetal force, a core commitment to all that is green and lives on terra firma. The fetishization of the land as a conceptual foundation or primitive term has limited the scope of ecocritical inquiry to terrestrial topics—the American West, Wordsworthian pastoral, Milton's and Shakespeare's woods and meadows. Terrestrial terminology (*ground* is also ubiquitous in ecocriticism) and imagery remain largely unexamined in spite of the polysemy of the term *land* (which can denote one's native country, dirt, or the physical landscape, just for starters), as well as its ubiquity in current scholarship. While an appeal to the land is useful shorthand for invoking the terminologically ephemeral ground of meaning of ecocritical inquiry (be it nature or the biophysical environment), this terrestrial bias also situates environmental scholarship and the subject of ecocritical inquiry on shore, banishing from view the sea and its intimate connection to terrestrial phenomena.

Almost entirely lacking from ecocritical scholarship is a critical approach to the global ocean—that immense, life-creating and biosphere-sustaining body of salt water in which all life came to be, to which some (marine mammals) returned after an evolutionary sojourn on dry land, and into which we continue to pour the detritus of our civilization and our lives: garbage, toxic waste, excreta, and sins of all kinds. While the rapid growth of ecocriticism beyond the confines of its traditional homes has led to a vast amount of new work, recuperative, revisionist, reactionary, progressive, critical, and experimental, the global ocean—and the work of marine scientists and marine environmental historians—has to date had no role in the scholarship. The best introduction to ecocriticism contains barely a mention of the sea or its denizens.[10] By splashing blue water onto literary scholarship, I would like to suggest that ecocriticism would do well to rethink its "primitive" terms and the preconceptions about the physical environment that accompany them.[11] Incorporating the literary history of the sea and the perspective of the marine sciences can greatly expand the horizons for ecocritical scholarship.

A glance at the major surveys and edited volumes confirms the ubiquity of the terrestrial bias in ecocritical scholarship. The land is at the heart of the matter, and it is everywhere. From scholarly monographs to emergent journals, articles, poems, essays in creative nonfiction, title after title refers to the land as a means of characterizing a scholarship that attempts to balance the aesthetic and the ethical.[12] Essay collections routinely invoke the land as a self-evident conceptual category serving as a presumably firm ground (if you will) of meaning. An appeal to the noun (*land*) or the noun phrase (*the land*) signals a set of values and concerns presumably shared by scholars committed to the study of environmental literature. Consider, for instance, the introduction to *The Ecocriticism Reader*, in which Cheryl Glotfelty notes that "ecocriticism takes as its subject the interconnections between nature and culture, specifically the cultural artifacts of language and literature. As a critical stance, it has one foot in literature and the other on *land*" (emphasis added).[13] For Glotfelty, announcing ecocriticism's coming of age in 1996, the land is shorthand for a host of environmental topics—and for the disposition of a new scholarship.

Not all invocations of the land are so casual. In the powerful and influential discussion of the land ethic with which he concludes his magnum opus, *A Sand County Almanac*, Aldo Leopold uses the term with considerable rigor. Leopold was primarily concerned with ecological balance; in his words, "Conservation is a state of harmony between men and land."[14] His groundbreaking theorization of a land ethic was partly motivated by his personal regret for having contributed, when he was a young man, to wolf-extermination programs in the mistaken belief that such killing would be good for deer populations. His life's work was to rethink terrestrial ecosystems in holistic and systematic ways, moving, in the words of his biographer Curt Meine, "toward a biotic view of the land."[15] As Meine points out, "Leopold's approach to education was closely tied to his broadening conception of 'land' in the late 1930s."[16] Leopold's famous theorization of the land ethic redefined the land as a much more complex substratum than any merely intuitive definition of the term, one based on his many years of experience as a field scientist. As he wrote, "The land ethic simply enlarges the boundaries of the community to include soils, waters, plants, and animals, or collectively, the land."[17] A more encompassing formulation would be difficult to imagine; a more influential one has never been penned.

In light of my argument about the (thoroughly unintentional) terrestrial bias of ecocritical discourse, two features of Leopold's formulations are especially worthy of note: first, humanity is signified by "men," which establishes a (thoroughly unintentional) gender normativity; second, the "waters" of the Earth are encompassed by the category of "the land." Perhaps because he was a scientist (not a word-obsessed student of language and literature) Leopold did not feel the need to scrutinize the basic terms of his discussion too closely.[18] They worked for him, just as they have worked for countless others whose work is inspired by Leopold's writings. Yet in the same way he uses *man* and *men* as normative terms for human beings, so too is *land* used to mean the natural environment. In the same way that we would, today, prefer a gender-neutral term to *men*, it seems apparent that *the biophysical environment* would be preferable to *land*. While I do not wish to take Leopold too sternly to task for employing terminology that held largely unchallenged normative significance in his lifetime, it would be a mistake to overlook their resonances, for built into Leopold's account of the land ethic (one that I find indispensible and inspiring) is an undeniable terrestrial bias, a privileging of terrestrial ecosystems that relegates the global ocean to a kind of conceptual netherworld. Leopold's definition of the land ethic as encompassing "waters" inverts biblical and classical cosmogony, in which the firmament and the *oikumene* are surrounded by "the deep," in one case, and Okeanos, in the other. In his view, water is secondary to land as well as part and parcel of it; nowhere is the specificity of the marine environment acknowledged.

It would be difficult to overestimate the influence of Leopold's writings on the discourse of ecocriticism, and it would be a terrible mistake to take an overly critical stance toward them. Yet in adhering to the letter more than the spirit of the land ethic, ecocritics have almost entirely overlooked how literally blue our planet is, as well as just how metaphorically blue it is becoming.[19] A truly encompassing land ethic would involve a perspectival shift in the conceptual categories by which we define our object of study; to accomplish this, we first need to acknowledge what Melville called "the watery part of the world."[20] Only by imagining the ocean in terms of mutuality and belonging—as an entity to which we belong, rather than vice versa—can we begin to conceptualize it and act more ethically toward it. Leopold's writings and the profound knowledge of terrestrial ecosystems that they contain have been immensely influential among scholars of environmental literature. Some of the conceptual and rhetorical power of William Cronon's field-changing study *Changes in the Land* (now two decades old and in its second edition) is no doubt owed to its author's brilliant insights into the constructed nature of the American landscape—its evolving plasticity at human hands.[21] Yet by describing American environmental history almost entirely in terms of land animals and flora, Cronon adds his notably powerful voice to the chorus of scholarly land-lovers.[22] Enormously influenced by Leopold and Cronon, ecocritics have followed suit, yet by characterizing the biophysical environment in terms of the land, we ignore the significance of nearly three-quarters of the Earth, impoverishing our understanding of the natural world and reinforcing the longstanding notion that the ocean is not subject to the constructions and depredations of humanity—that the sea is somehow not wholly a part of this world.

In *Ecological Literary Criticism*, Karl Kroeber proclaimed, "In calling for an ecologically oriented criticism I appeal to intensified awareness of the historicity of all our intellectual disciplines." To achieve this, he argues, "an ecological criticism must be historically more self-conscious, if only because ecology is a relative newcomer in the world of science. Such self-consciousness, moreover, is a requisite for any kind of useful interaction between scientific and humanistic studies. It is the dangers of metaphysical universalizing . . . from which ecologically oriented criticism principally offers to liberate literary studies."[23] Here Kroeber enunciates for us the crux of the matter, for "the land" has become a metaphysical term that has been hypostatized by overuse, even to the extent of authorizing the tendency of ecocritics to repress the ocean as a key feature of the Earth's biophysical environment. It is precisely the self-consciousness and interdisciplinarity Kroeber insists on (which means reading beyond disciplinary boundaries whenever possible) that ecocriticism needs if it is to remain vital. If it is to live up to the radical vision of those such as Kroeber, Leopold, and Cronon, whose work helped make environmentalism a viable approach to literary study (and if it is to live up to its own etymology and intellectual genealogy), ecocriticism—a bold neologism if ever there was one—needs a conceptual adjustment that acknowledges the existence of the global ocean and at some point strives to incorporate knowledge from the marine sciences. Ecocritics need a more encompassing and truly global approach to the relationship of literature and the nonhuman world, an expansion of the parameters of our interdisciplinary inquiry.

In a sense I am not arguing for anything new, for ecocritics have championed interdisciplinarity from the start. In the words of the distinguished ecocritic Glen Love,

> Interdisciplinarity, for all its difficulties and potential for misuse, seems the only rational method for bridging the gulf, first popularized by C. P. Snow forty years ago, between the two cultures of the sciences and the humanities.... The social implications of biological thinking and research are one of the great intellectual engagements of our time, and are sufficient to draw the attention and interest of all who are concerned with the place of humankind on the planet. Scientifically-informed ecocritics have an opportunity to reinvigorate the teaching and study of literature, and to help redirect literary criticism into a significant, widely relevant social and public role.[24]

My call for a scientifically informed thalassology can thus be seen as a logical extension of the work of prior generations of ecocritics, including Kroeber, Love, and Joseph Meeker, among others, who have blazed a trail toward broader interdisciplinary horizons—and thus, unwittingly or not, toward the shore and beyond.

There is a notable reason to let ecocritics and our intellectual forebears off the hook for their terrestrial bias. For if we have been all at sea in our efforts to conceptualize the totality of this blue planet, this situation is not the fault of particular scholars so much as the legacy of the longstanding cultural status of the sea in Western culture as a realm of chaos and radical alterity that can scarcely be conceived, much less domesticated. This is not a matter of mere oversight or willful ignorance on the part of a few humanities scholars; it is a feature of European culture derived from biblical and Hellenic cosmogonies and articulated in countless works of literature. From the book of Genesis to the English Romantic poets, the historicity of the ocean has been consistently denied, repressed, or erased. Liberal humanism exacerbates this tendency, defining literary study as an inquiry into the human condition; from this perspective the sea is nothing more than a colorful blue background against which the important action—war, desire, nation-formation—occasionally takes place. This approach defines the human condition as essentially static—both ahistorical and transhistorical—and separate from material and ecological circumstances, impoverishing our understanding not only of the biophysical environment but also of the innovative and sophisticated ways in which writers have imagined the human relationship to it. By ignoring the role of the ocean in constituting the Earth's biosphere, we continue to construct the category of the natural in terms of terrestrial life, consigning the sea to the realm of chaos, the primordial, and the nonhuman. We do so to our own detriment, confining our understanding of the natural world. That ecocriticism has inherited a terrestrial cosmology registers in the basic categories with which it defines its object of inquiry.

It is difficult to overstate just how radical is the idea that the marine environment is linked to human history. Patricia Yaeger theorizes what she calls "ecocriticism$" in terms of the historical exploitation of the oceans as a form of capital; thus, "the challenge of oceanic studies is to put the ocean's agitation and historicity back onto our mental maps and into the study of literature. The challenge of ecocriticism$ is to think through the literary and cultural implications of the complex ends for which seas are deployed."[25] At stake is the conceptual linkage of the sea and the idea of historicity itself. Western civilization has long defined the ocean as an unnatural (or prenatural) void forever evincing a hostile alterity, a void lying eternally outside—or on the margins—of human social constructs. This mythology runs through Western culture from its inception on the shores of the eastern Mediterranean to its current dispersal along every shore of this planet. As Antonis Balasopoulos has observed, water—particularly the salt water of a threateningly immense global ocean—has traditionally been perceived as "an entity whose nature paradoxically contravenes the very idea of a stability-conferring foundation."[26] The protean sea apparently undermines the human need for a solid ground of meaning. While some of the conceptual alterity of salt water may derive from its empirical qualities, it is also a culturally constructed notion, vividly described by Auden in his discussion of "the romantic iconography of the sea": "The sea, in fact, is that state of barbaric vagueness and disorder out of which civilization has emerged and into which, unless saved by the effort of gods and men, it is always liable to relapse. It is so little of a friendly symbol that the first thing which the author of the Book of Revelation notices in his vision of the new heaven and earth at the end of time is that *'there was no more sea.'*[27] On the Day of Judgment the deepest sea creatures, demonically hidden in their submarine lairs, will be brought to the surface by a wrathful God.[28] While it is associated with the divine, the deep stands outside of the creation as a secondary entity, anterior and inferior to the firmament.[29]

The second verse of the book of Genesis seems to suggest that the primal aquatic deep precedes the Creation: "and the earth was without form, and void; and darkness was upon the face of the deep. And the Spirit of God moved upon the face of the waters."[30] Strangely, the waters preexist the Creation itself. While the biblical deity organizes the cosmos by separating heaven from the outer waters and the land (firmament) from the lower waters, the waters both antedate the Creation and, later, frame it in a watery surround that reeks of the profane. As Adam Nicolson has observed, there is an implicit antagonism in this creation myth: "When, in the first chapter of *Genesis*, the Spirit of God was said to move 'upon the face of the waters,' those waters were clearly what God was not. The sea was the absence of all meaning, not its source."[31] Britons inherited the biblical paradigm of the timeless, sacred-yet-threatening deep. The translators of the King James Bible vividly rendered the idea in language that emphasizes the wonders of the creation as well as its contingency, environed as the firmament is by the chaotic waters that precede and surround it.

Biblical scholars "have pointed to the traces in Genesis and elsewhere of the notion of the sea's preexistence and autonomy from established divine systems," as Kimberly Patton tellingly observes. Even more revealing is her account of how widespread was the idea of the ocean's separateness from the divine in the ancient religions of the Cradle of Civilization:

> This ancient Near Eastern idea of the sea represents the prehistoric embodiment of formlessness and chaos that continues to threaten order even after it is divinely established, as one can see in the parallel ordeals of Marduk and Timat Baal and Yamm, or Yahweh and Leviathan. In nearly every narrative in which the ancient sea "pre-exists" the rest of the natural world and all later human cultural forms, it tends to symbolize the opposite of culture itself.[32]

Backs to the Sea?

This oppositional status of the marine environment imparts a complex combination of profanity and sacrality to oceanic space, for the divine is spectacularly manifest in its (His, Her) control over the deep and its denizens, such as Leviathan. The ocean is instrumental in manifesting providence, as the books of Genesis, Jonah, Job, and some of the Psalms make clear. Consider Psalm 107, verses 23–24: "They that go *down* to the sea in ships, / that do business in great waters; / These see the works of the Lord, / and his wonders in the deep" (emphasis added). The idea that the sea is "down," below and beneath the rest of Creation (if it is even part of the creation), echoes in literary history. In Coleridge's "Rime of the Ancient Mariner," when the eponymous seaman sets sail, his ship "drop[s]" "*Below* the kirk, *below* the Hill, / *Below* the light-house top" (emphasis added). Similarly, in Masefield's poem "Sea-Fever" (1906), long a favorite of English-speaking mariners (both professional and armchair), the speaker yearns, "I must go *down* to the seas again, to the lonely sea and the sky. . . ." (emphasis added).[33] Though bodies of water do tend to lie lower than the land, the idea that the ocean lies on a cosmological plane that is "down," and therefore in a timeless and unchanging space that predates the Creation, has been a perdurable one.

In Mosaic culture the sea is the sign and the instrument of divine wrath and providence alike; in Hellenic culture the case was somewhat different. For the Greeks, *Pontus* (the inland sea) was a universal solvent and cesspool, at once a literal and spiritual cleansing agent and the repository of filth and sin (*kaka*), while Okeanos, the encircling (and freshwater) world-stream, lay beyond the pale of *oikumene*, much like the biblical deep that precedes the creation. Both *Pontus* and *Okeanos* occupied a special position in the cultural imaginary of Greek civilization. The parallels between the waters in Hesiod's *Theogony* and the biblical deep are striking:

> Both *Pontus* and *Okeanos* are the children of Gaia, who came into existence just after Chaos. But Pontus, the open sea, the high sea, is the parthenogenetic child of Earth, born "without delightful love," and is himself appropriately fruitless, *atrugeton*: "the sterile main, raging in its swell. . . . "Deepeddying" *Okeanos*, though, is the child of Earth and her own offspring Heaven (*Ouranos*), who is a suitable mate because he is "equal to herself."[34]

For Homer, *Pontus* and *Okeanos* had different associations, the former a "theater of action and transformation" for the hero Odysseus, the latter (particularly in *The Iliad*) "cosmic, generative, and regenerative."[35] Both bodies of water were understood as being productive and destructive to life (like the biblical Flood), numinous as well as lethal.

Seawater itself, cleansing, renewing, mutable, and always lapping at the margins of human constructs, was for the ancient Greeks an objective correlative for spirituality itself. Its major function was cathartic, as Patton makes clear in her reading of Euripides' *Iphigenia in Tauris*. Thus, "the ancient Greek understanding of ritual purity featured the sea's unequaled capacity to wash away *miasma* ('stain' or 'defilement'), not only a moral condition but also a physical contagion that could contaminate other people."[36] Religious rituals of purification in ancient Greece almost universally involved immersion, literal or symbolic, in salt water. As one ancient Greek text affirms, "seawater is purifying by nature."[37] In her comparative religious study of the sea's association with purity and danger, Patton argues that seawater paradoxically cleanses human pollution and yet retains some of the spiritual burden of the filth it transports. The classical focus on the sea as a cleansing agent locates it both beyond and at the center of human civilizations: "As the uninhabitable, encircling matrix for the inhabited world, the religiously imagined sea—a forceful expression of 'space'—is a constant. It is the reference point for our land-based existence, nourishing that life at the same time as it threatens it and carries off its poisons. The sea, groundless, is our ubiquitous 'ground of being.'"[38] Both classical and biblical culture assigned the maritime realm to a different ontological and cosmogonic plain than solid ground, defining the sea as a space lying beyond the reach of human knowledge and control, and this alterity was conveyed in the major early English translations.

Gesa Mackenthun and Bernhard Klein note the traditional construction of the sea as an immense void: "Like the desert, the ocean has often been read as an empty space, a cultural and historical void, constantly traversed, circumnavigated and fought over, but rarely inscribed other than symbolically by the self-proclaimed agents of civilization."[39] The very notion of inscription seems incongruous when it comes to water—an incongruity that animates Keats's famous epitaph ("Here lies one whose name was writ in water"). The conceptual challenge of imagining the marine environment as anything but hostile and void, of course, was immense for a culture steeped in biblical and classical narratives. Balasopoulos argues that the early modern discovery—or conceptual assimilation—of the ocean as a global entity was inevitably framed in terms of biblical and classical precedents: "Lying simultaneously within the planetary imaginary and outside the bounds of 'the earth,' the oceanic realm constitutes the early modern world's most massive and politically consequential image of a nonplace."[40] Indeed, early modern legal discourse defined oceanic space as "a 'lawless,' antithetical 'other' lying outside the rational organization of the world, an external space to be feared, used, crossed, or conquered, but not a space *of* society."[41] Unlike some cultures in which the sea has not been traditionally defined as a hostile medium, early modern Europe approached the ocean with dread.

Construed as an asocial and ahistorical "space," not a place, the ocean was a dangerous void—as Herman Melville would later term it, "a chaos"—not an environment. Often depicted as a "sea of sin" by seventeenth-century Puritans, the newly discovered global ocean was the geographic, economic, and the aesthetic condition of possibility for the "modern world-system," in Immanuel Wallerstein's memorable formulation, an entity that fired the imaginations of artists and intellectuals to rethink the status of humanity in the *scala naturae*.[42] The peoples of the British Isles were particularly invested in rethinking the human relationship to the global ocean. As Claire Jowitt argues, "At the end of the sixteenth century the concept of a world economy was new and tentative, but recognizable. England was attempting to increase and announce its presence within a global economy through a surge of new textual and actual practices."[43] Arguments about the extent of human jurisdiction over oceanic space developed in the early seventeenth century as legal scholars debated the jurisdiction of national powers over coastal and offshore waters. International squabbles over control of maritime space (which would become the basis for modern international and maritime law) turned on defining oceanic space as either open or closed, *liberum* or *clausum*, in the terms established by the Dutch jurist Hugo Grotius and his English adversary John Selden. In 1608 Grotius wrote *Mare Liberum*, the treatise that is generally considered to have catalyzed modern maritime law and modern international law. For Grotius, the sea is a universal commons because of its spatial and material boundlessness: "The sea is common to all, because it is so limitless that it cannot become a possession of any one, and because it is adapted for the use of all, whether we consider it from the point of view of navigation or of fisheries."[44] Grotius had a strategic purpose in making such claims, specifically to lay the legal groundwork for Dutch encroachment on the Portuguese monopoly of the East Indies trade, while Selden wished to assert national-territorial claims over coastal waters. Grotius's claims about the limitlessness and freedom of *mare oceanum* have echoed right into the early twenty-first century: fundamentally limitless, the sea is defined in terms of a nearly infinite *copia* accompanied by an asocial savagery that permeates the waters and threatens to infect those humans who dare to cross it. Thus, the deep-rooted cultural tendency to define the ocean as a waste space to be traversed, not a place of human habitation, has a widespread intellectual legacy.

Grotius's ideas have an ancient religious basis that continues to shape our uninformed and occasionally disastrous marine policy. In his argument for the freedom of the seas, Grotius invokes ancient cosmology:

> The question at issue is the OUTER SEA, the OCEAN, that expanse of water which antiquity describes as the immense, the infinite, bounded only by the heavens, parent of all things; the ocean which the ancients believed was perpetually supplied with water not only by fountains, rivers, and seas, but by the clouds, and by the very stars of heaven themselves; the ocean which, although surrounding this earth, the home of the human race, with the ebb and flow of its tides, can be neither seized nor inclosed; nay, which rather possesses the earth than is by it possessed.[45]

Grotius emphasizes the sea's vastness and its protean inaccessibility as well as its availability as a universal commons that "can be neither seized nor inclosed," an entity that is either "the property of no one (*res nullius*), or a common possession (*res communis*), or a public property (*res publica*)."[46] By this argument the ocean cannot be possessed by humanity, for it is an entity fundamentally inimical to early modern ideas about private property. This idea continues to prevail in the twenty-first century: a recent book on piracy and lawlessness at sea by the journalist William Langewiesche, *The Outlaw Sea: A World of Freedom, Chaos, and Crime*, perhaps unconsciously evokes Grotius.

The interlinked ideas that human history transpires on land and that the ocean lies beyond the pale of historicity itself no doubt owe some of their durability to English Romanticism, which has long been fertile ground for ecocritics.[47] Romantic and Victorian poets tend to characterize the sea as a space of alterity, a source of the sublime, essentially ineffable. As Yaeger asks, with reference to the role of the surf in Matthew Arnold's "Dover Beach,"

Backs to the Sea?

"Doesn't the poem's ability to leap past the felt presence of the sea, to substitute the allegory of lost faith for a seaworthy material world, represent a habit of mind—a tendency to make the ocean sublime and thus available for sublimation?"[48] I would like to ask the same question of an earlier, Romantic articulation of the mythology of the timeless ocean that has been enormously influential both for scholars and nonacademic readers and continues to condition the way we—readers and ecocritics—respond to the global ocean, Byron's "Apostrophe to the Ocean," from *Childe Harold's Pilgrimage*:

> Roll on, thou deep and dark blue Ocean—roll!
> Ten thousand fleets sweep over thee in vain;
> Man marks the earth with ruin—his control
> Stops with the shore;—upon the watery plain
> The wrecks are all thy deed, nor doth remain
> A shadow of man's ravage, save his own,
> When for a moment, like a drop of rain,
> He sinks into thy depths with bubbling groan,
> Without a grave, unknell'd, uncoffin'd and unknown.[49]

These lines offer one of the most striking instances of what I shall call "the mythology of the timeless ocean." "The wrecks are all thy deed": the ocean can kill us, but we cannot mark it, much less transform it. For Byron the ocean itself is the agent of destruction. The sea's transformative power is unidirectional: "nor doth remain / A shadow of man's ravage, save his own." Beneath the surface, in the scarcely imagined depths, lies an alterity that the imagination can scarcely penetrate, and then only to recover a murky, half-glimpsed realm that can only be figured as negativity: "*un*knell'd, *un*coffined and *un*known" (emphasis added), a place where the musicality of the iambic pentameter modulates into a droning and shapeless "groan." Byron's watery plain is an infinite reservoir for the Romantic cult of the sublime precisely because it is fundamentally ahistorical. The rhetorical strategy of apostrophe, verbally addressing someone or something, implies the correlative response of *prosopopeia*, speech by an inanimate object. One half-expects the "deep and dark blue Ocean" that is the object of Byron's passionate verses to talk back, yet it remains silent.

By claiming that humanity's "control / Stops with the shore," the poet places great emphasis on the visual and acoustic impact of the medial caesura —amplified by a semicolon—that separates "the shore" from "the watery plain." This separation is definitive; the rupture enacts an irremediable boundary between land and sea, the one subject to "ruin," the other ineffable and indomitable. The descriptive language begins at the sea's surface, "the watery plain," and then moves to the depths, where all signs of humanity disappear. Figured as a tabula rasa both because of the monotony of its blue surface and because of its temporal featurelessness, "the watery plain" is immune to human influence. The speaker gets in touch with this primal "blue Ocean" by immersing himself in the surf and drawing inspiration from forces that engulf him. Finding "rapture" out of doors leads to a discovery of an inner correspondence—much like Wordsworth's correspondent breeze—between the self and Nature. The poet develops his personification of the Blue Ocean as "unchangeable" in the stanzas that follow: "Unchangeable save to thy wild waves' play / Time writes no wrinkle on thine azure brow— / Such as creation's dawn beheld, thou rollest now." These superb lines give exquisite verse form to the idea of an ocean untouched by "man's ravage" derived from cultural mythology.

Byron's "Apostrophe" moves from the apparently unchanging sublimity of the sea's surface to a vision of the seafloor as a productive, invisible place where "the monsters of the deep" are created:

> Thou glorious mirror, where the Almighty's form
> Glasses itself in tempests; in all time,
> Calm or convulsed—in breeze, or gale, or storm,
> Icing the pole, or in the torrid clime
> Dark-heaving;—boundless, endless, and sublime—
> The image of Eternity—the throne
> Of the Invisible; even from out thy slime
> The monsters of the deep are made; each zone
> Obeys thee: thou goest forth, dread, fathomless, alone.

Byron's vision of marine nature is decidedly one of surfaces; the depths are foreign. This vision is a Romantic one, but it is decidedly not an ecological one. Nor is it in any way sustainable, for the myth of the timeless ocean masks its radical transformation at human hands. If there is a grain of aesthetic truth to Bryon's verses, it is that many people do indeed respond to the ocean's immensity and grandeur with awe, and doing so can renew what Carson called "the sense of wonder" that people feel for the physical environment.[50] Byron, similarly, certainly got something right: imbibing the power of high-energy coastal ecosystems by entering the crashing waves washes us clean and reenergizes us. Like the poet, many of us are drawn to the shore for recreation, or to re-create, ourselves and our lives—spiritually, emotionally, and physically—and to reflect on the sea's apparent infinitude. Yet it is also true that the Atlantic Ocean itself is not in the least bit timeless. Although it has been vastly transformed—ecologically and chemically—by humans for centuries, the very idea of its historicity remains foreign to most scholarship in the humanities.

We do not tend to read poetry for its truth value. Figurative language differs from referential language in its emphasis on the medium over the message (if it did not, there would be no literature professors). Poetry does not so much convey information as give form to an emotional landscape; in doing so it emphasizes not the referent but the enunciation itself; any claims made about the world *out there* are less important than the faithfulness of language to the world *in here* (experience, perception). Thus, it is no doubt unfair to hold Byron accountable for perpetuating the misconception that the human impact on the environment "stops with the shore," but it is worth pointing out that the denial of the historicity of the sea is the very stuff of poetry. Byron's "Apostrophe"—judging him in wholly presentist terms—derives a great deal of its resonance by articulating a Romantic version of the timeless ocean reframed in the language of the sublime.

Not only does the perspective Byron celebrated condition our cultural notions of the ocean's appeal, it is closely linked to later iterations of the timeless ocean meme that can be located at the dawn of the modern biological sciences, including ecology, from which ecocriticism derives its inspiration, if not its methodology. Yet, as Yaeger asks, "What is the loss of faith compared with the loss of the living ocean?"[51] Ahistorical thinking about the ocean is not confined to the humanities; it also has a notable history in the development of the modern life sciences. Consider the role of the mythology of timelessness in the case of one highly influential nineteenth-century intellectual on the cutting edge of science. Not long after the publication of *The Origin of Species* in 1859, Thomas Henry Huxley, fondly remembered as "Darwin's Bulldog" for his energetic championing of evolutionary theory, was widely considered to be a scientific authority on marine affairs. In his role as chairman of a government commission on fisheries, Huxley rejected the complaints made by local inshore fishermen on Britain's North Sea coast about the destruction of fish stocks by steam-powered bottom trawlers. When British fishermen complained of having to sail farther offshore from their traditional fishing grounds each year, Huxley responded by advancing a classic argument that has bedeviled fisheries policy for as long as there have been "experts" producing it, articulating a version of what Deborah Cramer calls "the myth of inexhaustibility," the idea that overfishing is impossible, adding a scientific note to the mythology of the timeless ocean. Even as he played a pivotal role in popularizing Darwinian ideas, Huxley was still making the same argument for the ocean's infinite abundance in 1883, twenty years later, when as president of the Royal Society he gave the opening address to the Great International Fisheries Exhibition in London:

> I believe that it may be affirmed with confidence that, in relation to our present modes of fishing, a number of the most important sea fisheries, such as the cod fishery, the herring fishery, and the mackerel fishery, are inexhaustible. And I base this conviction on two grounds, first, that the multitude of these fishes is so inconceivably great that the number we catch is relatively insignificant: and secondly, that the multitude of the destructive agencies at work upon them is so prodigious, that the destruction effected by the fishermen cannot sensibly increase the death-rate.[52]

Huxley was wrong, but only recently have scientists and historians of the marine environment begun to determine just how wrong. As the environmental journalist Elizabeth Kolbert has recently written, "In an effort to figure out what ocean life was like before the modern era, marine scientists have, in the past few decades, cored through seafloor sediments, measured the size of fish bones tossed out at ancient banquets, and combed through the logs of early explorers." The evidence points to one inescapable conclusion, "that humans have been wreaking havoc in the oceans for centuries."[53]

The fishermen who had complained to Huxley about the impact of the new trawlers on fish stocks in local waters were right. Trawlers exemplify how human beings alter the marine environment: they devastate benthic habitat by smashing the undersea topography with metal beams or chains that scare up groundfish into moving nets.[54] Also known as "draggers," these vessels have the impact of a York Rake on the seafloor, pulverizing and thereby degrading the physical geography of the marine environment. As Charles Clover describes the process, "The weighted trawl and its chains, designed to beat flatfish out of the sheltering mud, smashes everything it does not catch, particularly the burrowing animals in the sediment. . . . EU scientists have calculated that up to 16 pounds of marine animals are killed by beam trawls to produce 1 pound of marketable sole."[55] Trawlers remove far more marine life from the water column than the fishermen using them intend; the unwanted species are known as "bycatch" or "trash fish." With this habitat destruction the entire marine food web is threatened, and biomass diminishes over time. This has been the story in the North Sea, the Gulf of Maine, the Caribbean, and many other once-fecund marine ecosystems where the supply of fish used to seem inexhaustible.[56] Fisheries not undertaken by trawlers, such as the herring fishery, often rebound when regulated. While the crash of herring stocks (not captured by trawling) in the North Sea has been reversed by recent regulations, the crash of cod stocks (trawled) on the Grand Banks of Newfoundland, once the most productive waters in the world, has not been ameliorated nearly twenty years after Canada unilaterally banned commercial fishing there. The destruction of the benthic habitat may be irreparable.[57]

Huxley's insistence on the infinite bounty of the sea was based on a mistaken analogy between an acre of farmed land and an acre of the sea floor. The latter, he claimed, produced more food than the former because of the ocean's miraculous abundance. This analogy is, in fact, built into the traditional terminology employed by fishermen to describe the best places to find fish: on fishing *grounds*. From time immemorial fishermen have pursued their quarry in places where the seafloor is known to be particularly abundant; these locales are often relatively shallow banks or shoals where a phenomenon known as *upwelling* occurs.[58] Yet an acre of the seafloor does not produce fish autochthonously, as it were, in isolation from the rest of the marine food web. Marine animal populations are in many instances linked across vast areas, and some species require a critical mass to spawn. Excessive removal of biomass—overfishing—weakens the entire ecosystem by rendering marine animal populations subject to boom/bust vacillations.[59] Just how profoundly wrong Huxley was in equating the seafloor with fertile farmland has become starkly apparent in recent years as scientists, fishermen, and policymakers begin to realize the massive effects that have resulted from the unregulated extraction of marine resources. While it may be unfair to use twenty-first century knowledge of marine ecology to bludgeon Huxley, it was certainly unfair of Huxley to pontificate without factual basis and ignore the fishermen who rightly noted a rising trend of scarcity in their waters.

An acre of ground at the bottom of the sea is much more like an acre of rainforest than it is like arable land, but even there the comparison is imprecise and misleading. Terrestrial comparisons are inadequate to represent the specificity of the marine environment. When we wish to describe what we mean by *the environment*, we are almost compelled to invoke the Arcadian imagery of pastoral or georgic images of hardworking farmers plowing the fecund earth. Neither of these traditions offers a compelling aesthetic lens for conceptualizing marine ecosystems. But it is an old habit: for many writers the sea has been a pastoral space (witness Milton's elision of the Irish Sea and "pastures new" in "Lycidas"); for many more it has been seen as a kind of watery forest where hunters wielding nets and hooks chase their scaly prey. In *A Brief Discourse of the New-found-Land* of 1620 John Mason wrote of the abundance of life to be found in the inshore waters of Virginia Americana: "For could one acre thereof be inclosed with the Creatures therein in the moneths of June, Julie, and August, it would exceed one thousand acres of the best Pasture with the stocke thereon which we have in England."[60] While the enclosure of common lands would indeed produce higher profits (and social problems) for early agro-industry in Britain, enclosing the sea seemed a fantasy.

Huxley's failure to imagine the specificity of the marine environment derives from a powerful literary legacy, for he was trapped by what amounted to a georgic vision of the sea, the bottom of which seemed essentially no different from the land worked by farmers. This literary legacy has in turn had a powerful influence on the way scientists have tended to write about the ocean, at least for popular audiences. Thoreau noted, astutely if inaccurately, "We do not associate the idea of antiquity with the ocean, nor wonder how it looked a thousand years ago, for it was equally wild and unfathomable always."[61] A century later Rachel Carson herself, an accomplished marine scientist and perhaps the most effective environmental writer of the twentieth century, articulated a version of the timelessness myth when she wrote, "To stand at the edge of the sea, to sense the ebb and flow of the tides, to feel the breath of a mist moving over a great salt marsh . . . is to have knowledge of things that are as eternal as an earthly life can be."[62] Here Carson's prose is more notable for its poetic timbre and cadences than for the value of its truth-claims, which were in any case far less dubious in her era than they are today. In her three-volume biography of the global ocean, Carson more than proves her understanding of the geologic history of the ocean, but it is a narrative that defines oceanic space as almost entirely divorced from human impact. In *The Sea around Us* she went so far as to claim that man "cannot control or change the ocean as, in his brief tenancy of earth, he has subdued and plundered the continents."[63] In fact, part of the stylistic beauty of Carson's magnificent sea trilogy (*Under the Sea-Wind*, *The Sea around Us*, and *The Edge of the Sea*) undeniably lies in its creative restatement of the mythology of the eternal ocean.

Carson wrote at a time when fishing yields were steadily on the rise, and she worked for government agencies charged with managing marine resources. She also learned her trade in Woods Hole, the home of the Woods Hole Oceanographic Institute, the National Marine Fisheries Center, the Marine Biological Laboratory, and other institutions at the leading edge of marine science. In 1955 Francis Minot, who directed the Marine and Fisheries Engineering Research Institute, cowrote a book with the symptomatic title *The Inexhaustible Sea*, in which he claimed that "we are already beginning to learn that what [the ocean] has to offer extends beyond the limits of our imagination."[64] It should be no surprise that a scientist should place such emphasis on the imagination, for science itself is driven by cultural narratives that are often buried beneath pages of data. For Minot, as for Huxley, the "myth of inexhaustibility" (Cramer's phrase) was simply a ready formulation for articulating an essentially Romantic belief in the limitlessness of the ocean. Was he really to blame? Was Carson? In the decades after the Second World War, the massive expansion of industrial fishing fleets seemed to promise an infinite bounty from the sea. It was not until the last decade of the twentieth century that the historical impact of humanity on the global ocean came into sharp focus.[65]

Scholars in the humanities remain attached to the mythology of the timeless ocean. While marine environmental historians such as Callum Roberts of the University of York and W. Jeffrey Bolster of the University of New Hampshire and marine scientists with an eye for history such as Jeremy Jackson of Scripps Institute and Daniel Pauly of the University of British Columbia have entirely dismantled the premises for claims of inexhaustibility, often quite spectacularly, some scholars continue to promulgate the mythos. In *Facing the Ocean: The Atlantic and Its Peoples, 8000 BC–*

AD 1500, the distinguished Oxford University archaeologist Barry Cunliffe frames his study in terms of a "timeless" seascape: "To stand on a sea-washed promontory looking westwards at sunset over the Atlantic is to share a timeless human experience." Cunliffe cannot make his point strongly enough: "We are in awe," he goes on, "of the unchanging and unchangeable as all have been before us and all will be."[66] Cunliffe exploits the mythology of oceanic timelessness rather more melodramatically and carelessly than does Carson, setting himself up for a fall. In response to Cunliffe's overblown (not to mention misleading and entirely out of step with the times) prose, Bolster quips, "This is a rather ahistorical opening to a history book."[67] Yet it is an appeal to the ahistorical nature of the ocean underwritten by much of Western culture.

Marine environmental historians have responded to the current global crisis of the marine environment by doing innovative, interdisciplinary work using data from the marine sciences, as well as from traditional maritime-history sources, to build a much more nuanced historical picture of the diachronic human impact on the sea.[68] They are not alone, yet as oceanographers, marine ecologists, geologists, paleontologists, political scientists, and historians actively transform our understanding of the relationship between humanity and the sea, past and present, modifying our knowledge of marine environmental history and our prognostications for an environmental future, ecocritical scholars frame their work in terms of a terrestrial nature largely derived from pastoral tradition and Romantic poetry, neither of which has much to tell us about the marine environment. No subfield or metafield of literary scholarship is immune to this criticism. Early modernists, for example, who in recent years have made great strides in historicizing the ecocritical project, still tend to exclude the marine environment from serious inquiry. With very few exceptions, even the most recent work has remained resolutely terrestrial.[69]

Keith Thomas's oft-cited study *Man and the Natural World*, surely one of the most influential works of historiography for ecocritics interested in Shakespeare, entirely omits any mention of the marine environment as such.[70] The basic terms of Thomas's study simply leave no room for it. Just as "Man" is for Thomas—as for Byron—the normative signifier for human beings, "the natural world" denotes terrestrial life. Marine biota are nonexistent. The few references to fish concern issues of freshwater angling, while early modern forensic, theological, protoscientific, and literary representations of saltwater fish, marine mammals, currents, winds, tides, and tempests are simply absent. That a cultural historian whose focus is the seventeenth century would fail to discuss, much less mention, the politics of herring, surely the most important species of saltwater fish in the period, universally consumed in the British Isles and the subject of political controversy with the Dutch, is staggering to contemplate. Even the marine animals mentioned specifically in the documents that Thomas discusses, including seals, penguins, and puffins, fail to elicit specific commentary as features of the marine environment. To the argument that could be offered in Thomas's defense, that his main interest was in the quotidian experience of "the natural world" for everyday Britons and not the exceptional experience of nature (such as going to sea), I would simply note the ubiquity of salt fish—cod, hake, and herring were utterly quotidian staples—in early modern England. On reading *Man and the Natural World* one would never know that it was about a people whose diet consisted largely of salt fish or that nearly every part of the kingdom contained at least a whiff of the sea.

Like the historiography that it invokes most frequently, ecocritical early modernism suffers from a severe case of what I call *chlorophilia*—an inability to look beyond the imagery of the land and its leafy green cloak. Green is indeed a vital color, but it is not nature's only shade, and it is not the color that hits the eye when one beholds the global ocean that covers the majority of the Earth's surface. To assume that green is the given color of the physical environment is to contribute, unwittingly, to the mythos of the timeless (hence unnatural, neither born nor dying) ocean.

Shakespeare scholars have almost entirely ignored salt water as a dimension of the environment. In his influential study *Green Shakespeare: From Ecopolitics to Ecocriticism*, Gabriel Egan makes the striking claim that "Shakespeare is indeed already green," an argument he develops in a series of short, clever, amusingly presentist takes on topics derived from current environmentalist discourse. In his laudable effort to nudge early modernists toward an environmentalist outlook and to guide ecocritics into "fresh Fields, and Pastures new," Egan takes admirable pains to avoid reinscribing a bardolatrous notion of the Swan of Avon as "Warbl[ing] his native Wood-notes wilde." But what is the specificity of the modifier "green" when juxtaposed with "Shakespeare"? Does it mean a love for what Shakespeare would have understood as the Creation and David Abram has termed the "more-than-human world"?[71] Is it the biosphere? Something more precise is wanting, for surely it was not the wild or uncultivated landscapes celebrated today and evoked by the term *green* that attracted Shakespeare.

Ecocritical discourse defines itself as "green" just as it fetishizes land and the ground. Yet the insistence on green—ubiquitous in the popular press—as the emblematic color of environmentalism and ecocritical inquiry imposes a categorical limitation on scholarly discourse. The terminology and accompanying imagery echo a thoroughly Romantic epistemology of the natural: nature's cloak is (essentially, fundamentally, transhistorically) green, so nature's poet must also be garbed in cloth of that color.[72] In Shakespeare's day good environmental policy consisted largely in the reclamation of "waste" (undeveloped, uncultivated) terrain.[73] The green space so treasured by the citizens of postindustrial nations today (including myself) held none of the edenic resonances for Britons suffering from grain shortages, floods, and overpopulation. Tudor and Stuart poets constantly reminded their audiences that Eden was an enclosed garden, a space of human control and cultivation.[74] In what way, then, does "green" describe the work of a poet-playwright for whom nature was more hostile than friendly and better exemplified by a blasted heath than a field of daffodils?[75]

Egan's answer is too general to be quite satisfying: "The plays are useful (and indeed infinitely pleasing) as interrogations of our ideas about our relations one to another and to the world around us."[76] What great literature fails to fit this definition? The formulation hinges on the legibility of two normative categories, "us" and "the world," which resemble *the land* in producing the appearance of semantic transparency. I cannot help but agree that the appeal of Shakespeare lies in his ability to render an interrogation infinitely pleasing, but what in the world is meant by "the world," after all? In what sense is Shakespeare's world "our" world? Egan seems an unlikely champion of the liberal humanist subject. Surely, environmental history, particularly the immense effect humanity has had on the biophysical environment of the past four centuries, complicates any notion of a stable, transhistorical "world around us," which apparently could equally describe the Bankside of early-Jacobean Southwark, the grounds of a chemical refinery, the dead puppies of Tudor-era Houndsditch, or the toxic petrochemical-and-steel landscape of a ship-demolition center on the Malabar Coast.[77] While Egan's study does, ultimately, offer some compelling reasons to harmonize the terms in the book's title, *green* and *Shakespeare*, his formulation for a bardic environmentalism leans on the cultural currency of imagery (*green* means pro-environment) that assumes a Romantic epistemology of nature that conflates a historically contingent cultural construction (the goodness of nature) with terrestrial imagery—green fields, woods, and gardens.[78] In the end (and it is a book deeply concerned with what the end of us all might be), *Green Shakespeare* fails to lay out a nuanced definition or comprehensive description of what "the world" might mean for ecopolitics or ecocriticism. The ocean is surely a ubiquitous presence throughout the corpus of plays and poems and a key feature of the playwright's discourse of nature. Yet water, much less seawater, has no role to play in Egan's book.[79]

It is not my wish here to play the part of an aquatic Lorax, kicking a pack of dusty Once-lers out of their high (ivory) towers with a denunciatory "J'accuse!" (although I must acknowledge a personal debt to Aquaman and DC Comics).[80] Nor do I wish to accuse the literary and intellectual forebears of ecocriticism of willfully misrepresenting the physical environment by neglecting the global ocean and all its seas, sounds, gulfs, bays, bights, harbors, and coves. Indeed, I appreciate the literary results of nearly any writing that attends to the oceanic dimensions of the biophysical environment. Byron's resonant claim, for instance, "Man marks the Earth with ruin," gives exquisite voice to humanity's concern over its own destructive tendencies, a concern that also animates ecocritical scholarship and is arguably one of the moral legacies of English Romantic poetry. As Jonathan Bate and others have argued, Byron and his fellow Romantics gave powerful voice to what we might call an aesthetics of human ecology—the idea that being part of nature is both beautiful and renewing.[81] Yet I linger on these articulations of the mythology of oceanic timelessness to locate an idea—call it a discursive formation, a habit, or a blind spot—that should be analyzed, historicized, and contested. By defining the natural world as a neglected and abused green garden, ecocritics remain hung up on Eden, that divinely demarcated site of terrestrial human habitation (and dominion).

The mythology of the timeless ocean, which relegates what Leopold terms "the waters" to a secondary place in the cosmos, is pervasive in Anglophone letters. As Yaeger argues in her reading of Pound's "Portait d'une Femme," a poem addressed to a nameless, timeless Woman, the sea and women both "remain base and marginal" in the cultural narratives of patriarchy.[82] Pound's profoundly sexist poem develops the conceit of Woman as Ocean, apostrophizing, "Your mind and you are our Sargasso Sea," and

> Idols and ambergris and rare inlays,
> These are your riches, your great store; and yet
> For all this sea-hoard of deciduous things ...
> there is nothing! In the whole and all,
> Nothing that's quite your own.
> Yet this is you.[83]

The apostrophized Woman, "you," is in her very essence derivative and illusory, a mere "Nothing." Yaeger accurately describes Pound's poem as "an avid portrait of woman as cheap pastiche," asking, "Should women have the right to vote? Should oceans have standing? Pound's poem does not ask these questions, but the answers echo in every line. The Sargasso Sea and the deciduous lady are secondary; they lack self-ownership."[84] In a peculiar way the poem seems to echo Byron's apostrophe to a primordial ocean on whose waves the poet flirts with the sublime and the timeless; in both instances the object of the apostrophe is, of course, silent. Yaeger rightly concludes that defining the sea, like women in patriarchy, in terms of an ontological "secondariness" "condemns oceanic commons to a shadow life."[85]

The narrative of the timeless and inexhaustible ocean continues to inform scholarly and popular notions of the marine environment, and it lies behind the terminology and conceptual apparatus with which we define our subject matter (and "object-matter" as well, to borrow Bill Brown's phrase) so as to exclude the global ocean.[86] This exclusion is not universal, and indeed the purpose of this book is to demonstrate the existence of a counternarrative in Western culture—a story about human and marine life that is far more mutual than the hegemonic mythology of timelessness. In the subsequent chapters I explore the contours of the Shakespearean counternarrative, which persistently represents human life and marine life as deeply interconnected.

But before turning to more developed readings of Shakespeare, I would like to close this chapter by offering a brief example of how a Shakespearean motif—slime—can be read (in a thoroughly presentist manner) as a commentary on the issues that I have raised in this chapter.

Daniel Pauly, who is widely regarded as the guru of fisheries science and policy, has somewhat facetiously suggested that we label the coming era of empty oceans the *Myxocene*, after the Greek word for slime (*muxa*).[87] For humans have removed so many edible species from the global ocean—fish, whales, turtles, crustaceans, and mollusks—that we have changed its biochemistry to such a degree that it has become a habitat of slime in which jellyfish, algae, microbes, and didymo ("sea snot") thrive. Shakespeare, too, was fascinated by slime, and he associated it with aquatic life forms. Clarence's nightmare foreshadowing his own drowning conjures the imagery of gems in dead men's skulls "which wooed the slimy bottom of the deep" (*Richard III*, 1.4.32; see chapter 3 in this work). Here the seafloor is figured as a watery grave, yet even in the depths a fearful beauty is born, and the verses resonate with a benthic aesthetic that fascinates Clarence and the audience. In his other plays Shakespeare several times evokes images of slime quickening in the mud: Antony, for example, swears "by the fire that quickens Nilus' slime" (*Antony and Cleopatra*, 1.3.68–69). For Shakespeare, slime matters; it is related to being human, a mediating term between the nonhuman world and the unfathomable nature of aquatic biota.

Slime was also present at the birth of ecology and in the early days of evolutionary biology. Born in the wake of Darwin's new theorization of species when thinkers like Huxley and Haeckel—and later Eugenius Warming—were attempting to conceptualize the relationship of the nature of species, their relationship to each other and their physical surroundings, the discipline of ecology is intimately connected to the nineteenth-century exploration of the ocean. Darwin's ideas, of course, were derived from his voyages aboard the *HMS Beagle*, whose purpose was to systematize the Royal Navy's knowledge of the ocean's physical geography. This was the moment when scientists dramatically expanded their scope of inquiry to include the open ocean and its depths. The American Matthew Fontaine Maury (1806–1873) contributed to the systematization of oceanography in *The Physical Geography of the Seas and Its Meteorology* (1856; see chapter 7 in the present work), and a great generation of British marine scientists was actively engaged in exploring the global ocean not in search of the riches that lay on its far shores but for the unknown life it contained. At almost the same time T. H. Huxley was advancing his now infamous claims about the infinite abundance of fisheries (in 1868), he reexamined some samples lying on his shelves which had been gathered from the bottom of the ocean a decade earlier from a depth of over one nautical mile (6000 feet) by scientists aboard HM frigate *Cyclops* of the celebrated *Challenger* expedition.[88] Huxley discerned a peculiar jelly-like substance lying in the alcohol at the bottom of the sample jar amid the benthic ooze. This substance seemed to fit the description of *Ur-Schleim* (ur-slime, protoplasm), the sought-for "primitive organism which might provide the missing link between inanimate matter and life" posited by the noted German biologist Ernst Haeckel.[89] Believing that "this was a living slime which carpeted the deep ocean floor, ingesting ooze and forming a rich layer of protoplasm that became a food supply for other life forms," Huxley named the substance *Bathybius haeckelii*, formalizing a terminological relationship between ecology and the deep sea.[90]

In fact the ooze-like "species" that Huxley named turned out to be a chimera, the result of the settling of matter in the sample jar (precipitation) and not, after all, the protoplasmic missing link between life and inorganic matter, but Huxley gave to slimy nothingness a name that holds an important if uncelebrated place in the intellectual genealogy of ecocriticism. For it was Haeckel who, in searching for the missing link between organic and inorganic matter, coined the term *ecology* in 1866, which he defined as "the knowledge of the sum of the relations of organisms to the surrounding outer world."[91] Huxley thus named his deep-sea slime at the historical conjuncture when Darwinian theory and oceanographic practice met to conceive of a new, holistic science of organisms' relationships to their physical environments. Like a kind of terrestrial unconscious, the ocean has been consistently repressed in order to erect ecocritical scholarship on seemingly firm ground.[92]

In a strange fashion, then, the global ocean—or a piece of it—was present at the birth of ecology, and *it was already being misrepresented*. This misrepresentation followed the prevalent cultural mythology of timelessness that defined the marine environment as an essentially ahistorical entity. We would do well to rethink this mythology. It remains to be seen whether the works of Shakespeare are pernicious, contributing to this mythology, or if they offer something more "rich and strange."

2

Consider the Crab

I prithee, let me bring thee where crabs grow.
CALIBAN

Barnacles cling at the low-water mark in the rocky intertidal zone of Massachusetts Bay, kelp fronds wave in the moving surge, and clumps of bladderwrack limn the granite shore. When wind and tide are at odds, white foam streaks the waves. The frigid water is fed by the Labrador Current, moving opposite to the east-flowing Gulf Stream far offshore, with nutrient-laden water from the Davis Strait. The shingle beaches of granite pebbles and crushed shell breathe with life at low water, tide pools chuckle, seaweed shifts and pops, and crabs scuttle in the shallows. At Flat Rock Beach, in my hometown, children motivated by what Rachel Carson called "the sense of wonder" delight in the sensory panoply of low water, poking along the rocky margin with eyes alight as they pick up seaweed and hunt for crabs.[1] Occasionally a child is bold enough to reach down and pinch the horny green carapace of a shore crab, lift the angry crustacean, and hold it aloft amid the pungent smells of mud and decaying organic matter above the clean scent of salt water. Scenes like this one create the impression of a timeless marine environment of the kind celebrated in the writings of Byron, Carson, and Cunliffe that I discussed in the last chapter. Yet that timelessness is an illusion.

An invisible change has come to Flat Rock Beach: the shore crabs that delight my two small children belong to a different species than the ones that I used to pick up in the same tide pools thirty years ago. Today we invariably encounter the Asian Shore Crab, *Hemigrapsus sanguineus*, which populates the shingle beaches where three decades ago my sister and I hunted the European Green Crab (*Carcinus minus*) and the Rock Crab (*Cancer spp.*). Until recently, *Hemigrapsus* was unknown in North American waters. First noted at Cape May, New Jersey, it was introduced in 1988 from the East Coast of Asia (from Hong Kong to Siberia), and since then has rapidly expanded its range along the United States Atlantic coast. In the early 1990s James Carlton, a marine ecologist and leading expert on marine bioinvasions, used to offer his students an ice cream sundae if they could find a sample of the new visitor on the Connecticut Coast.[2] A decade later he was making the same offer to students for finding any other species of shore crab on the same beaches.[3] In terms of its biotic constitution, then, the seashore where my children play is radically different from the one I knew as a child, with millions of introduced crustaceans occupying the rocky intertidal zone. This is not merely an instance of the "shifting baseline syndrome," whereby each generation defines its relationship to the environment in terms of historically contingent anecdotal touchstones (often in the form of fish stories); rather, it is an instance of sudden and radical ecological transformation hidden in plain view.[4] Even less obvious than the difference between *Hemigrapsus* and *Carcinus* is the role of human beings in causing the ecological transformation: it is a story that dramatically illustrates the historicity of the marine environment.

Marine bioinvasions are increasingly common as global trade and unregulated shipping increase. The large ships—bulk carriers, freighters, tankers, chemical tankers, "roll-on/roll-off" car transporters—that carry approximately 90 percent of the world's commercial goods ballast with seawater, which is pumped into ballast tanks when a ship is light and pumped out when the ship is laden. If a ship embarking "in ballast" (not fully laden with cargo) sucks up half a million gallons of seawater in Puget Sound and later dumps that water in Long Island Sound, myriad non-native species are introduced from one coast to another (which is most likely the way *Hemigrapsus* arrived).[5] Some will survive; some might even thrive. The ecological impact of species introduced to new ecosystems by human means, occurring at an ever-accelerating pace, is a major issue in marine policy.[6] What goes around comes around: the major species *Hemigrapsus* is displacing, *Carcinus minus*, was itself introduced to New England waters from Europe, probably over a century ago, and continues to be introduced elsewhere with drastic results to distant marine ecosystems.[7] When it comes to bioinvasions, it isn't turtles but crabs all the way down.

In her book *Sea Change: A Message of the Oceans,* the renowned marine scientist Sylvia Earle brought her vast experience to bear in demonstrating the extent to which human beings have been causing enormous ecological damage in the marine environment.[8] The idea of a global sea change affecting the marine environment runs entirely counter to the hegemonic cultural construction of the timeless ocean that I discussed in the previous chapter, a cultural narrative that defines oceanic space as an entity outside of history. Earle, who served as Chief Scientist for the National Oceanic and Atmospheric Administration (NOAA) from 1990 to 1991, was one of the earliest and most visible marine scientists to sound the alarm about the accelerating crisis of the marine environment.[9] The fact that she took the title for her book from Ariel's song is no surprise, for by the 1980s and 1990s *The Tempest* had become perhaps the best known of Shakespeare's plays in both scholarship and the public eye. While most attention to the play at the time concerned its refractions of European imperialism, increasingly the insight was offered that, as Jonathan Bate put it, "there is a larger sense in which *The Tempest* is a prologue to the whole thrust of technological modernity," and that "technological modernity" and "the modern world-system" were one.[10] Shakespeare's insular romance, thus, was seen as a rehearsal not only for the agon of imperialism and colonialism, but also for postcoloniality and, to some extent, postindustrial globality.

Earle's book title, thus, can be read as a gesture to the status of *The Tempest* as a touchstone in the cultural debate over the role of literature in mediating world history. Her appropriation of a phrase that has entered the language—a "sea change" now refers to a major change of course or significant transformation—was particularly clever, for she reanimated the maritime resonance that had evaporated over time. Earle put the "sea" back in "sea change" when she argued that modern technology and industrialization have dramatically augmented the human capacity for physically transforming—indeed destroying—the global ocean. Nowhere does Earle actually discuss *The Tempest,* much less explain the rationale for her title. But the implication is clear: a second sea change in the human relationship to the marine environment must take place if we are to keep from destroying it entirely. Like Earle, I make an intertextual gesture, in this chapter title alluding to

David Foster Wallace's celebrated essay on the human treatment of lobsters, which examines the morality of boiling crustaceans alive.[11] Wallace raised the issue of environmental ethics in one part of the American food system; in this chapter I hope to do something similar by examining the status of invasive species in early modern representations of the coastal environment.

Inviting Shakespeare to act as an expert witness in the case of invasive marine species might appear an extreme case of ecocritical tendentiousness, and certainly it would be a stretch to argue that anything he wrote evinces a full-scale encoding of an ecopolitical outlook or agenda. Nonetheless he did write a play in which European settlers have a transformative environmental effect on an island with a distinctively maritime setting: in *The Tempest* (in which Shakespeare coined the phrase "sea-change"), the change in question refers to the material power of salt water to transform matter as well as to the conceptual challenge of understanding marine phenomena and their relationship to what takes place on land. The word that Shakespeare employs to capture the combination of wildness and fascination that the ocean holds is "strange": the sea is "rich and strange," the home of the some of the strangest creatures the poet ever imagined (Caliban and Ariel, in particular), just as it is the home of some of the strangest life-forms on this planet (from our perspective as shore-loving bipeds). The memorable otherworldliness of the marine environment in *The Tempest* remains indistinguishable from the thematics of magic running through the plot. In this chapter I read passages in which Shakespeare imagines the relationship between the sea and the shore as allegories of the condition of literary scholarship in a time of epistemological sea change. Shakespeare's thematization of the ground as contingent terrain in Sonnet 64 and of intertidal life in *The Tempest* adumbrates the link between the physical environment and human political behavior that is the central preoccupation of ecocriticism.

In recent years environmental historians have gleaned much about the role of ocean voyages in importing new organisms from disparate ecosystems to new regions where they have often wrought havoc. When he made the novel argument (in the 1980s) that early modern European expansion around the globe constituted a kind of "ecological imperialism," Alfred Crosby noted that the consequences of the early modern human dispersion across the world's oceans included the ecological transformation of the settled regions.[12] Europeans brought with them to the Americas their flora, such as clover and dandelions; their fauna, including horses, pigs, rats, and cattle; and their microbes (including smallpox), much as the Polynesians had done in the previous millennium in their remarkable settlement of the far-flung Pacific archipelagos. In his discussion of weeds, Crosby cites John Fitzherbert's *Book of Husbandry*, which lists "divers maner of weeds, as thystels, kedlockes, docks, cockledrake," noting that such weeds "are as thick in Shakespeare's language as they no doubt were in his gardens at Stratford-upon-Avon." Crosby goes on to argue that "it is a sure bet that English weeds were rooted in North American soil while Shakespeare was alive": "John Josselyn, who visited New England in 1638 and 1663, scores of years after the first European fishermen began summering in Newfoundland and environs, and in all likelihood planting small gardens, made a list 'Of Such Plants as have sprung up since the English Planted and kept Cattle in New-England.' "[13] The ecology of Josselyn's New England was rapidly transforming because of European settlement and its attendant effects—deforestation, the removal of edible and marketable flora and fauna, and the introduction of new species (flora, fauna, and microbes).

While literature scholars have long remarked on the accuracy of Shakespeare's eye for flora, particularly weeds and wildflowers, what interests me here is Crosby's emphasis on the maritime history of English weeds, which were transported to the colonies (as one might imagine) not only by planters and farmers but also by fishermen.[14] The site of introduced European flora, the rocky shores of Newfoundland and New England were also the place where the European agents of the world's most productive fisheries processed their catch, drying and salting cod, haddock, and hake on small wooden stages known as "fish flakes." Today the inhabitants of coastal Newfoundland have discovered, in the words of Mark Kurlansky, "that they are on the wrong end of a 1,000-year fishing spree" which has completely transformed the once copious waters to a near-desert.[15] The cumulative effect of the massively increased resource extraction that accompanied European settlement became evident in the nineteenth century, when the extinction of the passenger pigeon and the near-extinction of the American bison made it clear that humans could indeed destroy the apparently miraculous copiousness of New World life in short order. Like the passenger pigeon, fish were to be found in such abundance that amazement became a standard topos of eyewitness accounts of the New World written by European travelers.[16]

While terrestrial ecosystems in regions of early modern European settlement were transformed by the introduction of myriad new species as well as by deforestation, water-diversion, and cash-crop plantations, the greatest impact on the marine environment was the removal of commercially viable species of edible fish, a process that took several centuries to reach a point where human beings began to recognize overfishing as a crisis. As the marine environmental historian Callum Roberts argues,

> Early European colonists of North America were surrounded by abundant wildlife, and for hundreds of years, if one species declined, they could just switch to others. The sea was a source of seemingly endless wealth to them, and the rivers and estuaries of the New World were equally important to the prosperity of the new colonies. But even in these first European centuries in the New World, there were already signs—below the surface, so to speak—of how rapidly fish and wildlife populations, once of an abundance hard to imagine, could be depleted.[17]

The signs of human overconsumption were urgent enough less than two decades after Shakespeare's death that the King himself attempted to regulate fishers. In 1631, a proclamation of King Charles I decreed, "The former abundance of fish is turned into such scarcitie an deareness, that ... our citie of London, and even oure owne Court, are many times unprovided for their necessary dyet ... therefore ... the nets heretofore called traules ... which is notoriously known to desctroy the said frie & spawne ... is ... forbidden by law."[18] London is a maritime town; the lower Thames is tidal to just upriver of the city. Setting dams across streams is an ancient method of fishing, described by Pliny the Elder and common in early modern Britain—"No more dams I'll make for fish," proclaims Caliban in his song of abbreviated freedom—but in Shakespeare's day this method was becoming politically sensitive in the overfished Thames (*The Tempest*, 2.2.173).[19] Fisheries were regulated on European rivers beginning much earlier than the seventeenth century, but in this instance they are an issue of national significance. The doomed Stuart monarch's concern about diminishing catches echoes through history: Jeffrey Bolster notes that as early as 1703 an Englishman lamented on coastal Newfoundland that "the fish grows less, the old store being consumed by our continual fishing."[20] By the middle of the nineteenth century, halibut, the iconic species of marine artists such as Winslow Homer, was nearly fished out in the Northwest Atlantic.[21]

Thoreau asked, apropos of the transformation of the New England landscape between the time when William Wood described its abundant glories in *New England's Prospect* (1633) and his own diminished era, "Is it not a maimed and imperfect nature that I am conversant with?"[22] While Thoreau was concerned with the extermination of the woodland predators of his home region, marine environmental historians and journalists are coming to grips with the historicity of a realm that has long been defined in terms of its timelessness, as if the ocean remained beyond the pale of human action. In the face of enormous evidence that the marine environment has been radically altered by human means, much as New England was between the seventeenth and nineteenth centuries (and even more so since), surely we must ask ourselves a similar question. It is also worth considering the possibility that contemporary artists aware of the European adventure in the Americas had something to say about it. As I will argue, Shakespeare does have something to say about an "imperfect nature" (if not a maimed one), which he locates in a coastal environment that owes much of its imagery to the New World.

Before turning to the theme of invasive species in *The Tempest* I would like to consider another superb instance of the poet's ability to evoke the dynamics of coastal forces: Sonnet 64. I turn to this sonnet here as an articulation of the relationship of nature and culture that employs the ocean to emblematize cosmic uncertainty and human contingency. The passage of time, figured in terms of the mutability of the terraqueous coastal landscape, is its central theme:

> When I have seen by time's fell hand defaced
> The rich proud cost of outworn buried age;
> When sometime lofty towers I see down razed,
> And brass eternal slave to mortal rage;
> When I have seen the hungry ocean gain
> Advantage on the kingdom of the shore,
> And the firm soil win of the wat'ry main,
> Increasing store with loss and loss with store;
> When I have seen such interchange of state,
> Or state itself confounded to decay,
> Ruin hath taught me thus to ruminate:
> That time will come and take my love away.
>   This thought is as a death, which cannot choose
>   But weep to have that which it fears to lose.[23]

This sonnet tells us that the works of humanity are precarious, the forces that rule this world dangerous and difficult to read, and art an imperfect seawall. We are led to consider the relationship between the ocean, the shore, and "time's fell hand," all of which are subject to the depredations of time—thus to face the historicity of the human relationship to a coastal landscape.

The "hungry ocean," which Shakespeare imagines as a massive material and metaphysical force forever impinging on "the kingdom of the shore," is clearly not the threatened ocean that we inherit today. If anything, the forces are now reversed: land-born (and occasionally sea-borne) humans, infinitely hungry for the fruits of the sea and increasingly capable of extracting its resources, have become a hungry ocean of consumers. With the passage of time, what once seemed a limitless, unfathomable, and infinitely copious realm of "store" is fast becoming an emblem of loss as the current explosion of knowledge about the mutual impact of the sea on human life and of humanity on the sea gives new meaning to Shakespeare's imaginative ecology. Nonetheless, in its ecological thrust Shakespeare's maritime imaginary is in significant ways like our own, in the twenty-first century. For Shakespeare the hungry ocean and the kingdom of the shore are interlinked features of the ecopolitical landscape. The hunger that impinges on "the kingdom of the shore" is no longer merely a void but a constitutive feature of the spatiotemporal setting of human life; no longer quite the ahistorical void of tradition, the ocean is one of the determining landscapes of human existence.

The representation of coastlines holds particular challenges. As Julie Sanders points out, "Shorelines and coastlines are only notionally fixed . . . they are permanently evolving boundaries, fluid frontiers, a contact zone between land and water that raises a pertinent set of issues relating to change, mutability, and drift."[24] The great Renaissance theme of mutability resonates in Sonnet 64. Yet it is not only in oceanic space that such mutability affects representations of space and place. If, as Garrett Sullivan has argued, "a landscape is a materialization of the external world, a way by which topography is brought into discourse and into knowledge," then in the terraqueous landscape of Sonnet 64 (and *The Tempest*, as I will argue), we find a shift in sensibility toward the ocean. "Landscape," argues Sullivan, "is profoundly ideological, for it simultaneously reflects and instantiates attitudes not only toward the land but to a whole range of social phenomena that are indivisible from the land." Here again we encounter the normative use of "the land" to describe the biophysical environment, but it is worth lingering on the suggestion that a poetic "landscape" that incorporates the "hungry ocean" is not merely aesthetically but ideologically (in this instance religiously and forensically) loaded.[25] Sullivan rightly stresses that landscape "simultaneously reflects and instantiates" our understanding of "a whole range of social phenomena"; in the case of Shakespeare's shifting coastline, these phenomena encompass the gradual shift in cultural attitudes toward the shore described by Corbin and evoking the idea that humanity could make claims upon maritime space. Sonnet 64 mourns environmental catastrophe and situates that mourning on the coast. Who controls "the kingdom of the shore"? This is the question that Shakespeare entertains in his sonnet of littoral cycles. Such questions as these were also, at the start of the seventeenth century, at the heart of the international debate about the jurisdiction of oceanic space.[26]

The Tempest, too, foregrounds the relationship between land, sea, and human survival in the context of a European colonial occupation of a landscape that bridges the Old World and the New, the Mediterranean and the Caribbean, and terrestrial and well as marine ecosystems. Any ecocritical reading is underwritten by an ecopolitics, just as every would-be regime on the magical island of *The Tempest* accompanies a particular ideology of territorial mastery. While scholars have long debated the relative merits of New World versus Old World approaches to decoding the play's setting and imagery, what has largely dropped out of the discussion is the observation—once front and center—that *The Tempest* is a play set in the marine environment—off the coast, in the water, on the beach, and in the intertidal zone.

Questions about the nature of landscape and environment preoccupy characters from the very first scene, when a ship full of Neapolitan nobles appears doomed to wreck on a looming lee shore. The old courtier Gonzalo complains, "Now would I give a thousand furlongs of sea for an acre of barren ground—long heath, brown furze, anything" (1.1.65–67). This is a richly nuanced appeal that puts into play several definitions of the land. Gonzalo's plea is for the solidity of dry land, in the first *OED* definition of the word, the solid part of the Earth. Gonzalo poses the *OED*'s second definition of "land," with emphasis on the (cryptic) "particular properties" of different kinds of territory, in conjunction with the first—"the solid portion of the Earth's surface"—as "anything" (anything solid). The third definition comes into play, too, in Gonzalo's precise terms of exchange: not only the sea but exactly a thousand furlongs of it are worth less to him than a mere acre of seemingly valueless soil. But behind Gonzalo's explicit wish for ground is a longing for epistemological surety. The sudden squall in which the Italian aristocrats find themselves threatens their persons and their knowledge of the world: they do not know where they are or what is happening to them. The loquacious counselor uncharacteristically finds himself incapable of explaining his own and his compatriots' circumstances; he is at sea, literally and figuratively. Thus, Gonzalo's plaintive lament for solid ground highlights the theme of disorientation that will be developed throughout the action that follows—a disorientation that is as much an intellectual condition as a physical one.

An ecocritical reading of this play should remain attuned to the early modern nuances of terms (*land, ground*) that are not merely literal descriptors of place but also conceptual categories. *Terra firma* has an altogether different semantic texture for a sailor just returned from a sea voyage than it does for a farmer plowing the back forty. Something of this distinction between the ground, as that which is distinct from the sea and the substratum on which human communities are built, is at work in Gonzalo's wonderfully enigmatic reference to several kinds of terrain. Leaving aside the ongoing editorial debate about what exactly "brown furze" means, or whether it should even be printed as such, the mere fact that a Jacobean audience would be expected to understand fine distinctions between types of terrain—the basis for different ecosystems—implies the existence of a highly nuanced discourse of the land as ground, earth, and terrain in Shakespeare's era.[27] As this example demonstrates quite spectacularly, the exact meaning of *ground* is a thoroughly textual matter. The ground of being and the ground of meaning, that which undergirds our existence and authorizes our ideas, are deeply political and aesthetic matters lying at the heart of *The Tempest*, a play about the human control over the biophysical environment figured in terms of a quasi-colonial occupation effected by visual control over a small piece of land awash in a vast ocean. Indeed, the entire play can be construed as an examination of competing definitions of land ownership as the basis for political authority. The plot of the play is driven by characters' attempts to master the terrain of the island. Prospero, Sycorax, Caliban, and the drunken mutineers Stephano and Trinculo all strive for ownership and control of the ground that saves them from the encircling and tempestuous sea.

Consider the Crab

Multiple tensions—between the natural and the supernatural, seawater and the seafloor, solid-matter versus fungible bodies—animate Ariel's song, which exquisitely captures the fantastical nature of the sea:

> Full fathom five thy father lies
> Of his bones are coral made
> Those are pearls that were his eyes
> Nothing of him that doth fade
> But doth suffer a sea-change
> Into something rich and strange
> (Sea-nymphs hourly ring his knell;
> Hark! I hear them, ding-dong bell).

Here the ready availability of the sea to evoke the twofold mystery of mortality and mutability is its chief aesthetic appeal. These lines capture the strangeness of the sea in the indeterminate nouns and syntactic suspension that give the song its otherworldly quality. "Nothing of him that doth fade" provides no clear referent, while the following two lines, "But doth suffer a sea-change / Into something rich and strange," resist clarity by pivoting between an invented nominalization, "sea-change," and an equally vague noun phrase, "something rich and strange." "Nothing" becomes "something" by way of a "sea-change," none of which stands on solid ground. The protean materiality of water becomes the stuff of language itself. Like the allegedly drowned king, an ineffable "something" that "fades" into otherworldliness while undergoing a benthic metamorphosis, the ditty is imbued with a murky fungibility.

As scholars such as Peter Hulme have observed, in *The Tempest* the notion of a sea change pertains to the human interaction with the marine environment on an individual and a historical level.[28] Not only were European habits of representing oceanic space transforming at a rapid pace in the sixteenth and seventeenth centuries, it was the sea that lay behind the transformation of the European world picture. The discovery of a vast global ocean was the condition of possibility for reconceptualizing the globe as an aquatic ball instead of an enclosed garden.

Many readers have remarked on the note of epochal change in Ariel's song, as if the sprite were singing not merely to one character about a local event, but to all of humanity of our condition of disorientation on a blue planet that we are perpetually in the act of discovering.[29] Whatever the documentary sources that fired Shakespeare's imagination about a magical island somewhere between the old world and the new, the playwright incorporated elements from various maritime locales—the Grand Banks of Newfoundland, Patagonia, the Bermudian islands—inaccessible to Europeans until at least the fifteenth century, locales that were only accessible by sea. Thus, Ariel's song stages the incorporation of the global ocean into the European imaginary as the aesthetics of the illusory, putting the disorienting power of art on display.[30] For the song misrepresents the fate of the Neapolitan king by exploiting his son's uncertain condition. The strangeness of the ditty, derived from its oceanic aesthetic effects, is a feature of Prospero's art: his thaumaturgy resides in the manipulation of natural phenomena, and his most spectacular tricks involve the sea. His agent Ariel is most at home in the fluid media of air and water, capable of shaping both with a magic at once pyrotechnic and aquatic.

Ariel's song enacts a carefully orchestrated coup d'état in which nature itself is enlisted for political purposes; it cannot help but evoke historical questions about the European ventures at sea in early modernity. The dramatic irony here—we know Alonso is high and dry elsewhere on the island—is heightened by the fact that Ariel's song is used as a magic charm, the performance of an illusion. Here the illusion is acoustic, not visual, and one that resides in the aquatic indeterminacy of the verses. Ariel *performs* this strangeness, exploiting the magical alterity of the maritime context in a disorienting aesthetic ruse and thereby suggesting that what happens on the seafloor is nearly impossible to fathom.[31] Ferdinand, the song's immediate audience, ultimately finds himself, Miranda, and his father again on the same shore where he imagines himself to be wrecked. The nature of this sea change is, if not providential, then at least benevolent. It is also illusory. Everything solid melts into air—or water, that denser fluid medium. Prospero acknowledges, in the end, that he is himself implicated in his creature's oceanic identity.

The sea is a transformative force in *The Tempest*, yet we know when viewing or reading the play that Prospero is behind the apparent tempest and the illusory wreck of the Neapolitan flagship. His control over winds and waves might be read as a prefiguration of the anthropogenic transformation of the global ocean; it certainly represents a European fantasy of mastery over nature. Mentz argues that "Ariel's 'sea-change' imagines the early modern sea astride the boundary between natural and supernatural" in part owing to the fact that "seventeenth-century English culture was in the early stages of the empirical and rational relationship to the natural world we call 'scientific,' but the sea remained the most magical part of nature."[32] Then as now, the sea is uncertain epistemological ground, bearing the potential to destabilize empirical claims and overturn positivistic definitions of nature.

Rob Watson makes much the same point about the nature of nature more generally in *Back to Nature*, arguing that nature was a slippery conceptual category and contentious issue in early modern culture. Watson claims that in the period he calls the late Renaissance, "the nostalgia for unmediated contact with the world of nature" was produced by "anxieties about mediation and the lost sensual past." Rapid historical and epistemological changes caused by "urbanization, capitalism, new technologies, and the Protestant Reformation," he argues,

> were already provoking skeptical critiques that alienated humanity from nature and discerned a fundamental indeterminacy in reality. The pursuit of empirical science forced one set of prominent Renaissance thinkers to confront epistemological doubts, while the . . . upheaval associated with Renaissance humanism threatened to produce a cognitive crisis among another set of thinkers by revealing that the world is less observed than constructed.[33]

This discussion helps us frame the coastal setting of *The Tempest*, for the empirical unavailability of marine phenomena—in Ferdinand's case, what happens on the seafloor—is a spectacular aesthetic instance of Watson's "fundamental indeterminacy." Indeed, Shakespeare consistently depicts the natural world as something "less observed than constructed," particularly where the sea is concerned. This is one lesson to be gleaned from Ariel's song and Prospero's magic: the sea casts a spell of strangeness that can be harnessed to produce magical effects, but that magic is itself a product of occultation. Ferdinand never sees his father's corpse; he only hears it described. Alonso never sees his son die; he only assumes he has, and only when he turns his back to the sea.

Consistent with the characterization of the ocean as a hostile void in biblical and classical culture (discussed in the previous chapter), the historian Alain Corbin has argued that the predominant early modern response to the seashore was one of horror and disgust mixed with a kind a lurid fascination, locating the genesis of this affective nexus in the biblical characterization of "the deep" as an ungodly (or pre-Jehovan) chaos diametrically (and perhaps dialectically) opposed to the "firmament" of creation:

> The ocean was [for premodern Europeans] the remnant of that undifferentiated primordial substance on which form had to be imposed so that it might become part of Creation. This realm of the unfinished, a vibrating, vague extension of chaos, symbolized the disorder that preceded civilization. A firm belief began to appear which held that already in antediluvian times, it was only with difficulty that the raging ocean could be contained within its bounds. Consequently, the ocean inspired a deep sense of repulsion.[34]

Corbin goes on to examine how the repulsion toward an inchoate element (the sea) and an indeterminate and often dangerous border (the coast) becomes, between the late sixteenth and eighteenth centuries, a source of fascination that eventually leads to a vogue of seaside vacationing, bathing, early beach culture, and marine art. The transformation in the cultural status of the seaside (and what lay beyond it) from the site of abomination to a place of aesthetic pleasure begins in the growing empiricism of representations of maritime space: Europeans at the shore found much to provoke the sense of wonder, and that wonder eventually turned to pleasure.

The historical transformation of coastal space from abomination to site of fascination traced by Corbin is a conspicuous feature of *The Tempest*, a play that both exploits and contests traditional constructions of the sea and the shore as monstrous and horrifying spaces inhabited by strange and hideous creatures, offering not an "ecophobic" vision of the marine environment as we might expect (given the claims of Corbin), but instead a terraqueous ecopolitics of indeterminacy and hybridity.[35] At times the poet depicts the ocean as a wild realm lying at the margins of civilization, suspended between the natural and the supernatural; at others the sea is, like the woods and wastes, a stark worldly reality—threatening, alluring, and largely unknown—lying just beyond the bounds of civilization (the city walls, the island nation). The aesthetics of indeterminacy and ontological hybridity characterize Caliban, an abominable creature (to his captors) of the strand who inspires repulsion and fascination, embodying what is strange about the seashore. His moral status remains at the heart of the scholarly discussion. The evocation of a human figure transformed by marine agency takes quasi-human form in a character whose initial impression recapitulates the idea of "something rich and strange"; Caliban is an ontologically indeterminate yet sensually powerful presence on the beach. Stranded by his European captors in a condition of servitude, he is also a kind of strand-dwelling (and beachcombing) merman, an apparently semihuman creature of the beach. In a rather burlesque way, he embodies what is alluring and baffling about the play's maritime setting.

The jester Trinculo, taking cover from the squally weather under Caliban's cloak, exclaims, "What have we here, a man or a fish? Dead or alive?— A fish, he smells like a fish . . . A strange fish!" (2.2.23–25). In repeating the adjective *strange*, a pivotal term in Ariel's song, Trinculo does more than merely emphasize Caliban's foreignness; the word that describes the seafloor here implies that Caliban is a conceptually foreign being belonging not to any recognizable civilization but to the maritime landscape. Consistent with the constant animalization of Caliban in the text (he is called "fish," "monster," "beast," "tortoise," and "devil"), Trinculo's first encounter with him on the beach suggests that he is a kind of washed-up merman.[36] Caliban is famously described in the Folio's cast of characters as a "salvage and deformed slave," which as many have noted defines him as savage or untamed. His strangeness inheres in the semantic overtones of the term *salvage*, which meant more than just an uncivilized creature. Derived from the Latin term for a wood or forest (*silvius*), "salvage" could be used to describe a landscape, an animal, or a human cast loose from society. The term is etymologically linked to the wild and, thus, to the *weald*, or *wold* (wood), a term that denoted not only woodlands but other kinds of undomesticated landscape.[37]

Caliban is, in short, quite wild—in a distinctly salty way; he is a sea creature cast upon shore and subject to an ocean of hungry colonists. From the perspective of Prospero and Miranda he is untamed, uncouth, and unrepentant, yet he forces them to reconsider their own occupation of the island. In his ontological association with the island landscape, he is a rather soggy instance of the wodewose, or man of the wood, who turns his back on civilization and thereby develops the ability to speak truth to power. Robert Pogue Harrison argues that these are the defining characteristics of a long line of characters who revert to a savage or outlaw state and in so doing occasionally discover a higher justice—natural law, the law of the forest— than what is available to the denizens of the court or the city.[38] Like Robin

Hood and other medieval and Renaissance literary outlaws who take to the woods, Caliban is scorned by those in power (particularly in the play itself) and revered by those on the side of emancipatory politics (particularly in the history of the play's reception). Yet the term *salvage* also suggests that he is a perpetual stranger, a piece of existential flotsam and a creature without a stable origin or home.

The *OED* lists 1645 as the earliest date for the use of "salvage" or "silvage" to mean "a payment or compensation to which those persons are entitled who have by their voluntary efforts saved a ship or cargo from impending peril or rescued it from actual loss; e.g. from shipwreck or from capture by the enemy." It is at least possible that the term's field of meaning could have encompassed this sense in a play written thirty-five years before. Caliban's wildness—his willful behavior as well as his status as a stranger to the imposed civilization of the Italian occupiers—is everywhere emphasized. As Alden Vaughan and Virginia Mason Vaughan note, "Each age has appropriated and reshaped him to suit its needs and assumptions, for Caliban's image has been incredibly flexible, ranging from an aquatic beast to a noble savage, with innumerable intermediate manifestations."[39] It would be strange indeed not to trace the genealogy of such a shape-shifter to a classical sea god, Proteus, or to medieval myths of mermaids and mermen.

As Prospero's "creature" who is, ultimately, redeemed ("This thing of darkness I acknowledge mine"), Caliban's condition is to be salvaged by the European occupier of his island (5.1.277–78).[40] His ontology is, etymologically and culturally, both maritime and wild, and his transformation from a speechless antagonist to an acknowledged "thing of darkness" makes him a politically fraught embodiment of the sea's strangeness. Perhaps the best explanation for the enduring scholarly debate over Caliban's existential provenance—whether Patagonian, Bermudian, Algerian, or otherwise—would be his existence as a hybrid product of the emergent modern world-system produced by European efforts to master the global ocean. Whether "aquatic beast" or New World indigene, Caliban is defined by an ontological hybridity whose condition of possibility is the sea.[41] Caliban's hybridity extends to his relationship to the coastal ecosystem he inhabits. Is he a sea creature or a creature of the land? Perhaps, like a crab, he is something of both.

I would like to end this chapter the way it began—with some observations on crabs. Here, however, I am not interested in literal crabs such as *Hemigrapsus* but in more elusive textual ones that might not even be crusta-

Consider the Crab

cean in nature. In Act 2, Caliban promises to reveal the gustatory delicacies of the island to his newfound "master," the tippling butler Stephano, in a passage laden with terms that have baffled readers and editors for centuries:

> I prithee, let me bring thee where crabs grow,
> And I with my long nails will dig thee pignuts;
> Show thee a jay's nest and instruct thee
> How to snare the nimble marmoset; I'll bring thee
> To clustering filberts and sometimes I'll get thee
> Young scamels from the rock. Wilt thou go with me? (2.2.1253–58)

The physical detail with which Caliban describes how he "will with [his] nails dig pignuts for you" evokes hunter-gatherers as well as primal tilth. The imagery of long-nailed fingers pulling sustenance from earth is particularly striking in a play that begins amid storm-tossed waters and shifting sands. Caliban earns the sobriquet hurled at him by an angry Prospero, "Thou earth, thou!" In his proximity to the island's obscure provender he becomes something more than just a slave—he is a native species. Or is he the offspring of a prior bioinvasion?

The local foods that Caliban enumerates are famously indeterminate, their nature as strange and unclear as the island's geography. What kind of land is this, and what is the nature of its fruits? The question of whether "scamels" derives from a compositor's error for "sea-mew," meaning seagull, or some obscure vegetable produce has long been a textual crux. Part of the import of this question—I don't have a simple answer—pertains to determining just how carnivorous Shakespeare wishes Caliban to appear. "A monster half-fish, half flesh," he is both an earthy creature and a fishy one, ontologically proximate to animals and part of a local food web that he wishes to introduce to his liberators at the moment he imagines being freed from the Milanese tyrant he serves.[42] His visceral description of gathering food is a key part of his characterization as an island indigene. If we read his reference to "crabs" in light of this imagery, the crabs would seem to be located, like the pignuts, on the ground or just under its surface—not on trees cultivated for their fruit. Moreover, the wild harvest he describes is part of the coastal topography of a thoroughly marine environment. The ambiguity of the terminology with which he describes food gathering raises important questions. Does he intend to lead Stephano into an edenic interior replete with trees laden with forbidden fruit, or are the fruits of the island part of the intertidal zone where all of the action up to this point in the play has transpired? Is Caliban promising the newly masterless Europeans a salad of wild produce for a mostly vegetarian palate, or is he serving up mixed meats—the nutmeat of filberts and pignuts, the flesh of marmosets and scamels (most likely avian), and the meat of intertidal crabs? It is this last question that I would like to entertain here.

What is the nature of Caliban's crabs? Are they to be found "grow[ing]" on trees located on higher ground, or do they "grow" under intertidal rocks? Do they belong to the animal kingdom or the vegetable? Do they have claws and an exoskeleton or skin and sour flesh? Shakespeare refers to crabs of both varieties, animal and vegetable, more than a dozen times in his oeuvre. It is clear in some instances that he means the sour apples that were eaten roasted or boiled; in at least one instance he means the marine crustacean proverbial for peevishness and walking sideways (also eaten roasted or boiled). Yet in some instances he seems to mean both kinds of crab, using the word to describe any ill-natured character, but even that association fails to differentiate animal from vegetable, for both are notable—and were, in early modern Europe, proverbial—for their ability to pinch. Sour crab apples cause the eater's mouth to pucker, while sharp claws could lacerate flesh or sever a digit; both had antisocial connotations. Both kinds of crab were common foods in early seventeenth-century England, the one harvested in green fields and the other on the coast. Making this ambiguity all the more tantalizing is the recent archaeological evidence from Southwark indicating that the animal variety of crab was a popular snack at the open-air theaters.[43] Fishwives and apple-wives were frequently mentioned in late-Elizabethan and Jacobean plays, and theater historians teach us that both made up a sizable percentage of audiences at the open-air theaters, where fishmongers and costermongers plied their wares. For a playwright much given to metatheatrical gestures, to mention crabs would seem to strengthen the case for the topicality of the crustaceans.[44]

When it comes to decoding Shakespeare's crabs, then, clearly we are not out of the woods—indeed we may be deep within them (or all at sea, which may amount to much the same thing). In some of Shakespeare's metaphors the two kinds of crab are strangely indistinguishable. What is consistent, however, is Shakespeare's tendency to link crabbiness with human life: crabs symbolize a limited set of associations based on their physical qualities.

Consider the Crab

Only the crustacean was known for its peculiar form of locomotion: as much as their tendency to pinch, they were useful symbols for walking backwards. (Prince Hamlet invokes these qualities when he mocks Polonius's old age.) In *The Tempest* it is the European overlords, not the crabs gathered by their salvage subject, who are the invasive organisms in a brave new coastal ecosystem. A crabby subaltern himself, Caliban shares an obscure kinship with the other denizens of his environment. By imagining a "creature" whose salvage ontology puts into question the relationship between colonialism, invasive species, and both marine and terrestrial ecosystems, Shakespeare offers a terraqueous model for conceptualizing the biophysical environment, a space where "the hungry ocean" is conspicuously part of "the kingdom of the shore."

3

Shakespeare's Benthic Imagination

> Heave him away upon your winged thoughts Athwart the sea.
> SHAKESPEARE, *Henry V*

European intellectuals and artists have long employed the metaphor of human life as a sea voyage. Embarkation, passage, and shipwreck have long been popular topoi for the vicissitudes of human existence. In the sixteenth century the classical metaphor "the ship of state" gained new currency as the fates of European nation-states turned increasingly on sea power. Five hundred years later the metaphor remains alive. In the second half of the twentieth century the German philosopher Hans Blumenberg argued, perhaps hyperbolically, that "humans live their lives and build their institutions on dry land. Nevertheless, they seek to grasp the movement of their existence above all through a metaphorics of the perilous sea voyage."[1] Whether or not we accept the universality of such a claim, the sea voyage provides a powerful metaphor for thinking about the trajectory of a human life.

Literature scholars likewise see the voyage of life as a powerful and ubiquitous metaphor. Philip Edwards has called "the traditional metaphor of the voyage" across the water "perhaps the commonest metaphor in literature, going back beyond Horace ... and going on beyond Hardy's 'Convergence of the Twain.'"[2] It would be a surprise, then, if William Shakespeare did not employ this readily available topos—as indeed he does. Shakespeare imagines the ocean as (1) a mirror of human ontology, culture, and civilization; (2) the space of transit, an undomesticated boundary between realms, a threat to cosmic and social order; (3) the arena of providence; and (4) a transitional space between the supernatural and the protoscientific. Sea voyages occur frequently in Shakespeare's plays; these voyages offer a latent challenge to the idea of a terrestrial human ontology. Shakespeare's characters traverse the waters, become wrecked (literally and metaphorically), are immersed, lost, and washed ashore. In the elegant words of Steve Mentz, "Human bodies plunge into hostile seas, and poetic forms attempt their salvage" in the Bard's works.[3] In the last chapter I played on this formulation by suggesting that, for Shakespeare, to be alive on this planet is to be a kind of ontological salvage—in both early modern senses of the term. *Salvage* (from Sp. *salvaje*) meant savage; at some point in the seventeenth century it came to mean redeemed flotsam as well. Characters who embark upon the ocean often get lost and rediscover themselves as salvage, or salvaged, beings. In this chapter I examine the role of sea voyages, both horizontal excursions across the surface and vertical passages into the depths, in the figurative construction of what I call an "oceanic subjectivity" throughout Shakespeare's dramatic corpus.

The wildness—danger mixed with uncontainable slipperiness—that characterizes Shakespeare's ocean is nothing new, derived as it is from Western culture's earliest narratives and intricately linked to the sea's construction as an entity that exists outside of time. Shakespeare's representation of the ocean as a vast blue wilderness follows religious and cultural tradition, portraying it as an ancient, chaotic, and dangerous entity set off from civilization and distinct from the "firmament" established by the logos. At the same time that Shakespeare employs this construction of the chaotic deep, however, he also talks back to it, reimagining and reshaping the traditions he exploits for his imagery. The result is a strange brew: the aesthetic appeal of the protean depths contains the potential for a "brave new world" in which human life and marine life harmonize in new ways (*The Tempest*, 5.1.186). The cultural construction of the sea as a wilderness derives partially from longstanding cultural habits of describing the ocean as a realm that stands outside of time, a point that Patton emphasizes in her encompassing account of spiritual and literal pollution in various global religious cosmogonies: "As is often the case with other primordial forces in myth, Ocean is construed as wild, unruly, and undifferentiated because it is (constructed as being) timeless. Its chaotic nature is somehow implied by the facts of its endless past and equally endless future. Apparently nothing so old can be imagined as ordered."[4] Traditionally constructed as an ahistorical realm of lateral and vertical passages in Western culture, the ocean—much like the desert and the forest—has long been perceived as a quintessentially wild space, dangerous, foreign, untamable, and inimical to the more domestic notion of place.[5]

Pulled between the mythopoetic ocean of biblical and classical culture and the emergent empirical sciences, Shakespeare consistently depicts the ocean as a strange, wild realm lying between the natural and the supernatural. The earliest plays and the latest seem especially preoccupied with the role of the sea in disrupting the plans of those in power. In the late plays, diverse characters mingle on a briny commons, accidents happen, characters go overboard (literally and figuratively), lives and families are blown off course, plans founder, and providence becomes manifest. In the romances, with their incessant saltwater voyages and thematic preoccupation with storms, shipwrecks, and providence, the sea catalyzes the action and provides a reservoir of metaphor for reflecting on the contingencies of human life. Humans are not entirely at home there, and in venturing upon the waters or merely imagining the depths, characters are confronted with the question of how to conceive of their place on this blue planet. Their fate often turns on passages across the waters, while the theological overtones of the deep provide somber atmospherics.

The view of human life as an extended voyage is prevalent in the plays with Mediterranean settings. In a famous speech in *Julius Caesar*, Brutus refers to "the affairs of men" as "all the voyage of their life," articulating a version of the classical ship of state topos in terms of individual lives (4.3.2229, 2231). In *The Comedy of Errors*, also set in the Mediterranean, Egeon, whose name suggests an existential connection to the Aegean Sea, refers to "the always-wind-obeying deep," personifying the ocean and ascribing an agency to it that will appear time and again in passages throughout the rest of Shakespeare's career (1.1.63). In the same play, Antipholus of Syracuse likens human life to "a drop of rain" engulfed in the ocean; he does so in a manner that differs markedly from biblical and classical precedent as well as from Romantic and post-Romantic effusions about the sea's ineffable sublimity. Salt water and human life are mutually determining. The Syracusan Antipholus soliloquizes:

> I to the world am like a drop of water
> That in the ocean seeks another drop,
> Who, falling there to find his fellow forth,

> Unseen, inquisitive, confounds himself.
> So I, to find a mother, and a brother,
> In quest of them, unhappy, lose myself. (1.2.35–40)

The idea of the self as a drop lost in a greater body of water is the source of fear and anxiety: jumping in, he worries, he will be like a drop of water that "confounds" or destroys itself utterly. In *The Comedy of Errors* the ocean is intricately involved in human history. A force of change, separation, and reunion, its briny power both threatens human life and offers the potential for rediscovery and renewal.

Nautical metaphors appear at unlikely moments in the tragedies, often to liken human existence to a sea voyage. In a soliloquy on the eve of Duncan's murder, Macbeth employs the imagery of fishing and navigation to describe his anxieties about regicide, dimly foreseeing in his imagining that the consequences of the crime, an act he himself understands to be unnatural, will be of oceanic enormity:

> If it were done when 'tis done, then 'twere well
> It were done quickly. If th'assassination
> Could trammel up the consequence, and catch
> With his surcease success: that but this blow
> Might be the be-all and the end-all, here,
> But here upon this bank and shoal of time,
> We'd jump the life to come. (1.7.1–7)

The nautical imagery, "here upon this bank and shoal of time," gestures to the ubiquitous sea voyage topos, for Macbeth is embarking on dangerous but also potentially productive waters: in killing Duncan, figured here as an act of existential fishing, he has much to gain and everything to lose. A mariner in his own mind, Macbeth has run aground upon "this bank and shoal of time." Here a human figure casting a net into the sea of time becomes a trope for radical alienation. A trammel was a net commonly used for fishing and birding. Used as a verb—"trammel up the consequence"—it suggests an attempt to capture the results of one's own actions, as if the future could be quarry.

Reinforcing the maritime metaphors in this passage, the language Macbeth employs upon accomplishing the murder is even more vividly oceanic: "Will all great Neptune's ocean wash this blood / Clean from my hand? No, this my hand will rather / The multitudinous seas incarnadine, / Making the green one red" (2.2.58–60). Here the playwright imagines seawater in vital colors, green and red, and he also imagines its transformation from one to the other by human means. When Shakespeare penned such lines as these he could not have had in mind the anthropogenic impacts on marine ecosystems that I have discussed in the opening chapters of this book. Nevertheless, the suggestion that human hands can change the color of the "multitudinous seas" from green to red gives us a striking image of human agency affecting the global ocean. Even if such a transformation is cast as impossible, it is undeniably evoked, articulating a spatial relationship between human life and the untamable ocean. Characters in Shakespeare who find themselves in terribly difficult circumstances, like Titus, Macbeth, Lear, and Hamlet, often describe their own circumstances in maritime imagery, and they do so with striking vividness.

Beleaguered characters also not infrequently escape across the water and return that way as well. In *The Winter's Tale* the Mediterranean functions as both a barrier and a means of connection between far-flung characters and locales. Camillo's fear that Perdita and Florizel are embarking on "a wild dedication of yourselves / To unpathed waters, undreamed shores" paints the sea as a pathless region and expresses fear of straying from customary routes (4.4.554–55). Setting sail is a "wild" thing to do, and the young lovers, it is implied, are acting willfully by embarking offshore. The sea is a force and a space where their own wildness finds some kind of resonance with the watery wilderness on which they embark. This is consistent with descriptions of the ocean throughout Shakespeare: the "wild ocean" is invoked in *The Two Gentlemen of Verona*, and in *Henry V* it is called "the wild and wasteful ocean." Robert Macfarlane's explanation of the etymological connection between wildness and willfulness is particularly suggestive here:

> The etymology of the word "wild" is vexed and subtle, but the most persuasive past proposed for it involves the Old High German *wildi*, and the Old Norse *villr*, as well as the pre-Teutonic *ghweltijos*. All three of these terms carry implications of disorder and irregularity, and . . . they bequeathed to the English root-word "will" "a descriptive meaning of . . . willful, or uncontrollable." Wildness, according to this etymology, is an expression of independence for human direction, and wild land can be said to be *self-willed* land.[6]

Shakespeare's Benthic Imagination

The wildness of the watery path that Perdita and Florizel will take has an ontological component: their embarkation indulges an inner willfulness. Their willingness to transgress Polixenes' proscription of their love is literalized when they give themselves over to an uncontrollable element that matches their own condition. The sea becomes the objective correlative of their willful, desiring state of being.

In literally or figuratively running away to sea, Shakespeare's characters often acquire a kind of psychosocial depth not unlike what happens to his characters who retreat to the woods. In this, Shakespeare's ocean resembles Robert Pogue Harrison's description of the forest as a space that mirrors and shadows the constructs of humanity, perpetually challenging our definitions of nature and culture and compelling us to rethink and redraw the line between the two.[7] Unlike the forest, however, the global ocean is not integral to the symbolic and literal construction of civilization but genuinely marginal, a borderland that defines the *eschatia*—the spatial, conceptual, and spiritual limit—of the social order. Like the forests in Harrison's study of medieval and early modern European literature, Shakespeare's ocean is a "landscape," albeit of a peculiar blue-green, a feature of the physical environment that is real and imagined, preexisting and constructed, natural and anthropogenic. Like the woods in Dante and Spenser, the sea in Shakespeare constitutes a contingent wildness always susceptible to paradox, reversal, and transformation. The sea is a space of invisibility and unknowing, where the limitations of sight undermine epistemological certainty; its reaches belong to the epistemological limits, lying beyond the conceptual pale but exercising a powerful influence on human life.

Shakespeare's sea voyages are frequently imagined as horizontal passages that emblematize the life trajectories of such characters as Egeon, Ferdinand, Miranda, Florizel, Desdemona, and Othello; other characters, however, notably embark on vertical passages, moving down from the surface—the region of life and light—to the depths, where death holds sway. It is the second kind of voyage that I turn to here, for the aesthetic allure of the depths complicates and deepens our understanding of how Shakespeare and his contemporaries set about fathoming (both measuring and understanding) the figurative possibilities of the sea.

The Greek word for the bottom of the sea, *benthos*, is used in the marine sciences to describe marine life on the seafloor; benthic organisms live and feed at the bottom of the water column. The historian of science Helen

Rozwadowski notes that "before the last quarter of the eighteenth century, understanding of the ocean's depths derived mostly from the imagination."[8] Shakespeare's imagination was drawn to the bottom of the ocean throughout his career, perhaps because the benthic realm lacks visual accessibility, and in this it is a challenge and a barrier, a geographical mystery and a license to invent. The depths represent an otherness that cannot be intellectually or linguistically domesticated; they are "wild" in the etymological sense. They are also profoundly related to human life.

I call Shakespeare's penchant for imagining the depths and for bringing the reader into their murky otherworldliness his "benthic imagination," which is frequently signaled by two terms, *sounding* and *fathoming*, that the playwright employed often to describe the human relationship to the ocean. Shakespeare employed both words in the literal sense to refer to the measurement of the depth of a body of water; he also uses them in the abstract sense of attaining understanding or conceptual mastery. How do we fathom that which is fathomless? How grasp that which is unavailable to the senses? Shakespeare turns to the ocean to interrogate human efforts to fathom the natural world, offering a poetics of the seafloor that can be seen as an instance of figurative technology. His many references to fathoming and sounding suggest an analogy between the act of literally measuring the depths and *poesis*, the act of making what is discovered resonant in figurative language. For Shakespeare, poetry performs a technological function which, if not quite exactly analogous to the depth-measurement today done by side-scan sonar and Doppler radar, nevertheless attempts to take the measure of the ocean.[9]

Fathoming, the act of measuring the depths (known in the sailor's idiom as "taking soundings")—so often evoked in Shakespearean drama—suggests a profound conceptual link between human life and the sea. The playwright exploits the semantic resonances of sounding and fathoming, verbs central to early modern navigation, to create a consistent association between human encounters with the sea, epistemology, and ontology. Derived from an Old English word for "the embracing arms," the ancient form of the word *fathom* encompassed the notion of "grasp, power" as well as "the object of embrace." The infinitive "to fathom" connects physical reach (the length of a person's two outstretched arms) with conceptual grasp or understanding. The *OED* cites Shakespeare for coining the use of *fathom* in the abstract, to mean "understanding," in *Othello*: "Another of his fathom they have none /

Shakespeare's Benthic Imagination

To lead their business" (1.1.153–54). *Sounding*, a word that shares much with *fathoming* in its maritime meaning and poetic resonance, is defined as "ascertaining the depth of water by means of the line and lead or (now usu.) by means of echo; an instance of this" (*OED*).

Early modern navigators relied on the use of the lead line, a length of cord with a weight or plummet attached, to find their way in coastal waters. John Locke described the use of the lead line in *An Essay Concerning Human Understanding*: "'Tis of great use to the Sailor to know the length of his Line, though he cannot with it fathom all the depths of the Ocean. 'Tis well he knows, that it is long enough to reach the bottom, at such Places, as are necessary to direct his Voyage, and caution him against running upon Shoals, that may ruin him."[10] The lead line was an essential piece of equipment for sixteenth- and seventeenth-century mariners. For writers and intellectuals it provided a wonderful metaphor for the limits of the human grasp of the physical world. The frontispiece of *The Mariners Mirrour* clearly demonstrates the centrality of the lead line for sailors (see figure 1, also discussed in the introduction). Flanking the title page are two mariners, both with lead lines coiled in one arm and a plummet hanging approximately a fathom and a half from the other hand toward the sea's surface beneath them. Beneath the mariners' feet, symmetrically placed on each side of the page, are dividers and a compass adjacent to the pendant plummet. Above the figures and in the center five men and a boy peer intently at a large globe, which is conspicuously blank (perhaps awaiting their cartographic labors), while the arts of cosmography and cartography are emblematized by a sky map on one side of them and a world map on the other. Hanging from a quadrant in both upper corners is an astrolabe; beneath each of these is a pendant weight. In the foreground is a full-rigged ship (a carrack) bowling along in a fair breeze under the main and fore courses (the largest and lowest square sails).

The importance of the lead line in early modern navigation can hardly be overstated. Drawing on contemporary navigational writings such as *The Mariners Mirrour* and Sir Henry Mainwaring's *Life and Works*, Falconer explains the use of the lead line: "On 'coming into soundings,' that is, on reaching water of a hundred fathoms or less, the mariner had to look out for dangers from rocks, shoals and currents, and had to try the depth of water and find the nature of the ground for, 'according to the depth and ground.... when we can see no land yet we know where we are.'"[11] Depths could be measured in fathoms by a line cast off a vessel's bow and then measured or "told" by reading the fathom marks close to shore; those farther out were "fathomless." While the idea of measuring depth is manifest at a glance, less obvious is the fact that soundings were a crucial means of ascertaining location. Medieval and early modern mariners found their way in coastal waters by sampling the seafloor with a smear of tallow on the plummet. Sailors determined their location on a known coast by keeping track of soundings to form a mental picture of the underwater topography—the threatening "shelves and sands" in *The Rape of Lucrece* indicate two kinds of seafloor—and also by sampling the materials picked up on the plummet (especially useful in fog). Thus, long before the development of sophisticated means of ascertaining longitude, orientation at sea was a function of vertical measurement—at least in the waters above the continental shelf that borders the continents and major islands of the world. Benthic sampling provided empirical evidence of what lay on the bottom of the sea and clues to a mariner's location on the vast blue plain that encircles the globe.

The ubiquity of the lead line in any kind of coastal navigation inevitably caught the attention of our playwright. When Edgar, as Tom o'Bedlam, shouts, "Fathom and half, fathom and half!" in *King Lear* (3.4.38), he plays the part of the "leadsman"—a mariner standing in the bows and throwing a lead line ahead of a vessel—who indicates a depth of nine feet. The language of soundings is not just incidental. The imagery of sounding the depths partakes of an elaborate thematic structure in which balanced social relations—between aristocrats, peasants, kings, and subjects—are a matter of environmental justice. This is also the case in *Richard II*, which contains a striking instance of the playwright's benthic imagination. In the first scene the king employs a striking metaphor in demanding of Gaunt, "Tell me, moreover, *hast thou sounded him*, / If he appeal the Duke on ancient malice, / Or worthily, as a good subject should, / On some *known ground* of treachery in him?" (1.1.8–11; emphasis added). Here the king uses the language of navigation to ask if Gaunt has measured the depth of Bolingbroke's claims against Mowbray. "Hast thou sounded him?" The monarch's question depicts Bolingbroke as a body of water and the questioning as casting the lead line. For this metaphor to work, the vehicle must be conceptually available to playgoers—much less certain today than it was for Shakespeare. While the tenor of Richard's metaphor is immediately apparent, less obvious is the specificity of the historical practice on which the vehicle depends. Not only does the metaphor suggest that the king is uncertain of the depths, it also implies that he is quite lost—all at sea—and on a voyage that will end in shipwreck.

In using the language of soundings Richard emphasizes his own wish to get to the bottom of things, to find the "known ground" on the coast of his own realm where soundings can be taken and deeper waters left behind. The search for evidence of any "known ground of treachery in him [Mowbray]" thus describes both litigants in the language of coastal navigation. The litigants Bolingbroke and Mowbray are figuratively on the edge of the kingdom, and their condition is to be navigated by throwing the lead line of courtly custom into the ocean of their souls. Yet providing a context that helps to explain a metaphor only takes us so far in our reading of this scene. The evocation of the seafloor contributes to the theme of territorial mastery in a play that justifies the accusation that the monarch is "landlord, not king." By conjuring up the image of the bottom of the sea, Richard's appeal to a ground of knowledge modulates into questions about loyalty to the kingdom that implicate the king himself. The "known ground of treachery" that the king invokes foregrounds the problem of knowing and managing the land, a kingly role that Richard consistently botches. He is, ultimately, responsible for the murder of Gloucester and for the kind of financial mismanagement of which Mowbray stands accused. Figuratively, Richard does a poor job as captain of the ship of state; he is also a poor navigator, for he fails to keep a good reckoning of what his lead line brings up from the depths.

The association of king, subject, and the depths takes a different form in *Richard III* where Shakespeare imagines the bottom of the sea as a benthic mingling of death, wealth, the natural, and the supernatural. Clarence has a vision of the deep that emphasizes the sea's intense combination of strangeness and lethal power:

> As we paced along
> Upon the giddy footing of the hatches,
> Methought that Gloucester stumbled, and in falling
> Struck me—that sought to stay him—overboard
> Into the tumbling billows of the main. (1.4.16–20)

Clarence frames his nightmare vision of what lies on the seafloor in terms of "the giddy footing" of a pitching deck. He likens himself to the standing rigging that holds up a mast—he seeks to "stay" Gloucester, appropriately enough since the latter is known by the nickname "Crooked Dick" and presumably could use some stays and shrouds to straighten him—and in so doing is sent overboard to a watery grave. Neither he nor we are on solid ground in this description, and no amount of contextual background can put us on an even keel. The bottom of the sea as it is figured in Clarence's prophetic dream is a benthic mix of the natural and the supernatural.

In the richly descriptive passage that follows we are transported downward through the water column to depths characterized by an eerie mix of the lethal and the alluring:

> O Lord! Methought what pain it was to drown,
> What dreadful noise of waters in my ears,
> What sights of ugly death within my eyes.
> Methoughts I saw a thousand fearful wrecks,
> Ten thousand men that fishes gnawed upon,
> Wedges of gold, great ouches, heaps of pearl,
> Inestimable stones, unvalued jewels,
> All scattered in the bottom of the sea.
> Some lay in dead men's skulls; and in those holes
> Where eyes did once inhabit, there were crept—
> As 'twere in scorn of eyes—reflecting gems,
> Which wooed the slimy bottom of the deep
> And mocked the dead bones that lay scattered by. (1.4.21–33)

In this passage the aestheticized depths hold a half horrifying, half mesmerizing mixture of riches and death. Measureless opulence marks a watery graveyard: the corpses on the bottom are not merely adjacent to "wedges of gold, great ouches, heaps of pearl, inestimable stones, unvalued jewels" but are materially tangled up in treasure. Eyes replaced by "reflecting gems" that "wooed the slimy bottom of the deep" evoke a demonic agency, and the whole vision oozes with a glittering alterity. "Inestimable stones" reflect the gaze of the mind's eye so as to mock the desire for visual mastery.

Clarence's dream imagines the seafloor as a graveyard filled with the corpses of drowned sailors and as a crystal ball foreshadowing his own imminent death. His ultimate end in a butt of malmsey seems appropriate enough after the nearly hallucinatory imagery of the benthic realm.[12] Clarence foretells Richard's treachery and bloody career by figuring the usurper's ontological wildness as a form of landlessness; Richard is as anarchic and destructive as the ocean itself, and because of him Clarence will soon join the "ten thousand men that fishes gnawed on." The seafloor here is not a downward limit but a liminal space, for Clarence moves in his dream from a vision of the underwater topography to hell, passing directly through the watery depths to the fiery pit. Blumenberg's notion of the shipwreck as "metaphor for existence" seems particularly germane here, for Clarence's dream asks us to imagine a particularly sophisticated scenario of the "shipwreck with spectator" as an oneiric phantasmagoria of prior shipwrecks, viewed in the mind's eye by a troubled spectator at one remove.

A murky otherwordliness is not all that we encounter in Shakespeare's eerie vision of the deep. In Clarence's dream vision Shakespeare imagines a mutually transformative relationship between humanity and the sea. The landscape of the seafloor is littered, Ozymandias-like, with mementoes of human hubris, "a thousand fearful wrecks" and heaps of unused treasure. The human figures that populate this submarine landscape are in turn being actively transformed by the malign agency of sea creatures gnawing on corpses. Something more than the fate of one character seems to be adumbrated in this description; indeed, the metaphorical resonances of shipwrecks, imagined or imminent, impart a dimension of existential reflection to Clarence's dream. Littered with memento mori, Shakespeare's benthic imagination gives form to the notion of a deep providential reminder of Clarence's butt of malmsey (1.2.146). Clarence's oneiric (and oeniferous) demise is multiply redeemed later in the playwright's career in the thematic association of human existence with sea voyages. The "rotten carcase of a butt" that both threatens to drown Prospero and Miranda and carries them to an unknown shore gives closure to Clarence's nightmare.

The seafloor often symbolizes despair in Shakespeare's works. In tragedies such as *Titus Andronicus* and *Macbeth*, oceanic vastness gives weight to the condition of characters experiencing radical alienation, and the immensity and indifference of the sea are invoked by outcast characters who have sunk to the depths. For instance, when in *Titus Andronicus* the eponymous old soldier finds himself in a desperate and worsening situation, he announces to those loyal to him, "*Terras Astraea reliquit*" (The goddess of justice has forsaken [or abandoned] the world). He then turns to the ocean for imagery with which to express his sense of the futility of human action:

"You, cousins, shall / Go sound the ocean, and cast your nets. / Happily you may catch her in the sea; / Yet there's as little justice as at land" (4.3.4–9). The imagery evokes the sounding of a body of water for a missing person (or corpse). To "cast [one's] nets" or "sound the ocean" in this context is to engage in a futile search for the personified figure of Justice.

For Shakespeare the seafloor is a phantasmagorical place where death, history, and untold riches mingle promiscuously in a murky supernatural ooze. The playwright revisits the bejeweled benthic fate that Clarence imagines in *Richard III* much later in his career, in the first of the romances, *Pericles*, in a passage that evokes a similarly sinister association between death and the depths. In the beautiful lines delivered by the eponymous hero upon learning that the ship's crew wishes to sacrifice his wife's body to propitiate the storm that threatens to sink them, Shakespeare has the Prince of Tyre return to the dazzling seafloor of Clarence's dream, with the addition of a whale:

> Th'unfriendly elements
> Forgot thee utterly, nor have I time
> To give thee hallowed to thy grave, but straight
> Must cast thee, scarcely coffined, in the ooze,
> Where, for a monument upon thye bones
> And aye-remaining lamps, the belching whale
> And humming water must o'erwhelm thy corpse,
> Lying with simple shells. (lines 55–63)

Here the depths are associated with a threateningly large example of marine life, "the belching whale" that will with the "humming water" "o'erwhelm thy corpse." This vivid evocation of the seafloor depicts a realm of sensory overload, a kind of primal chaos that mocks the very idea of a burial monument. It also figures the sea voyage of human life as a vertical passage into the depths.

The allure of the unfathomable and the desire to be either ontologically or epistemologically associated with it—to be profound and unknowable—animates Henry Hotspur's boast, in *I Henry IV*, that he will "dive into the bottom of the deep / Where fathom line could never touch the ground" (1.1.204). Here the hotheaded warrior claims he is capable of a superhuman feat, likening himself to a blue-water navigator jumping "off soundings," or sailing beyond the coastal zone. In putting it thus he boasts of his own courage and claims to be a singularly bold leader. Like a parodic Columbus or a Cabot, Hotspur is eager to proclaim his willingness to leave the epistemological comfort of the shore. Such passages are numerous and form a large body of allusion to early modern navigators. Hotspur's tendency to construe cartography too literally makes him look foolish, yet elsewhere, the same impulse is an index of a character's sagacity—or even his profundity. The same nautical imagery lies behind Prospero's promise, "And deeper than did ever plummet sound / I'll drown my book" (5.1.56–57). In doing so he will not only consign his art to a watery perdition; the act of immersion implies a relationship between deep-sea navigation and occult knowledge.

The desire to be ontologically associated with the oceanic depths is linked to Renaissance cartography: both navigation and cartography attest to a cultural preoccupation with measuring the reaches of those heretofore unknown realms, the sea and the human psyche. While such deft allusions suggest an intimate and longstanding knowledge of seamanship on the part of Shakespeare, they also invite an analysis of the relationship between subjectivity and geography, not merely the relationship of early modern selves to particular places, but also the role of place-based writing and the spatial arts—cartography, geography, chorography, cosmography—in the constitution of a subject born of a relationship with a watery globe. The corpus of Shakespeare's works is charged with a spatial energy derived from incorporating the spatial arts that flourished with the early modern transformation of the world picture from a Eurocentric, terrestrial model to an oceanic one.

The association of characters whose motives and psychology are inscrutable or unfathomable—Hamlet, Iago, Malvolio, and others—with oceanic vastness and benthic depths produces what I call an oceanic subjectivity. The language of navigation employed by the ill-fated King Richard and the imagery of the murky oceanic depths both resurface later in the corpus, with even more complex resonances. At a crucial moment in *Hamlet*, just after the protagonist has "caught the conscience" of Claudius by angling for a royal response to *The Mousetrap*, a tense exchange transpires between Hamlet and Polonius:

> *Hamlet:* Do you see yonder cloud that's almost in the shape of a camel?
> *Polonius:* By the mass and 'tis, like a camel indeed.
> *Hamlet:* Methinks it is like a weasel.

Polonius: It is back'd like a weasel.
Hamlet: Or like a whale.
Polonius: Very like a whale. (3.2.345–51)

Here a natural phenomenon tests the limits of representation. The whale threatens intelligibility. Unlike the camel and the weasel, which might be said to walk on solid empirical ground because of their phenomenological availability (they can be seen as distinct totalities), the whale represents an amorphous aquatic entity at the margins of knowledge, available only through legend and lore. In a world before scuba gear and underwater cameras, whales could only become manifest to human perception in two forms: as a shapeless mass of blubber washed up on the beach or as the dark, arching back of *something* glimpsed on an undulating surface.

This exchange elicits uneasy laughter because it undermines all epistemological certainty. The shifting similes end up at a sort of hermeneutic reductio ad absurdum: camel, weasel, and whale all have an arched back, but they occupy vastly disparate orders of visual accessibility. Clouds become camels become weasels become whales: nature is, to borrow a clever phrase, "as you liken it."[13] The largest inhabitant of the sea is, in this exchange, the ultimate instance of such slipperiness.[14] Hamlet tricks Polonius into agreeing too much. By cornering him into seconding a groundless affirmation, Hamlet exposes the fatuousness of the old courtier's prying machinations and develops the theme of the limitations of human knowledge in accounting for the "things in heaven and earth" (1.5.168). Hamlet gives Polonius a crafty lesson: figurative language, the very stuff of imaginative literature, only functions to the degree that it rests on solid epistemological ground. For the simile to work, either the tenor or the vehicle must be conceptually stable at some level: if a cloud is "like" something else, that something must have enough intelligibility to anchor the comparison. Perhaps this is Shakespeare's point: to foreground the sea as the part of nature that can never be fully domesticated.

The joke here is partly on the audience, for there is no actual cloud present to provide an ekphrastic anchor to our understanding. Clouds by nature are amorphous and protean; they also exist offstage.[15] Scholars' varied attempts to explain the symbolic status of the animals in this passage fail to account for the seaward drift of Hamlet's similes. By taking his chain of similes out to sea, as it were, Hamlet reveals that neither he nor Polonius knows what he is talking about, and that natural phenomena are as mutable as language can make them. He also reveals the limits of "our philosophy," which becomes increasingly less credible when we attempt to fathom natural phenomena, particularly of the marine variety (1.5.169). One way to construe this brief exchange is in a historicist mode, as an instance of the epistemological unavailability of the sea and its denizens to early moderns. Another is in a presentist mode: it provides a paradigm of general human ignorance about the sea. The early modern sea was several centuries from being sounded by the new philosophy, and whales were seen to embody its mystery. In choosing a whale to baffle one who attempts to fathom (or sound) his own condition, Hamlet likens himself to a sea creature. Faced with "a sea of troubles," the angry prince adopts a strange and unfathomable guise.

The metaphor of sounding the human mind appears again in *Hamlet* wrapped in a more developed and also more vivid nautical metaphor. When Guildenstern informs Claudius of the distracted Prince Hamlet's disposition, "Nor do we find him forward to be *sounded*, / But with a crafty madness keeps aloof / When we would bring him on to some confession / Of his true state," the schoolmate-cum-spy claims that he cannot take the measure of Hamlet's mental condition (3.1.7–10; emphasis added). As does the reference discussed earlier about taking soundings in *Richard II*, this passage portrays an ineffectual monarch who wishes to peer into the deepest recesses of a subject's soul. Here the notion of sounding the prince describes the effort to gauge the depth of Hamlet's rebelliousness, which figures the spies as coastal navigators and the prince himself as a body of water through which they are making their way. But they are out of their depth. As Falconer explains, "'unsounded depths' and all that 'the profound seas hide in unknown fathoms' fill the mind with an overwhelming sense of the unreachable." Hamlet, too, is navigating a course through the sea of sin that surrounds him; he does so by donning an unfathomable guise. In this he resembles Junius Brutus, in *The Rape of Lucrece*, who tells the bereaved Collatinus, "Let *my unsounded self*, supposed a fool, / now set thy long-experienced wit to school" (lines 1819–20; emphasis added). "Unsounded" here means something like "deep" would mean today (to describe one with wisdom and experience). Hamlet and Junius Brutus both claim to possess a personal interiority marked by suffering; they contain hidden depths.

A historical explanation of the importance of soundings in coastal navigation is as far as traditional scholarship on Shakespeare and the sea tends to go in interpreting the language of such scenes as this, yet several decades of intense scholarly focus on the rhetorical construction of subjectivity suggest that much more is at stake. The exchange between Claudius and Guildenstern is not merely an allusion to the navigator's habit of taking soundings; it is a carefully constructed metaphor that figures the subjectivity of the prince in terms of oceanic depths. Earlier in the play Hamlet has claimed to have "that within which passeth show— / These but the trappings and the suits of woe," a psychological interiority that cannot be fully fathomed (1.2.85–86). Guildenstern confirms this inwardness, which fuels the suspicion of the usurping Claudius, provokes Polonius to beleaguer the prince with unsubtle angling, and helps to drive Ophelia mad. Faced with "a sea of troubles" and the likelihood of a watery grave, Hamlet has adopted a strange and unfathomable guise, much to the dismay of those around him who cannot take his measure. The metaphor of sounding the waters of his soul is carefully chosen. Like the deep sea, he wishes to be perceived as ultimately unknowable—unreachable, ungraspable—to those who would take his measure, and in this he is at least temporarily successful.

The psychological effect of an immense global ocean inspired Shakespeare to produce a mix of maritime metaphors when Guildenstern tells Claudius that Hamlet "with a lofty madness keeps aloof" (3.1.8). The standoffish disposition of the prince is described by the metaphor of the ship of self: Guildenstern invokes a tactic of coastal shipping. According to the *OED*, the word *aloof* derives "from the idea of keeping a ship's head to the wind, and thus clear of the lee-shore or quarter towards which she might drift"; thence "came the general sense of 'steering clear of,' or 'giving a wide berth to' anything with which one might otherwise come into contact." The first three definitions are all literal: "1) The order to the steersman to turn the head of the ship towards the wind, or to make her sail nearer the wind; 2) Away to the windward; 3) Of position: Away at some distance, with a clear space intervening, apart." These literal definitions lead to the figurative ones: "7) At a distance; distant; hence, detached, unsympathetic." Holding himself (metaphorically) upwind is a tactic Hamlet borrows from naval warfare; he is out of reach of others.

Hamlet repeats the metaphor later in the play when he says, "I stand aloof, and will no reconcilement" (5.2.258). To stand aloof in the early modern idiom meant something more than it does today, for the metaphor is now a dead one. Yet as Jonathan Raban summarizes the purport of the metaphor, "*Aloof* (that most English of postures) is *a-luff*. Guildenstern's description of Hamlet's behavior alludes to the practice of 'rounding up' into the wind to avoid collision at sea when faced with heavy shipping traffic. Faced with a suspicious prospective father-in-law and the impertinent enquiries of friends-turned-spies, Hamlet has luffed up into the wind to gain sea-room away from them."[16] By standing aloof in his sea of troubles, Hamlet becomes the figurative shipmaster of his own soul, wisely giving himself room to maneuver in a predatory and martial world of metaphorically heavy shipping (the court). The danger of standing aloof (also referred to by sailors as "luffing up") is the possibility of losing all headway and thereby losing the ability to steer one's vessel—a predicament referred to by sailors as "being caught in irons." Standing aloof is a risky tactic, particularly in crowded waters.

Hamlet's inscrutable behavior—neither Polonius nor Claudius has much of a clue as to his motives—is that of an oceanic self. The maritime imagery produces an aura of the immeasurable by associating subjectivity with the deep sea, in the form of unfathomable depths, and with navigation. By figuring Hamlet's psychic condition in nautical language, Shakespeare also produces a lurking feeling that the prince is in imminent danger of shipwreck. Throughout the play he certainly finds himself beleaguered by pirates of various kinds. Hamlet's wildness manifests itself in a kind of oceanic subjectivity constructed in terms of an unfathomable nature. Hunted by a ruthless monarch and his henchmen, Hamlet becomes an aquatic being, a piece of marine life, both ship and princely whale, capable of cloaking his thoughts in a soundless alterity; he is as unapproachable as a sounding whale. Often whales respond to the presence of humans and ships by diving; since the sixteenth century the infinitive "to sound" has been the standard term for this behavior (*OED*). Early modern cetological inquiry emphasizes the intellectual challenge of animals that seem to epitomize the strangeness and immensity of the sea (as I discuss more fully in chapter 5). Here the whale becomes an emblem of unknowing: Shakespeare figures the indeterminacy of marine phenomena as a challenge to visual, conceptual, and rhetorical domestication. As his shifting similes demonstrate, whales have long symbolized the sea itself; emblems of marine ontology, they have been seen as embodying the inaccessibility of the deep. For Hamlet the whale acts as a test case for our ability to understand, control, exploit—in the mariner's idiom, to sound—nature.[17] Being associated with the ocean's profundity and inaccessibility is both a key feature of the rhetorical construction of Hamlet's interiority and a potentially lethal feature of his social interactions. By assigning what amounts to a pop quiz about how to read natural signs, Hamlet in effect turns the tables and sounds Polonius himself. By too readily agreeing with the suggestions proffered, the courtier proves himself superficial and thereby fails the prince's test; he soon suffers the consequences of his inability to fathom Hamlet's oceanic inwardness.

The desire to get to the bottom of things by careful, even ingenious, forms of measurement was widespread in early modern protoscientific thinking. In her history of the marine sciences in Europe, the historian Margaret Deacon identifies what she calls "the seventeenth-century movement towards a science of the sea," tracing the early modern fascination with the depths to the rediscovery of Aristotle: "Aristotle put forward the idea that the oceans occupy the deepest parts in the surface of the earth, which he knew to be a glove. Later geographers, from their ideas on the possibility of the sea's silting up, would seem to have shared this view. They had no knowledge of the sea's actual depth."[18] Intellectuals in the European Renaissance, for whom "much of the thinking about the sea was still rooted in the tradition of Aristotle and Pliny which had survived unbroken from the Middle Ages," began to advance the importance of accurate measurements to understand physical geography.[19] In the fifteenth century Cardinal Nicholas of Cues (Cusanus) advised in *The Idiot* that the sea would best be measured with a modified lead line (first English translation, 1650):

> It might bee done with a piece of Lead, made after the fashion of the moon of eight dayes old, yet so, that one horn of it be heavier, & the other lighter, and on the lightest horn let an apple, or some other light thing be made fast, with such an instrument, that the lead pulling down the apple after it to the bottom, and first touching the ground, with the heaviest part thereof, and so laying itselfe along accordingly, the apple then loosed and freed from the horne, may returne up again to the top of the water, provided that thou have first the knowledge how long such a lead will be sinking, and the apple rising in a water of known depth.[20]

Although far ahead of its time, this plan for a sounding machine highlights the energy and ingenuity going into efforts to produce new forms of measurement. Shakespeare's poetic attempts to measure the depths produced—instead of technological innovations useful to mariners—vivid evocations of the depths of the human and the humanity of the depths.

The pervasiveness of sounding and fathoming the depths in Shakespeare's writings suggests a powerful linkage in the poet's imagination between technology and representation—a connection that extends to other navigational technologies as well. Two developments linking figurative and technical production in the sixteenth century converged to link humanity with the global ocean: (1) the discovery of the Western limit of the Atlantic Ocean and the existence of the Pacific by European navigators; and (2) the increasing sophistication of the spatial arts with which intellectuals pieced together a new blue world picture. In his study of "cartographic latency" in early modern French literature, Tom Conley identifies "a history that sees the birth of the subject at a moment that coincides with the extraordinary growth of cartography in print culture. The time (1460–1660) roughly parallels that of the coming of autobiography, thus hinting that mapping is responsible for the consciousness that leads to the production of the fashioned self. The creation of the subject is buttressed by the subject's affiliation with the mapping of the world."[21] That the discursive construction of a distinctly modern subjectivity should not simply be an effect of discourse but also in part an effect of cartography should come as no surprise, as Conley, Gillies, and others have argued, for sixteenth-century European culture everywhere bespeaks a fascination with the global ocean.[22] The development of spatial technologies, from cartography and surveying to navigating on the open ocean, only contributed to this transformation in the early modern world picture. As John Gillies argues:

> Shakespeare's awareness of the new geography of the sixteenth century—a geography that owed at least as much to mariners' accounts as it did to tradition—was current and thematically developed. Shakespeare is demonstrably conversant with quite a variety of geographic discourses and a variety of cartographic genres. An irresistible corollary is that he was also well acquainted with the new geography in the sense of knowledge of new lands and seas as revealed by new discoveries and explorations. This, of course, is the very aspect of the "new map" to which Shakespeare draws attention in *Twelfth Night*.[23]

Gillies rightly emphasizes Shakespeare's awareness of new developments in geography and cartography at the turn of the seventeenth century, but he fails to discuss what is perhaps the most striking feature of Maria's allusion to the latest transformation of the English *imago mundi*: the comparison of a diagrammatic image, a world map, to a human face. Malvolio is rendered, by Maria's description, a cartographic being.

The growing empiricism of early modern representations of oceanic space is reflected in Shakespeare's ludic examination of the idea of a cartographic subject, a self that is rhetorically constructed using the language and imagery of the globe. In the previous chapter I argued that Caliban can be seen as the personification of the strange new world picture that confronted early modern Europeans in conceptually incorporating the global ocean. As a creature of maritime modernity he strangely resembles Maria's famous description of the ill-used Malvolio in *Twelfth Night*: "He does smile his face into more lines than is in the new map with the augmentation of the Indies." The "new map" in question is a specific one, referring to the *Hydrographiae Descriptio* of the mathematician Edward Wright (figure 2), a nautical world map specifically produced for navigation and the first successful planispheric version of the Mercator projection. For a writer to mention a specific map is striking enough—it tells us at the very least that the visual projection of the global ocean fired the playwright's imagination—but less obvious is the specific reference to the "lines" that traverse the map: they are rhumb lines, used by cartographers to represent given courses from which mariners could plot their own voyages across the open ocean (which sailors call *blue water*).

Maria's gesture to cartography is more complex than at first it appears, for in making himself the hypocritical butt of anti-Puritan sentiment, Malvolio makes a global fool of himself and is lured into producing a spectacular display of it. His "aspect," as Gillies puts it, is likened to a tableau of the globe traversed with innumerable lines. The implication is that Malvolio, who is actively engaged in plotting a course for Olivia's bed as well as her estate, is defined by a will to power that connects him with other speculators and adventurers embarking on similar courses across the ocean. The image of Malvolio's grotesquely smiling face as a world map inevitably reminds the audience of the *Fool's Cap mappa mundi*, which the editors of *The Norton Shakespeare* have chosen for their cover illustration. The *Fool's Cap* is a metamap (figure 3), at once a map of the world and a commentary on mapping the world. Like Shakespeare's metatheatrical works, it defies a gaze

Shakespeare's Benthic Imagination

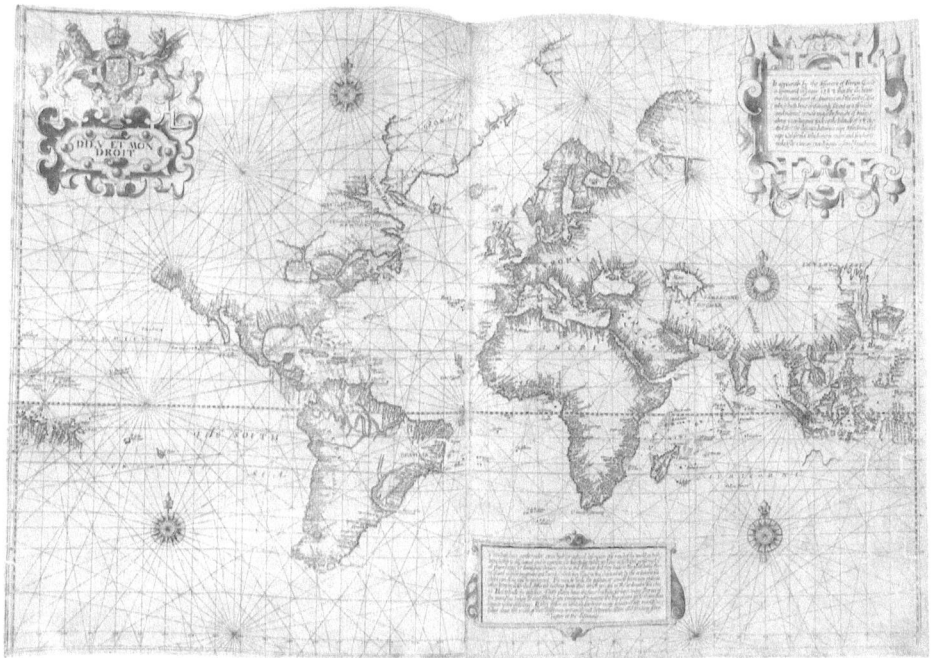

FIGURE 2. Edward Wright, *Hydrographiae Descriptio*, 1599. (University of Virginia)

that would assign it a singular meaning. This particular map is thoroughly theatrical. It "personates" the world, to use an early modern idiom; it is the image of the world personified. The map is a bust wearing the traditional garb of the fool, and for a face it has the image of the world. On its head are a fool's cap and bells. A metatheatrical trickster, the fool makes the viewer or reader of a play aware of his or her own position vis-à-vis the text or play by using language to reflect the viewing subject. The world map stares back at the viewer as a kind of mirror image.

The charge of the visual joke lies in its personification of the globe. The globe becomes the reflection of a fool looking in a mirror. The word *speculum*, Latin for mirror, was another term for a map at this time. The subject gazing at the *imago mundi* is the emergent cartographic subject. At the top of the tableau, the telling words "NOSCE TE IPSUM" saturate the map with irony, suddenly exposing it as a joke, a vanity. To whom does the text address itself; who is *"te"*? The map apostrophizes a viewer whose gaze is returned by the image of a foolish world, an echo of the picture of "We Three" referred to

Shakespeare's Ocean

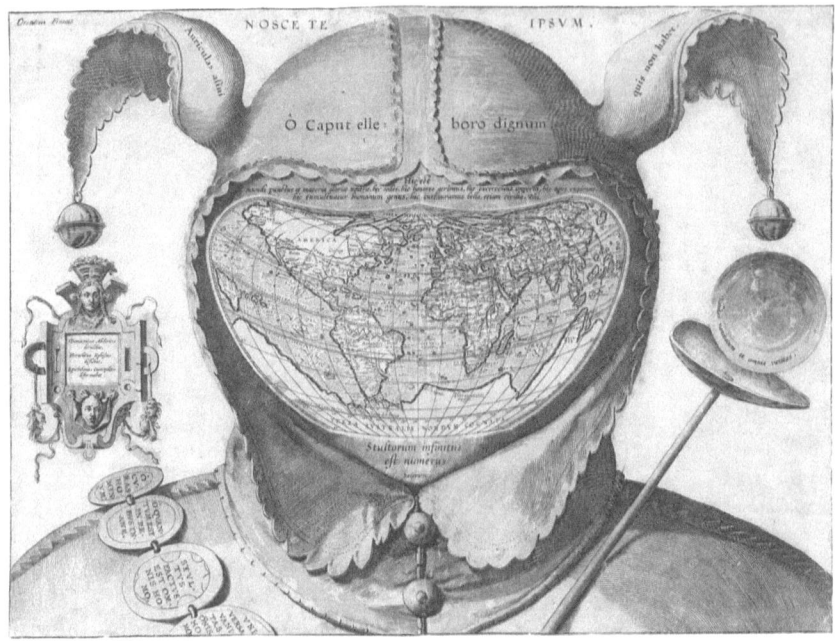

FIGURE 3. *Fool's Cap*, 1590. (Bibliothèque Nationale de France)

by Feste in *Twelfth Night* (Act 2, scene 3). Feste refers to a trick picture that portrays two fools, leaving the spectator puzzled about its title and becoming, thus, the third fool caught in the act of looking. "Know thyself," enjoins the caption at the top of the tableau. By reflecting the viewer's position as part of the message encoded within the composition, the world becomes the emblem of our own gaze. All the world's a fool. But the joke does not end there: it implicates the viewer in a globally foolish project by suggesting that the image of the world that we see is to some extent a projection of the cartographic subject, a selfhood defined in terms of its relationship to a diagrammatic image of the world. A symbolic portrait of both the European *vanitas* of global knowledge and the *hybris* of the Renaissance global projects of cartography, exploration, and discovery, the *Fool's Cap* uses a theatrical ruse to comment on cartography, and theater and cartography to comment on the visually constituted subject. The cap and bells and the admonitory Latin text also suggest another meaning that goes beyond the joke played at the expense of the viewer. They imply that this is, truly, a fool's world. The role of an oceanic *imago mundi* is a subtly encoded theme running through the Shakespeare corpus, figuratively connecting human and marine life.

Passages in which Shakespeare poetically sounds the depths offer a skeptical take on the human relationship to the physical environment, and the seafloor, a landscape at once supernatural and empirical, forms a kind of shorthand for cosmological uncertainty in the face of the global ocean. Shakespeare invites his audience to contemplate profound—and perhaps unanswerable—questions that speak to the core of Western cosmogony. What part of us belongs to the world of nature? To what extent is nature alien? To what extent are we alien to ourselves? Do we really know what we're doing here? Do we know what is in store for us? In raising such questions as these, Shakespeare offers poetry itself as an apparatus for fathoming the vastness and the depths of an ocean that would in four centuries become, like the diminishing rainforests and the melting polar regions, another depleted and devastated feature of this blue planet, further complicating the relationship between human constructs—history, ideology, structures of power—and the "more than human world."[24]

4

Tidal Bodies

> We are of the sea, and the sea is of us.
> DEBORAH CRAMER

The nature of the material relationship between the human body and the physical universe was a particularly pressing topic for early modern poets. As Philip Hardie notes, "The early seventeenth century saw a great output of poetry containing cosmological allusion, but the advances in science which were largely responsible for this interest were also creating the conditions of a division between poetic and scientific discourses that has lasted to the present day."[1] For Shakespeare, writing at precisely this moment of discursive and epistemological divergence, and often writing *against* such a divergence, cosmology—knowledge of the order of the physical universe—remained a central preoccupation of poetry. As I argued with reference to the metaphorics of sounding the depths in the previous chapter, many of his maritime descriptions suggest that Shakespeare understood *poesis* as a potent spatial technology for investigating the relationship between human life and the physical universe. His efforts to depict a human connection to the sea are even more evident in his fascination with the tides, those fluctuating streams of saltwater that represented opportunity—the moment of embarkation on life's sea voyage—for humans before steam power and internal combustion engines transformed the fluctuating rhythms of navigation.

Tidal metaphors are a major part of the discourse of nature in Shakespeare's writings: from the narrative poems to plays spanning his career, an imaginative linkage develops between human ontology and the physical environment through comparing human emotions with the tides and moving water—currents, eddies, floods. The poet not only writes of tides as metaphors, he also demonstrates a thorough awareness of tides as a very literal, physical force exercising a powerful influence on history. Indeed, Shakespeare invokes the tides so frequently that their metaphorical significance appears, at first glance, almost too obvious, their flux and reflux the basis for easily legible metaphors for the moment of opportunity, a change of momentum, the fluctuating dynamics of crowds, and the raw power of natural forces acting on human bodies. Douglas L. Peterson has noted Shakespeare's use of tides as metaphors for time in his study of the late romances, but by relegating their significance entirely to the metaphorical, without directing any attention to the playwright's sophisticated protoscientific familiarity with the range and complexity of tidal phenomena, he collapses the significance of time and tide, elevating the tenor of tidal metaphors (time) while neglecting the vehicle (tide). While Peterson anatomizes the nuances of temporality in the romances, making distinctions between metaphorical time, durative time, occasion, and other temporal variations, he fails to note the parallel complexity of Shakespeare's descriptions of and allusions to tidal phenomena.[2]

A close look at Shakespeare's tidal metaphors reveals the persistent tropological evocation of a deep bond between human beings and the physical environment, both driven by the same hydraulic forces. Shakespeare's characters are frequently overwhelmed by emotions that rise and fall like the tides, and in their powerful coenesthetic experience—the sum total of sensory perceptions—of these cosmic forces on their own lives, characters often rediscover themselves as aquatic beings violently transported or carried away, their fates shaped in obscure ways by the same forces that control the sea.[3] In this chapter I argue that Shakespeare imagined an ontological connection between human life and the ocean that is as much material as it is metaphorical, an insight he shares with modern ecologists, environmental ethicists, and a handful of ecocritics. I explore the significance of the playwright's knowledge of tides and currents in several plays and narrative poems, contextualizing my readings in the history of early modern marine science, largely preoccupied as it was with understanding the causes and effects of tidal movement.

No systematic theory explaining the cause of the tides and their local differences on the various coastlines of the world emerged until the seventeenth century. One of the hallmark achievements of scientific modernity (by which I mean the post-Baconian triumph of empiricism and inductive logic) is the ability to predict the tides—and their local effects—with great accuracy.

In England, Shakespeare's contemporary William Gilbert (1544–1603) offered the most compelling and prescient discussion of the tides. Gilbert is credited with a theory of magnetic attraction between celestial bodies that closely anticipated Newton's theory of gravity. *A New Philosophy of our Sub-Lunar World* was not published until 1651 but was written much earlier. Gilbert came perhaps the closest of any Renaissance thinker to a modern conception of the tides, suggesting that the planets are held in their orbits round the sun by the same force with which the moon influences the seas.[4] The Englishman John Wallis (1663) most clearly recognized the importance of the moon in his early contribution to the Philosophical Transactions of the Royal Society, *An Essay of Dr. John Wallis, exhibiting his Hypothesis about the Flux and Reflux of the Sea*:

> The sea's ebbing and flowing has so great a connexion with the moon's motion, that in a manner all philosophers have attributed much of its cause to the moon, which either by some occult quality, or particular influence which it has on moist bodies, or by some magnetic virtue, draining the water towards it, which should therefore make the water highest where the moon is vertical . . . that it would seem very unreasonable to separate the consideration of the moon's motion from that of the sea.[5]

Wallis is essentially correct in insisting on the moon's effects on "moist bodies," and indeed high tide does occur when the moon is at its zenith. These efforts culminated with Newton's theory of gravity in the *Principia Mathematica* (1687). So important was Newton's explanation of the tides that historians often dismiss earlier theories. For this reason the pre-Enlightenment knowledge of tides is often relegated to the historical slag heap of superstition, when in fact many forms of quite practical knowledge existed. Cartwright opines that pre-Newtonian models "were all completely replaced in the light of Sir Isaac Newton's gravitational theory presented in 1687."[6] This is not to say, however, that historical haziness as to the precise causes of the tides and their mathematical prediction meant that premodern and early modern thinkers were ignorant on the matter.

Knowing something of the tides has long been essential for sailors and useful for landlubbers engaged in coastal or transoceanic travel. In his history of the systematic conceptual mastery of the tides, the physical oceanographer David Cartwright suggests, "The daily pulse of the tide has always been familiar to those who live by a sea exposed to the oceans. Both the rise and fall at the shorelines and the swing of the currents offshore are obvious."[7] In the maritime regions of the world, "seafarers of all kinds have always made their own observations of the tides along the coasts they frequent, and have devised their own practical 'rules-of-thumb' for rough predictions."[8] This is especially true of regions such as the British Isles, where tidal ranges are high and greatly varied, producing significant coastal effects, such as currents, eddies, and standing waves, that any mariner must be aware of to survive. In a nation bordering the North Sea and settled by Norse tribes who crossed it, where the tides average 22 feet, we might expect a high cultural awareness of these phenomena. In the English language, "the close alliteration of the Anglo-Saxon words *Zeit, Gezeiten*, Time and Tide (which 'wait for no man'), testifies to early awareness of the tide's regularity by North Sea coastal dwellers, fishermen, navigators and pirates."[9] That tide and time are etymologically connected is clear from a glance at the etymology of the word *tide*. The OED cites its earliest usages in the English language to refer to a moment, occasion, or "any definite time in the course of the day, as even-tide, morrow-tide, noon-tide."

That the tides represented danger as much as opportunity is a tension ubiquitous in English literary history, extending as far back as the seventh and eighth centuries, when the Germanic tribes from across the North Sea known as the Anglo-Saxons settled in Britain. Tidal flats protected Jarrow, the ancient home of the Venerable Bede, who wrote a book on the measurement of time, *Opera de Temporibus*, before producing his celebrated *Ecclesiastical History of the English People*. In the *Opera* the observant cleric explicitly connected the cycles of the moon with tides: "But the most admirable thing of all is this union of the ocean with the orbit of the moon. At every rising and every setting of the moon the sea violently covers the coast far and wide, sending forth its surge, which the Greeks call *reuma*; and once this same surge has been drawn back it lays the beaches bare, and simultaneously mixes the pure outpourings of the rivers with an abundance of brine, and swells them with its waves."[10] For those like Bede who live near tidal flats, where rising water can engulf a human body in a matter of minutes, knowing something of the tides is a matter of life and death, and because different bodies of water fill and drain at different times, knowing how to calculate the ebb, flood, and slack water (the "stand" between the two) is essential for piloting a boat through the Thames Estuary as it is for sailing "down Channel" to the open sea.[11] "Knowing the tides"—a colloquial expression still used by sailors—has been one measure of seamanship from time immemorial.

In the General Prologue to the *Canterbury Tales* Geoffrey Chaucer frames his description of his competent Shipman in terms of his knowledge of the tides:

> But of his craft to rekene well his tydes,
> His stremes, and his daungers hym bisydes,
> His herberwe, and his moone, and his lodemenage,
> Ther nas noon swich from Hulle to Cartage.
> Hardy he was and wys to undertake;
> With many a tempest hadde his berd been shake.
> He knew alle the havens, as they were,
> Fro gootlond to the cape of Fynystere,
> And every cryke in Britaigne and in Spayne. (GP, lines 401–9)[12]

The poet demonstrates an admirable technological mastery of late medieval navigation. Knowing the "tydes," like knowledge of "stremes" (currents), "herberwe" (harbors and safe havens), "his moone" (lunar cycles associated with the tides and—inaccurately—with the weather), "and his lodemenage" (use of the compass, or managing its lodestone), joins the crucial geographic knowledge provided by late-medieval *portolani*, the harbor-finding charts upon which European navigators depended.[13] The Shipman not only knows each landmark and harbor in Western Europe, he also knows about the tides and their effects ("stremes," or currents), just as he knows of "his daungers him besides." Thus, while he may lack gills, his beard has been "shake" by "many a tempest."[14] He is a thoroughly aquatic being. Here Chaucer associates tides with contingency, risk, and the knowledge shared by an international cabal of mariners bound by their intellectual mastery of the forces that made ships sink or swim.

Like Chaucer's Shipman, Shakespeare had a thorough understanding of the tides as well as of the marine environment's "daungers him bisydes," not only for mariners but for landsmen as well. The sole instance of the playwright's invoking tides nonmetaphorically, in referring to a specific feature of

Tidal Bodies

the English coastal geography, stresses the lethal nature of the tidal flood in a low-lying coastal region. In *King John* Philip the Bastard protests:

> Withhold thine indignation, mighty heaven,
> And tempt us not to bear above our power!
> I'll tell thee, Hubert, half my power this night,
> Passing these flats, are taken by the tide;
> These Lincoln Washes have devoured them;
> Myself, well mounted, hardly have escaped. (5.6.2618–23)

The Wash is a bay on the north side of East Anglia, near Boston and King's Lynn (Chaucer's place of birth, as it happens); its tidal flats have been notoriously dangerous for centuries. This amply demonstrates an awareness of environmental contingency. Navigational hazards haunt Shakespeare, occurring in *Twelfth Night*, the sonnets, *Hamlet*, *Macbeth*, *The Merchant of Venice*, *Pericles*, and *The Tempest*, to name just a few of the most obvious works. In Shakespeare, the tides hold several different yet interrelated meanings pertaining to the cosmic forces that dictate the terms and conditions of human lives, signifying opportunity, the rise and fall of seawater relative to a body of land, and the cosmic force that exerts an invisible yet palpable influence over distant bodies.

The moment at which a tide is "full" has from time immemorial been the time to embark ("the fullness of tide," just before the start of the ebb). Not only is the turning of the tide a relatively peaceful moment, known as "slack water," but this moment has a longstanding association in folk history and folklore with death. That Shakespeare knew of this tradition is evident in the death of Falstaff, who dies, reports Mistress Quickly, "even at the turning o' the tide" (*Henry V*, 2.3.12). Such a reference would have been immediately meaningful to an early modern London audience, for the tides in the Thames were for centuries calculated by rules of thumb and in published tables notable for their accuracy.[15] The pervasiveness of tides as metaphors in Shakespeare's writings suggests that they were especially meaningful for the poet.

The most famous oceanic metaphor in Shakespeare is a tidal one. Brutus's speech in *Julius Caesar* exhorting the conspirators to act at the proper moment, when "Our legions are brim-full, our cause is ripe" (4.3.2226–27), exploits the etymological nexus of time and tide:

Shakespeare's Ocean

> There is a tide in the affairs of men,
> Which, taken at the flood, leads on to fortune;
> Omitted, all the voyage of their life
> Is bound in shallows and in miseries.
> On such a full sea are we now afloat;
> And we must take the current when it serves,
> Or lose our ventures. (*Julius Caesar*, 4.3.270–76)

The conceit is easily grasped: the conspirators find themselves, like mariners wishing to embark on a perilous voyage ("on such a full sea are we now afloat"), aboard ship "at the flood," ready to "take the current when it serves." High tide is the right time to catch the ebb (the falling tide), while low tide (when natural forces are spent) is to be avoided. In an era when the only auxiliary propulsion for seagoing vessels was the use of oars (nearly useless on the carracks and galleons of Shakespeare's day), catching the tide was vital.[16] Less obvious in Brutus's lines is the set of distinctions made between different features of the marine environment, tide, flood, and current, all of which denote distinct phenomena. The tide itself is an invisible force which drives the "current" that will float the conspirators away from the "shallows" and "miseries" that will otherwise bog them down. "The flood" refers to high tide; "the current" is the actual flow of water that will bear them to the open ocean. That the playwright seamlessly integrates these terms with complete accuracy has often been remarked; what has not received adequate attention, however, is the sophistication of his figurative use of tides, throughout the corpus, to suggest a profound interconnection between the human body and the physical environment—ocean, tides, currents, and lunar influence.

Antony refers to Caesar as "the noblest man / That ever lived in the tide of times" (4.3.267). In *Troilus and Cressida*, another of the plays set in the classical world, Diomedes tells Achilles, "I have important business, / the tide whereof is now" (5.1.74–75). Elsewhere Shakespeare develops a deeper connection between human ontology and seawater. In the second act of *The Two Gentlemen of Verona*, multiple metaphorical possibilities for the tides are operative. The aptly named Proteus exclaims, "The tide is now: nay, not thy tide of tears; / That tide will stay me longer than I should" (2.2.580–82). These lines pivot between the longstanding metaphorical (and etymological) association of tide with time and establishing a somatic link between rising seawater and human tears. In the first instance, Proteus means, "this is the moment of opportunity"; in the second, "thy tide of tears" suggests that the time of departure draws forth a different kind of human tide. His language is as protean as his understanding of time and tide is subtle. Later, Panthino warns, "You'll / lose the tide, if you tarry any longer" (2.3.629–30). In the following scene the same polysemy appears: "Launce, away, away, aboard! Thy master is shipped / and thou art to post after with oars. What's the / matter? Why weepest thou, man? Away, ass! You'll / lose the tide, if you tarry any longer" (2.3.627–30). To "lose the tide" refers, quite simply, to the possibility that a sailing vessel or passenger might miss the opportunity to leave port on the falling tide, yet once again the occult forces that determine human destiny also draw forth a physical response to the emotional moment—an upwelling of tears.

Shakespeare frequently gestures toward the chemical link between seawater and human blood, sweat, and tears, particularly in the early plays. This association occurs again in *Two Gentlemen*, but more poetically in *1 Henry VI*: "Were our tears wanting to this funeral, / These tidings would call forth their flowing tides" (1.1.87–88). Characters in Shakespeare who find themselves in exceptional emotional circumstances, flooded by passion beyond their control, are often figuratively associated with the sea and its hydraulic forces (as I mentioned in the previous chapter). Seawater and tears bespeak an occult interconnection between the forces that control the ocean as well as human lives, which is why we would expect to see the two forms of salt water linked in the most thoroughly maritime of Shakespeare's early plays, *The Comedy of Errors*. And so we do. Smitten by Luciana, Antipholus of Syracuse pleads,

> Are you a god? Would you create me new?
>   Transform me, then, and to your power I'll yield.
> But if that I am I, then well I know
>   Your weeping sister is no wife of mine,
> Nor to her bed no homage do I owe.
>   Far more, far more to you I do decline.
> O, train me not sweet mermaid, with thy note
>   To drown me in thy sister's flood of tears.
> Sing, siren, for thyself, and I will dote. (3.2.39–47)

The dramatic irony here is that Antipholus, a twin, is in a sense not himself ("if that I am I"), or at least not the self he appears to be in Luciana's eyes, metamorphosed into the cipher of a self as he and his family have been by the cosmic agency of the sea. His calling Luciana "sweet mermaid," then, mirrors his own condition as a merman of sorts, a human who has been transformed by the sea. The "flood" he describes might seem to describe high water caused by a superabundance of tears, but it could also be meant to invoke—and I find this sense more precise—weeping as a rising tide. As John Smith describes the flood in *A Seaman's Grammar*, "Flood is when the water beginneth to rise, which is young flood as we call it, then quarter flood, halfe flood, full Sea, still water, or high water."[17] In this case it refers not to an excess of water but to the rising sea.

The tendency to associate human bodies, especially (but not exclusively) the female body, with the tides is evident in the narrative poems, where both desire and weeping are frequently compared to the rising tide. In *Venus and Adonis*, Venus is physically tied to natural forces:

> Here overcome, as one full of despair,
> She vail'd her eyelids, who, like sluices, stopt
> The crystal tide that from her two cheeks fair
> In the sweet channel of her bosom dropt;
> But through the flood-gates breaks the silver rain,
> And with his strong course opens them again. (lines 955–60)

Unlike Luciana in *The Comedy of Errors*, Venus in this epyllion really *is* a goddess ("are you a god?"), but paradoxically one incapable of making her love object "yield"; hence her tears. The exquisite metaphor of tears as a "crystal tide" develops the metaphorical pattern of association between human bodies and topographies that is so arresting in this poem.[18] Venus attempts to stop her tears by closing her eyes, only to have them forced open by a new upwelling—or shower—of tears, which falls like "the silver rain": "Whereat her tears began to turn their tide, / Being prison'd in her eye like pearls in glass" (ll. 979–80). Both kinds of body that the poem maps in exquisite topographical detail, geographic and somatic, are traversed by analogous forces. Venus is a tidal being. If we recall Botticelli's magnificent depiction of her in *The Birth of Venus* we realize how fitting is Shakespeare's figurative association of the tears of Venus with the seawater from which—according to the etiological mythology of Greece and Rome—she first emerged.

While the traditional link between Venus and the sea would seem an inescapable figurative reservoir for the poet, Shakespeare's tidal imagery does not always bespeak such a harmonious flow of forces between nature's cycles and the body. In *King John*, for example, the physical analogy between human and geographic bodies, both subject to tidal forces, is depicted as antagonistic:

> Upon thy cheek lay I this zealous kiss,
> As seal to this indenture of my love,
> That to my home I will no more return,
> Till Angiers and the right thou has in France,
> Together with that pale, that white-faced shore,
> Whose foot spurns back the ocean's roaring tides
> And coops from other lands her islanders . . . (2.1.309–16)

Here a human cheek, given a farewell kiss, is figuratively linked to "that pale, that white-faced shore," the cliffs of England's south coast (the basis for the Latin name Albion). While here again human and geographic bodies are both subject to the sea, "the ocean's roaring tides" are depicted as a threatening exteriority.

Everywhere in Shakespeare's writings, moving water bespeaks uncontrolled cosmic forces that surround and traverse human lives, metaphorically and materially connected to those internal forces, the passions—lust, rage, overwhelming grief—which have the power to subvert reason but also to be channeled to one's own advantage. Shakespeare consistently associates vicissitude, loss, calamity, and mourning with being overwhelmed by a rising tide. This is a particularly striking rhetorical feature employed by characters in—if you will—dire straits. In *Richard II*, for example, on receiving bad news, York exclaims, "God for his mercy! What a tide of woes / Comes rushing on this woeful land at once!" (2.2.98–99). Yet the plays and poems with Mediterranean settings most frequently employ the tides to describe characters in extremis.[19]

The young king in *Henry V* similarly uses the tides as a metaphor for the fluctuating fortune of war (4.1.95–96), and also to illustrate English anxiety over leaving the Scottish border unguarded:

Shakespeare's Ocean

> For you shall read that my great-grandfather
> Never went his forces into France
> But that the Scot on his unfurnish'd kingdom
> Came pouring, like the tide into a breach,
> With ample and brim fullness of his force,
> Galling the gleaned land with hot assays,
> Girding with grievous siege castles and towns (1.2.291–97)

The young English king imagines his historical adversary to the north biding its time and, when the army is abroad, suddenly "pouring, like the tide into a breach." As in Sonnet 64, where "the hungry ocean" impinges on "the kingdom of the shore," here the force of the opportunistically invading "Scot" is figured as a nearly inevitable feature of the wartime landscape. The Scot becomes a rising tide ready to pour "into a breach" if given the chance, flooding the English land "with hot assays." While this vicissitude threatens his French campaign, by demonstrating his awareness of this exigency King Harry shows his subjects that he knows how to navigate the ship of state across the Channel while keeping a weather eye out for storms on the domestic front. It is interesting in this context to note that the playwright ascribes the ability to manipulate the tides to Sycorax, of *The Tempest*. In describing Caliban, Prospero claims, "His mother was a witch, and one so strong / that could control the moon, make flows and ebbs, / And deal in her command without her power" (5.1.272–74).

Shakespeare's contempt for those who see inevitability where they in fact have choices to make concerning their own circumstances is apparent in Octavius's description of the fickle crowd in *Antony and Cleopatra*, which he compares to a flag floating on the surface of the sea, passing back and forth with the rising and falling tides: "This common body, / Like to a vagabond flag upon the stream, / Goes to and back, lackeying the varying tide, / To rot itself with motion" (1.4.47). Here the social "body" becomes a "vagabond flag" controlled by forces beyond its power to control and unable to remove itself from their clutches. Cleopatra herself is similarly equated with vagrant flotsam in the greater ocean of a destiny she cannot control: "Her tongue will not obey her heart, nor can / Her heart inform her tongue,—the swan's down-feather, / That stands upon the swell at full of tide, / And neither way inclines (3.2.1649–52). The conventional misogynist topos of women's fickleness is here emblematized as the regal "swan's down-feather"; like the fluc-

Tidal Bodies

tuating feather, Cleopatra's will is not fully under control. It is impossible to see this rather shopworn patriarchal metaphor without recalling what is perhaps the most famous description of Cleopatra:

> Age cannot wither her, nor custom stale
> Her infinite variety. Other women cloy
> The appetites they feed, but she makes hungry
> Where most she satisfies (2.2.240–43)

Here Enobarbus describes the Egyptian Queen as a (sexual) force of nature.

In *Troilus and Cressida*, Agamemnon enjoins Patroclus to keep watch on the Greek champion: "yea, watch / His pettish lunes, his ebbs, his flows, as if / The passage and whole carriage of this action / Rode on his tide" (2.3.121–24). The language of lunar cycles, typically reserved for misogynist broadsides (such as those leveled at Cleopatra), is here leveled at the greatest of the Greek warriors.[20] Agamemnon explicitly associates Achilles—an unstoppable force of nature whose rage overwhelms the mightiest Trojan just as it determines the success or failure of the Achaian invaders—with tidal forces. Achilles is of the sea, Agamemnon implies, in part a lunatic (subject to the cycles of the moon), as evidenced by his emotional instability, and yet also the vehicle of war on which the entire Greek "action" rides. The Trojan War, "this action," is compared to a ship or naval fleet whose course depends on the hydraulic forces of the sea; that sea is figured in this instance as Achilles himself. Ascribing to his unpredictable champion the immense power of a leviathan imbued with more-than-human power to float or sink the Greek cause, Agamemnon charges Patroclus to act as a go-between, just as Claudius does with Rosencrantz and Guildenstern, whose task is to spy on a dangerously oceanic subject.

The effect of Agamemnon's language is not unlike that produced by the tidal imagery in *The Rape of Lucrece*: like Achilles, whose inability (or unwillingness) to control his own "folly" leads to monstrous violence, Tarquin is a force of nature. It is in this sense, as a roaring, raging hydraulic power linked to monstrous and scarcely containable human drives, that the poet metaphorically employs the tides in *The Rape of Lucrece*. In this early narrative poem on Roman history Shakespeare crafts a highly developed figurative association between aquatic forces and human beings—the body and the passions—in a metaphorical pattern developed over the entire poem. In her reading of "*the transfer of desire* to the audience in the form of total *absorption* in the work," Marion Wells demonstrates the "destructive power" of the rhetorical figure of *enargeia*, defined as "emotionally charged visual description."[21] The vividly visual rhetorical strategy, linked to ekphrasis, absorbs the reader in a manner dangerously akin to Tarquin's absorption in Lucrece's idealized femininity. The poem's enargeia "causes the hearer or reader to be 'carried away' by the force of the description." This seems particularly fitting for a poem about rape, the Latin word for which, *raptus*, means a carrying-away that is also an act of theft.[22] This etymology is evoked by the poem's imagery of characters threatened by rising tides of adversity, which consistently carry them—and their ability to control themselves—away.

Critics have long described the emotional economy of the poem in terms of its figurative transference from character to audience and back again. As Katharine Eisaman Maus observes, for many readers "the rhetoric of *The Rape of Lucrece* conceals, confuses, overwhelms," an effect that has shaped the poem's modern critical reception.[23] Indeed, the experience of reading the poem is not unlike the overwhelming emotional agon endured by the characters themselves, so much so that its effects are perhaps best described not in terms of absorption but as a kind of tidal *raptus*—a captivation and emotional transportation by physical forces analogically connected to the tides. The emotional and physical struggle staged by the poem spills over the borders of print. What has not been noted is the source of this spillage, a series of carefully constructed and interlinked metaphors connecting bodies and emotions to oceanic forces—tides, storms, piracy, and shipwreck. Following Joel Fineman's well-known discussion of "the liquid temporality of rape" in the poem, which seems an apt (if unwitting) description of the poem's predominant tidal imagery (tides are "liquid temporality" literalized), my reading examines just how thoroughly Shakespeare evokes a human ecology of hydraulic forces by likening characters to the sea and their emotional transport to the effects of rising and falling tides.[24]

Tarquin Sextus is the first character in the poem to be subject to what I shall call "the tidal economy of emotion," a narrative hydraulics that powerfully affects each of the three major characters (Tarquin, Lucrece, and Collatinus). In deliberating with himself on the eve of his crime, Tarquin consistently compares his own maleficent intentions to natural forces that cannot be contained. The passions that move him, he tells himself, inexorably subvert human reason. Tarquin figures himself as a mariner when plotting and executing the assault and rape: "Desire my pilot is, beauty my prize, / then who fears sinking where such treasure lies?" (279–80). Lucrece becomes a merchant vessel and her eventual rapist a privateer or pirate intent on capturing a "prize."[25] Here the invocation of piracy sets in motion a complex metaphorical structure of maritime imagery in which the rape is figured as an act of piracy, Tarquin the pirate, and the body of Lucrece his "booty"; the imagery subsequently modulates into a series of rising and falling emotional tides that traverse the bodies of the poem's leading characters. The effect is to locate uncontainable forces associated with the marine environment squarely within the emotional and somatic constitution of the characters themselves. In brief, Tarquin, Lucrece, and Collatine become tidal beings linked not only by a horrific crime but by the cyclic flows that determine their language and their emotional condition.

The imagery of the rapist as pirate repeats at the moment Tarquin, on breaking into Lucrece's chamber, pricks his finger on a needle and draws blood. Instead of taking the accident as a warning against further transgression, he instead chooses to interpret it in terms of the inevitability of nature's "lets":

> "So, so," quoth he, "these lets attend the time,
> Like little frosts that sometime threat the spring
> To add a more rejoicing to the prime,
> And give the sneaped birds more cause to sing.
> Pain pays the income of each precious thing
>   Huge rocks, high winds, strong pirates, shelves, and sands
>   The merchant fears, ere rich at home he lands." (lines 330–36)

By invoking the spring, with its frosts that can nip the new buds, Tarquin attempts to naturalize his own ungovernable will. At the same time, he imagines himself as a pirate and pirates as a natural feature of the maritime landscape, equating the needle that has just drawn his blood with the navigational hazards that threaten seagoing vessels, "huge rocks, high winds, strong pirates, shelves, and sands." Like other hazards that threaten sailor's lives, pirates cause "pain [that] pays the income of each precious thing," just as the spilling of blood is, to Tarquin, a "let" that will only heighten his pleasure. But instead of naturalizing his behavior, this rhetoric backfires: listing "strong pirates" along with the natural hazards of the marine topography foregrounds just how out of place pirates are among the natural features of the seascape. Like a pirate, Tarquin appears monstrous and human at the same time. It is no wonder that Lucrece refers to his "rocky and wreck-threat'ning heart" (590).

Rationalizing his decision not to heed the inevitable consequences of the rape that he plots, Tarquin convinces himself of the uncontrollable nature of his criminal desire: "But nothing can affection's course control, / Or stop by the headlong fury of his speed" (ll. 500–501). "Affection" dictates his course, impelling him with "headlong fury" toward an oceanic condition beyond reason, decorum, and domestication. The tendency to think of his own lust in terms of the inevitability of rising water characterizes Tarquin at the height of his violence. His unrelenting nature is vividly emphasized by the maritime imagery employed when Lucrece pleads with him: "Her sad behaviour feeds his vulture folly, / A swallowing gulf that even in plenty wanteth" (556–57). The appetitive "gulf" of Tarquin's "vulture folly" then takes a metaphorical turn to the self-descriptive metaphor of his own will as a flood tide:

> "Have done," quoth he; "my uncontrolled tide
> Turns not, but swells the higher by this let.
> Small lights are soon blown out; huge fires abide,
> And with the wind in greater fury fret.
> The petty streams, that pay a daily debt
>   To their salt sovereign, with their fresh falls' haste
>   Add to his flow, but alter not his taste" (645–51).

Tarquin here insists that his passions are, like the forces that move the ocean, not subject to reason or persuasion but "uncontrolled."[26] His will—which bears "the paronomastic possibility of invoking both 'desire' and 'genitalia'"—is wild and oceanic, swelled by the "let" that resists it.[27] The paradox is that, in claiming his own nature to be as unchangeable as the sea, Tarquin invokes the proverbially changing tides so often employed in misogynistic discourse (I will return to this later) to symbolize fickleness and superficiality. As if glimpsing the slipperiness of his own rationalization in mid-declamatory stream, he immediately returns to the self-aggrandizing metaphor of himself as "the salt sovereign."

Tidal Bodies

Tarquin is not alone in describing his motives in terms of the marine environment. Moved by her assailant's rising tide of rhetorical violence, in the following stanza Lucrece takes up the maritime metaphors, cleverly but ineffectually pleading her case by turning his own metaphor back toward him in diminished form. Lucrece attempts to use Tarquin's own maritime metaphorics in a kind of verbal defensive action, modifying them to channel and temper the hydraulic flow of his will.[28] The imagery of Lucrece's resistance as a "petty stream" of fresh water incapable of altering the salt ocean turns into the moral question of "staining" his honor when she reimagines the impending crime in terms of the pollution of Tarquin's noble blood by "lust, dishonour, shame, misgoverning":

> "Thou art," quoth she, "a sea, a sovereign king,
> And lo, there falls into thy boundless flood
> Black lust, dishonour, shame, misgoverning,
> Who seek to stain the ocean of thy blood.
> Of all these petty ills shall change thy good,
> Thy sea within a puddle's womb is hearsed,
> And not the puddle in thy sea dispersed." (652–58)

Pollution is a matter of scale.[29] If her attacker really is like the sea in the way that he claims, Lucrece argues, then the stains of "lust" and "dishonour" cannot possibly dilute his blood; if they can do so, then he is nothing like the boundless ocean but merely a minor sea "hearsed" in a "puddle's womb" and thus easily stained by any drop of sin. Puddles are not subject to tidal fluctuations (neither are some seas, including the Mediterranean and the Baltic); the effect of comparing him to a puddle is to imply that Tarquin is not as oceanic as he claims. The imagery of containment persists in the evocation of the rape: Tarquin "entombs her outcry" in the "white fleece" of "the nightly linen that she wears" and thereby "pens her piteous clamours in her head" (679, 678, 680, 681). The moment of the rape itself is figured as a turning of the tide: Tarquin's "flood" is met by "the chastest tears / That ever modest eyes with sorrow shed" (682–83). The poet is moved to comment, "O deeper sin than bottomless conceit!" a comparison that modulates the maritime imagery from the surface effects of streams and floods to an emphasis on Tarquin's depths.[30]

Fineman argues that "Tarquin and Lucrece both speak the same language, a point already clear enough from the equivalent tonalities and diction, the shared motifs, the stichomythian back-and-forth rhythms, through which the two of them conduct their formal argument."[31] Telling though this analysis may be, it fails to account for the peculiar metaphorical give and take between the two characters, which is more than a "shared language." This "back-and-forth" rhythm is consistently figured in tidal imagery; hence, what the two share is less a language than an affective response to the metaphors they employ, an economy that also operates at a metatextual level. The imagery is etymological: the word *metaphor* is a compound derived from the Greek meaning "to carry over or transfer."[32] The Elizabethan rhetorician George Puttenham asks, "for what els is your metaphor, but an inversion of sens by transport?"[33] Shakespeare takes this etymology (almost) literally in Tarquin's case: his psychic condition mirrors his transgressive physical progress into Lucrece's chamber. He persistently gets carried away by his own metaphors, allowing himself to be *transported* by figures of speech and insisting on his own inability to resist what moves him. As Maus argues, "Tarquin's characteristic mode of self-justification does not involve arguing directly for the rightness of his action. Rather, he elaborates metaphors that allow him to establish a clear, if perverse, hierarchy of priorities."[34]

Even after Tarquin's flood of will reaches its highwater mark, turns, and begins to ebb (at which point he slinks away), the poet continues to develop his theme and variations on the tidal dimensions of human emotion. The response of Collatinus to his wife's horrible narrative of her rape is likened to a tide, if anything in even more violent imagery than that which precedes it. Succumbing to an "untimely frenzy" of grief, he can scarcely contain himself:

> As through an arch the violent roaring tide
> Outruns the eye that doth behold his taste,
> Yet in the eddy boundeth in his pride
> Back to the strait that forced him on so fast,
> In rage sent out, recalled in rage being past;
>   Even so his sighs, his sorrows, make a saw,
>   To push grief on, and back the same grief draw. (1667–73)

Here the simile evokes a tide running at full tilt under a bridge, the flowing water channeled by "an arch" into an "eddy" that swirls out from the main stream and back again. The arch's "let"—which, as Fineman notes,

Tidal Bodies

here signifies an impediment—only serves to make the flow more forceful and chaotic. In being likened to water, Collatinus's breath becomes tactile and fluid, joining the other bodily flows and fluids. Shakespeare employs the same imagery of a channeled current in *Coriolanus*: "Ne'er through an arch so hurried the blown tide, / As the recomforted through the gates" (5.4.3781–82). The metaphor would likely have been a vivid one to Londoners, for (as I have noted already) the Thames is tidal well upstream of London, and the many arches of London Bridge undoubtedly produced spectacular eddies and standing waves.[35]

The final gesture to tidal flows in *The Rape of Lucrece* occurs at the moment of her suicide, the climax of the ongoing narrative of violence: "the crimson blood / Circles her body in on every side, / Who like a late-sacked island vastly stood" (1738–40). As the blood, "bubbling from her breast," flows from her self-inflicted wound, the poet calls it a "fearful flood" (1741). Here again we might interpret the "flood" as describing an excess of liquid like the biblical flood that temporarily overruns the firmament, but the specificity of the imagery—upwelling blood "Circl[ing] her body in on every side," and her body an island—suggests a rising tide or a storm surge. This is precisely the imagery employed to describe Collatinus's emotional response to her death immediately thereafter. After bathing his face in "Lucrece' bleeding stream," Collatinus pronounces the name of Tarquin several times, "through his teeth, as if the name he tore," evoking the earlier image of the tide racing through an arch (1787). In this pause before tears he is likened both to a storm and to a turgid sea: "This windy tempest, till it blow up rain, / Held back his sorrow's tide to make it more. / At last it rains, and busy winds give o'er" (1788–90). It seems more than likely from this passage that the poet was aware of the phenomenon now described as a "storm surge," whereby a rising tide is heightened by the effects of low pressure and powerful winds, making it all the more dangerous. Collatine's voicing of sorrow and anger is like a "windy tempest" that blusters until the rain falls, then becomes calm, with the double effect of holding back "his sorrow's tide to make it more" and preceding his rain of tears. Fineman observes that "erotic Time (*tempus*) takes place within him when the 'windy tempest' (*tempestas*) overflows."[36] Collatine is profoundly moved, transported by the hydraulic forces that course through the poem.

The imagery that illustrates the emotional economy of *The Rape of Lucrece*, then, is generally maritime and specifically tidal, following a cyclical pattern of waxing and waning passions that flows from character to character in a series of exquisitely crafted metaphors linking human affect with rising and falling seawater. Tarquin's tide of "folly"—an uncontainable mixed passion of lust and self-love—rises to a flood of criminal action and, the crime over, falls, at which point he slinks off. He is the poem's first tidal persona, transported both by Collatine's verbal blazoning of Lucrece and by his own oceanic metaphors. Lucrece then becomes the central tidal character as her passion rises in her retelling of the rape; at its height her condition is literalized by the flood of blood that courses from her body. Collatinus then becomes the central bearer of this fluctuating emotional hydraulics, powerfully moved as he is by his wife's story and her death. He responds to the emotional tide in turn, but with the assistance of Lucius Brutus channels his rage into effective action. The entire poem is structured on an analogical relationship between human characters as embodiments of forces that ebb and flow and the marine environment. *The Rape of Lucrece* contains the most developed tidal conceit in all of Shakespeare's works, a metaphorical inquiry into the relationship of the ocean to violence and emotional transport. Is it any surprise that Lucrece compares "my tears, my sighs, my groans" to a "troubled ocean"? (588, 589)

Another of the most vivid evocations of a tide of woes appears in what may be the most violent of Shakespeare's plays, *Titus Andronicus*, which has much in common with *The Rape of Lucrece*—a Roman setting, monstrous characters, and a central rape. When Marcus discovers his niece Lavinia in the woods after she has been raped and tortured by the monstrous Chiron and Demetrius, her hands cut off and her tongue cut out, he brings her to his brother, the embattled Titus. On encountering his daughter thus devastated, emblematically stripped of all agency in the loss of tongue and hands with which she might tell her story, the old soldier describes his own condition of mourning in vivid imagery moving from the forest to the sea:

> It was my dear, and he that wounded her
> Hath hurt me more than had he killed me dead;
> For now I stand as one upon a rock
> Environed with a wilderness of sea,
> Who marks the waxing tide grow wave by wave,
> Expecting ever when some envious surge
> Will in his brinish bowels swallow him. (3.1.93–97)

Tidal Bodies

Each calamity that Titus suffers is another "wave" that hems him in as he awaits an "envious surge" to "swallow him" in "his brinish bowels." Titus's "waxing" tide of misfortune seems animated by a hostile cosmic agency, a leviathan with a personal animus toward the old warrior. The "surge," described as a monstrous and malignant adversary intent on destroying him, becomes in this passage a watery version of what Marcus calls "some Tereus" who "hath deflowered thee." The rape and disfigurement of Lavinia, like Tarquin's actions in *The Rape of Lucrece*, can only be likened to the inexorable force of the rising tide.

There is something cosmically arbitrary and ecologically cruel about tidal violence in these examples, as if the worst kind of misfortunes humans can endure were those caused by a wholly uncaring nature. Like Brutus, who insists on taking the "tide in the affairs of men" that he instigates, the villainous Tarquin appeals to the inevitability of such forces to convince himself that he cannot possibly stop in his course of action, while others, such as Lucius Brutus after his daughter-in-law's rape and Titus after his daughter's rape and disfigurement, choose not to be wholly impelled by those forces but instead to channel them, when the opportunity presents itself, to the furthering of their own purposes. The implication in each case is that understanding tidal forces is a kind of hydraulic technology akin to the knowledge of human nature. The conceptual mastery of the tides allows characters to make the most of opportunities in which they could, if unwary, be wholly victimized. As the Earl of Worcester points out, in the first part of *Henry IV*, "think how such an apprehension / May turn the tide of fearful faction / And breed a kind of question in our cause" (4.1.66–68). Human lives, both individual and collective, are like the ebbing and flowing ocean, subject to powerful forces that cannot be fully controlled but must be understood to be navigated.

The examples I have discussed from *King John, Henry V, Julius Caesar, Antony and Cleopatra, Titus,* and *Lucrece* all center on the fate of individuals in relation to the emergent empire or nation-state. *Titus Andronicus* and *The Rape of Lucrece* contain the most developed comparisons of a hydraulic economy of flux and reflux. It strikes me as no accident that both works are centrally concerned with the relationship between the victimized female body—the dismembered Titus and Lavinia, the raped and self-destroying Lucrece—and the absolutist state (in both cases Rome). *Lucrece* is an epyllion, generically and topically related to epic; hence it offers a perspective on the heroic classical past that is in some sense teleological, or at least proleptic. It is thus a poem that in its critical examination of tyranny looks forward to the Roman Republic (in this again it resembles *Titus*). Shakespeare's metaphorical use of tides is often imperial, or at least national-political in scope. To return to Hardie's discussion of *Cosmos and Imperium* with which I began my discussion of the tides in Shakespeare, I submit that for our poet, the relationship to cosmic forces and their conceptual mastery (cosmology) has a national-political dimension, the causes and effects of the tides deeply connected to human history. A healthy state is one in which the body politic and private bodies are in some sense harmonized with the commonwealth—and both live in harmony with the physical environment. England's emergence as a major player in the early modern geopolitical arena put new pressures on intellectuals to explain the physical relationship between self, state, and world. As a major maritime power coming into its own after 1588, England understood its own historical role as one intimately connected to the ocean. In the works of Shakespeare, then, we witness a poetic mediation of the historical and the natural that we might call an ecopolitical cosmology—a *poesis* that attempts to fathom the deep connections between the environmental forces and the political structures that rule the individual and the social body. When those forces slip their bounds, as Cleopatra puts it, then "Sink Rome" (*Antony*, 3.7.15).

5

Royal Fish

SHAKESPEARE'S PRINCELY WHALES

> This is the generation of that great LEVIATHAN, or rather,
> to speak more reverently, of that mortal god, to which we
> owe under the *immortal God*, our peace and defence.
>
> THOMAS HOBBES

On Wednesday, February 24, 2010, the Sea World trainer Dawn Brancheau was pulled by the hair from the shallow end of a pool and drowned in deeper water by a male orca named Tilikum.[1] The media coverage of this dreadful event emphasized not merely the literal circumstances of the drowning of the human victim but the psychology of the cetacean perpetrator: what, people wondered, was going on in "Tilly's" mind? In an article published two days after Brancheau was killed, a *New York Times* journalist noted that "questions about the mammal's intent continue to linger."[2] Was the young male cetacean "acting violently, possibly because of stress from captivity? Or was he just playing?" By ascribing intentionality to this particular "wild animal," the journalist put his finger on precisely what differentiates whales from most other species in the popular imagination: like humans, whales are endowed with consciousness, and hence intentionality (or private motives). The fact that Tilly was implicated in two prior killings, the first of another trainer and the second of a homeless man who somehow got into the whale's pool, seemed to imply that this particular whale's consciousness is not a healthy one. Either Tilly is a serial killer whose psychopathology bears investigation, or he is just too playful for his own—and others'—good. Playfulness and monstrous force: both qualities are emphasized in the Western cultural narrative of the cetacea. Orcas, long referred to as killer whales, are the extreme case of a narrative vacillation between monstrosity and kinship.

Shakespeare's Ocean

Interest in the psychology of whales—their capacity to think and communicate among themselves and with humans—has been a hallmark of the modern environmental movement. In *A Whale for the Killing*, his impassioned plea for the ethical treatment of whales, Farley Mowat notes an evolutionary kinship between both kinds of mammal: "Whales and men trace the same ancient lineage through creatures born in the warm waters of the primal oceans who exiled themselves to the precarious environment of the dry land."[3] The relatively large brains of both humans and whales have preoccupied environmental ethicists, ethologists, and the American public at least since the 1960s. "Such studies as we have made," argues Mowat, "suggest that the more advanced whales have brains comparable to and perhaps even superior to ours, both in complexity and capacity. It is clear that their power to think has steadily increased, even as ours has." Whether Mowat is correct in linking brain size with cognitive function, the ontological relationship that he implies (whales and humans share unique traits that put us on the same level) and the ethical conclusions he later draws articulate the idea of interspecies kinship. This special relationship motivates the members of Sea Shepherd Foundation (the subject of the Discovery Channel program *Whale Wars*) to risk their lives to prevent the commercial and "scientific" killing of whales, and it is a sentiment that lies behind the popularity of such films as *Free Willie*, *Whale Rider*, and (more recently) the Oscar-winning documentary *The Cove*.

While I do not pretend to know anything about the psychology or consciousness of whales (although I confess to finding Mowat's position compelling), in this chapter I suggest that when it comes to speculating about a special kinship between whales and humans, Shakespeare got there first. In his plays I find a consistent pattern of association between human beings and the *cetacea*, reflecting classical ideas about frolicsome dolphins as well as biblical constructions of a threatening and monstrous leviathan. The neglect of marine animals in Shakespeare studies is especially surprising given the significance—indeed, the prominence—of whales in Shakespeare's maritime imagination.[4] Living and writing roughly half way between the publication of Machiavelli's *The Prince* and Hobbes's *Leviathan*, Shakespeare frequently entertained the idea of a special relationship between princes and whales, more than once negotiating the humanity of royals and aristocrats by comparing them with enormous sea creatures capable of doing great harm. As Falconer noted in the 1960s, Shakespeare's metaphorical and emblematic use of whales demonstrates a familiarity with them that exceeds his familiarity with most other marine animals.[5] Absurd as such an assertion might at first appear—after all, what could a Renaissance English poet know about whales, and why should he care about them?—it is evident from his writings that Shakespeare not only knew something of cetacean ethology (the study of animals in their environments), he also gave us a prescient model for thinking about the behavior of the kings of the sea in terms of the passions and behavior of those who rule on land.

Shakespeare frequently negotiates the humanity of princely characters by comparing them with whales, which are emblematic of immense power and of sovereignty, of grandeur and huge appetites. In perhaps his most striking description of cetacean behavior, he employs the unusual metaphor of a stranded whale to describe the emotional constitution of the wayward Prince Hal in *II Henry IV.* Misunderstanding his own son's cagey behavior, the king tells his retainers how they should deal with the wayward prince:

> Chide him for faults, and do it reverently,
> When you perceive his blood inclined to mirth;
> But being moody, give him line and scope
> Till that his passions, like a whale on ground,
> Confound themselves with working (4.3.37–41).

Here Shakespeare serves up a mixed marine metaphor, comparing the prince to a hooked fish easily lost with a taut line ("give him line and scope") and equating him to a whale stuck in the shallows ("like a whale on ground"). Too tightly managed, the prince will break the line and swim off; given "scope," his struggles will eventually "confound" themselves, in the sense of "to defeat utterly," and also "to waste, consume, or spend" (*OED*).[6] In both cases "to confound" is to use up: that which makes the prince "moody" will be consumed if his counselors allow the royal passions sufficient "scope" to work themselves high and dry. "Confound" derives from the Latin *confund-ere*, to pour or mingle together, mix up, confuse, confound (*OED*). In a sense, then, the prince has already been confounded—confused by his father with a stranded whale.

Shakespeare was particularly fond of the word *scope*, employing it both in its literal sense of "room for exercise," and in its abstract meaning, "reach or range of mental activity" (*OED*).[7] At once a hooked fish and a doomed whale, the passionate prince is ascribed an oceanic subjectivity, his characteristic behavior best explained in sea metaphors. The courtiers must angle delicately in their efforts to work with the royal fish: only by letting the prince reel himself in, as it were, can they be certain that his passions will work themselves out without causing undue damage to the court. The trope implies, however subtly, that courtiers should emulate not merely fishermen but, more specifically, whalers. Yet his father misunderstands the heir apparent: far from being dominated by his passions, Hal is consistently depicted as rational, calculating, and indeed cold-blooded throughout the three plays Shakespeare devoted to him. The scenario that the first Lancastrian monarch describes is the reverse of what will take place in his son's court: the young king will consistently fish for his subjects' motives and passions, with great success, while hiding his own.

In describing Prince Hal as a royal fish, his father takes up an idea that had considerable currency in Shakespeare's lifetime. Tudor jurists argued that whales stranded on the coast by right belonged to the monarch. Whatever "wreck" washed ashore was subject to the monarch's dominion over flotsam as well as the seafloor and coast. Royal salvage included the corpses of animals, captured by hardworking fishermen, brought to shore to be butchered.[8] A lively debate over crown properties rumbled throughout the reign of Elizabeth I and those of James I and Charles I. The claim that the Crown is the owner of the foreshore and the seabed under territorial waters was argued by Thomas Digges in 1568–69 and supported by Robert Callis and Sir Matthew Hale in the seventeenth century. This Elizabethan debate over royal claims to the foreshore continues to shape modern coastal zone law in the United Kingdom. Royal rights to stranded whales are still a feature of British Coastal Law: a beached whale over twenty-five feet in length is defined as a "royal fish" and remains the property of the Crown.[9]

In comparing his son's emotions to the struggles of a stranded whale, the Lancastrian king makes an obvious pun, for the young Hal is the Prince of Wales, the customary title used to describe the heir apparent to the English throne since the early fourteenth century. Melville would later echo the pun in describing his character Queequeg, an heir apparent (in his own fictional Pacific island kingdom) turned whale hunter and harpooneer, as "this sea-prince of Wales."[10] In *I Henry IV*, the pun is more subtle, even implied, in the passage linking the behavior of the prince to that of a stranded whale. The echo of "whales" in "Wales" seems, on the surface, to be a simple gag; in fact, it alludes to a longstanding cultural association between the English royal family and a particular region of the kingdom (as well as, figuratively, with marine mammals).

In England and in France the heir apparent has traditionally been given a cognomen establishing a geographic relationship to the kingdom.[11] In England the tradition began in the late Middle Ages after Edward I undertook a military campaign to "pacify" Wales. The historian Sandra Raban notes, "In 1301, Prince Edward, who had been born amid the building works at Caernarfon in 1284, received the king's Welsh lands as an appanage, together with the title of Prince of Wales, thereby beginning the traditional association with the heir to the throne."[12] This association was both conventional and practical. As Peter Saccio has argued, "the title 'Prince of Wales,' bestowed upon the English heir apparent since Edward I's conquest, was no idle decoration. Those portions of Wales not held by marcher lords like Grey and Mortimer were ruled as a principality from Chester."[13] This historical-geographic connection between Wales and the English royal family is central to much of Shakespeare's second tetralogy, particularly *I and II Henry IV*. Although Shakespeare paints the young prince as a wayward soul who keeps the dubious company of John Falstaff, Pistol, and Nym, as Saccio points out, "Hal himself, at the age of sixteen, was king's lieutenant for Wales," hardly the office of an idler.[14]

Between the end of the thirteenth century and the start of the fifteenth, various claimants to the title emerged on both sides of the ongoing disputation between the Welsh leaders and English royalty. A century after the establishment of the tradition of naming the English heir apparent the Prince of Wales, the last indigenous claimant to that title, Owen Glendower, was declared Prince of Wales (*Tywysog Cymru*) by a Welsh parliament gathered for that purpose. Glendower is depicted by Shakespeare in *I Henry IV* as an ineffectual rebel much given to mysticism and self-aggrandizement, but in fact he represented a serious threat to the first Lancastrian monarch (Henry IV) and his heir. While several English princes claimed the title of Prince of Wales in the century before Glendower, it was the hero of Shakespeare's second tetralogy, Prince Hal (later Henry V), who consolidated the claim for the English royal family against the Welsh claimant to the title of national leadership. In his military victory at Shrewsbury, somewhat fancifully depicted in *I Henry IV*, all disputes about the rightful bearer of the title are symbolically resolved, and Hal becomes fully enfranchised as *Princeps*

Wallie. Shakespeare's pun on Whales / Wales thus alludes to a particularly fraught chapter in the history of the British Isles in which dynastic claims, regional jurisdiction, and the symbolic presence of marine mammals intermingle. In a strange way, whales and dolphins are deeply (if subtly) encoded in a discourse of national identity and princely powers that lies at the heart of Shakespeare's second tetralogy.

This symbolic bouillabaisse has a less obscure history on the other side of the English Channel. From the fourteenth century the French crown prince was known as the Dauphin, literally the Dolphin, and has been, like the Prince of Wales, symbolically associated with a particular region that bears his title. The Dauphiné ("dolphinage") is in the southern Alps, now part of southeastern France. Between the eleventh and fourteenth centuries this region was an independent state, and until 1457 it preserved a separate political identity from France. After that date it became the particular region of the heir apparent. In *Henry V*, the young English king's main adversary is the Dauphin. Throughout the play Shakespeare emphasizes the Dolphin's sportive disposition; he is unable to take his enemies or his office seriously. The French prince is also consistently characterized by an affection for horses, which further suggests a not quite fully human constitution. Ultimately, the French army is defeated at Agincourt and King Henry makes good his claims to France. Thus, it makes perfect historical sense that in a series of highly nationalistic history plays the playwright would figure the English crown prince as a larger cetacean than the French heir apparent, whose belittling is the cause of so much humor in *Henry V*. The English whale-prince outweighs the French dolphin, whose military prowess is no match for the larger animal.

To claim as I do that a pattern of metaphorical association between princes, whales, and dolphins constitutes a discourse of the marine environment might seem to be a case of ecocritical hubris, yet it is precisely this claim with which I begin my analysis of human-cetacean kinship. Shakespeare's references to whales tread the line between conceptions of the whale as an emblem of epistemological uncertainty and as an instance of strange kinship. Not only does Shakespeare associate whales with royalty, aristocracy, and the passions of the great, grand, and gross, he also ascribes to them a princely subjectivity that undermines the distinction between land animals and the social hierarchy of sea creatures. His frequent references to whales suggest a special relationship between humankind and marine animals; they also demonstrate the poet's familiarity with some cetacean ethology.

Recent studies of human-animal relations have opened up new vistas for early modern ecocriticism. Bruce Boehrer, Erica Fudge, and Karen Raber, in particular, have advanced our understanding of the significance of terrestrial animals in early modern culture generally and Shakespeare specifically. Boehrer has argued that "the ways . . . we think of the natural world are, in a fundamental sense, the ways . . . we think of ourselves."[15] This is certainly true of how Tudor and Stuart writers and intellectuals negotiated the border between human and animal. As Erica Fudge has argued at length (in two separate studies), the category of the human was discursively constituted by what Fudge calls "brutal reasoning," the construction of animal nature as an ontological condition into which humans were in danger of falling by succumbing to our passions, appetites, and sinful nature. In early modern literary negotiations of the human as a conceptual category, the bestial side of human nature was explicitly and elaborately formulated in terms of a spectrum linking human passions to their emblematic animal counterparts. Lust, gluttony, greed, wrath: all had their animal corollaries manifest in human beings with the weakening or loss of reason. Fudge demonstrates that humanity was seen as a tenuously held condition from which it was always possible to lapse.[16] In succumbing to alcohol, humours, or the devil, men and women could sink to the level of apes, goats, pigs, dogs, shrews, and any number of other animals. If the "lower bodily strata" were, in the Bakhtinian paradigm, a reservoir of antiauthoritarian sentiment based on bodily functions, in the emergent paradigm of early modern human-animal studies, it is not the grotesque that creates social solidarity but the bestial that threatens to abase rational beings by reducing them to a nature that is always latent in the human constitution.[17]

In his theorization of "the post-human," Cary Wolfe argues that a violent "speciesism," by which animals are to be sacrificed at the altar of the human, is one way humanism constructs its subject:

> The humanist concept of subjectivity is inseparable from the discourse and institution of speciesism which relies on the tacit acceptance . . . that the full transcendence of the "human" requires the sacrifice of the "animal" and the animalistic, which in turn makes possible a symbolic economy in which we

can engage in a "non-criminal putting to death" (as Derrida phrases it), not only of animals but of *humans* as well by marking *them* as animal.[18]

Early moderns saw the line between human and animal as a boundary constantly under threat and in need of shoring up in acts of discursive articulation centered on establishing and maintaining a firm boundary between human and brute beast. This boundary was iteratively constructed in contradistinction to correlative beings on a "lower" ontological plane—animals that could be killed without penalty.

Compelling and analytically powerful as such discussions have been, strikingly absent from the scholarship is any mention of marine animals in the system of brutal reasoning. While scholars have illuminated the complexity of Shakespeare's penchant for depicting human-animal metamorphoses, they have not considered the special place of marine animals in performing this kind of figurative work. Boehrer argues that "Shakespeare toys with the slippages—between woman and beast, for example, or man and monster—that ground the system of meaning of which he is part."[19] As in most early modern literary scholarship, the ocean is erased (or merely forgotten), along with its cultural history. Yet in early modern forensic discussions, natural history, prose descriptions of whale strandings, emblem literature, and Dutch seascapes, the human relationship to whales is depicted in terms of a shared ontology: in our behavior and appetites, we may be like them—and they us—in profound and unsettling ways. Whales perform crucial figurative work in constructing Shakespeare's natural world and defining the human relationship to it, and an ecocritical assessment of their meanings must pay particular attention to the instances in which whales and other sea creatures perform figurative work, however obscure. They are an unusual instance of the "brutal reasoning" that uses animals to construct the category of the human (as Fudge and Boehrer argue). For in comparing exemplary humans —princes and nobles—to whales and in so doing emphasizing their passions, lusts, and appetites, Shakespeare implies the obverse of the conventional scenario of humans slipping down the chain of being to the level of beasts; to the contrary, in their outsize and dangerous appetites, the princes of the sea may differ little from those who lead humanity.

From the biblical leviathan to stars of the screen, stage, and recording studio, whales are the protagonists in one of Western culture's great narratives of interspecies kinship; they also hold a particularly privileged place in the environmentalist movement of the half century preceding the current study. By *whales* I mean the entire family of cetaceans, the *mysticeti* (baleen whales) and the *odonticeti* (toothed whales); the latter category includes dolphins (family *Delphinidae*) such as Flipper (genus *Tursiops*) and killer whales, *Orcinus orca*, (Shamu, Willie, Tilly). Western conceptions of these marine animals have undergone a centuries-long (and only partial) transformation, moving from portraying them as the object of fear and awe to seeing in them the subject of self-recognition. Whales feature prominently in cultural narratives—not only Greek and Hebraic but also Maori—in mediating the relationship of humanity with nature, and they do so under the weight of a cultural history that vacillates between a threatening alterity and a mirror of ourselves: whales are both monstrous and strangely familiar.[20] As the largest inhabitants of the global ocean and proximate to the Judeo-Christian deity, whales have long been associated with the power and brutality of monarchs.[21] In late Renaissance England this tension (or vacillation) surfaces frequently in multiple discourses—forensic, protoscientific, and poetic.

The Bible recognizes a special connection between the human, the divine, and the largest creatures of the deep. In the books of Genesis, Jonah, Job, and the Psalms, the leviathan has a special relationship to the Lord. Throughout the Bible leviathan is a divine sea creature, the instrument of the deity's wrath and providence in the book of Jonah and the symbol of divine omnipotence in the book of Job. As the first creature named in Genesis—"and God created great whales, and every creature that moveth, and the waters brought forth abundantly, after their kind"—the whale holds a conspicuous place in the biblical creation myth that names Adam and Eve as the stewards of every creeping, flying, and swimming thing. Speaking to Job from the whirlwind, the God of the Israelites asks,

> Canst thou draw out Leviathan with an hook? or his tongue with a cord which thou lettest down? Canst thou put a hook in his nose? or bore his jaw through with a thorn? Will he make a covenant with thee? wilt thou take him for a servant forever? . . . Canst thou fill his skin with barbed irons? or his head with fish spears? . . . None is so fierce that dare stir him up: who then is able to stand before me? . . . He maketh the deep to boil like a pot: he maketh the sea like a pot of ointment. . . . Upon earth there is not his like, who is made without fear. He beholdeth all high things: he is a king over all the children of pride.[22]

These verses describe leviathan as God's subject and yet "king over all the children of pride." At the same time that the leviathan is a terrifyingly powerful and fearless sea monster, it is also the deity's special pet: the third verse asks, "Will he make many supplications unto thee? will he speak soft words unto thee?" This special relationship between sea creatures and the divine also animates Psalm 104: "There go the ships: *there is* that leviathan, *whom* thou hast made to play therein."[23] Again we encounter a vacillation between the whale as monstrous embodiment of the deep and as God's creature.

In Greek culture dolphins are similarly playful: in the myth of Arion, music causes the playful dolphins to carry a human ashore on their backs. Commenting on the symbolic role of fish in early Christianity, Brian Fagan observes, "Fish and sea mammals had profound symbolic importance going back to Homer's time. Many species, especially dolphins, carried a cultural association with the dead, carrying such mythic heroes as Achilles on their backs."[24] In the *Halieutica* (second century CE), which Fagan accurately describes as "a five-book didactic poem on sea-creatures and how to catch them," Oppian (Oppianus) of Cilicia writes

> The hunting of dolphins is immoral. . . .
> for equally with human slaughter the gods abhor the deathly doom of the monarchs of the deep;
> For like thoughts with men have the attendants of the god of the blooming sea;
> Wherefore they practice love of their offspring and are friendly one to another.[25]

Oppian's exhaustive poetic descriptions of the creatures of the sea often employ personification but rarely to such a degree as in these lines, where an iconic marine animal clearly occupies a different order of being than other inhabitants of the sea. Dolphins are "the monarchs of the deep," and they play a special role as the attendants of King Neptune himself; they also resemble humans in their social behavior, in that "they practice love of their offspring and are friendly / one to another." Oppian echoes and develops the image of the sociable dolphin in the myth of Arion, whose music caused a group of dolphins to carry him safely to shore.[26] Oppian's emphasis on parental affection and friendliness foreshadows the modern cultural status of

Royal Fish

dolphins: in the *Helieutica* we are not so far from Flipper, the bottle-nosed dolphin whose friendship with a group of American children in the 1960s television show made him a familiar and beloved national pet—Lassie of the Everglades (in a wetsuit)—whose playful and noble behavior in episode after episode constituted a foil for the (un)ethical behavior of humans.[27]

Classical ideas of human kinship were followed by the demonization of whales in medieval Europe. For centuries associated with the demonic and the unknown, whales were less familiar than monstrous, evidence of primal chaos and the punitive Flood. The sea animals in *Beowulf*, for example, are monstrous foes of the *eschatia* (limits, wastelands and waters) who, like Grendel and his mother, must be vanquished for the human social order to survive. By the late Renaissance a transformation in the cultural significance of whales gradually took place along with the transformation of the sea's status from a blank space to an object of fascination. Alain Corbin notes in *Territoire du Vide*, his history of European attitudes toward the seashore, that "in the figure of Leviathan . . . the Bible established the monstrous nature of fish."[28] Yet the prevailing conception of marine animals as universally monstrous eroded rapidly in the sixteenth century as Europeans grew increasingly familiar with mariners' accounts of real whales encountered at sea and whales' corpses on the beach.

Motivated variously by the Reformation, Counter-Reformation, and national-political realignments (in France, the Netherlands, Britain, and elsewhere), late Renaissance cultural production transformed the status of the sea from the supernatural deep to a place where humanity might—in part—belong. This was the case in the British Isles as much as on the continent: whales were a special preoccupation of writers and artists attempting to take stock of the natural world at a time when the human intervention in nature—in the form of grafting, gardens, and countless instances of the social negotiation of the categories of human and animal—as well as anthropogenic crises—war, famine, the overexploitation of resources—loomed large.

The late Renaissance religious fixation on whales has at least a partially religio-economic basis. Were they fish or were they flesh? As Emma Phipson noted over a century ago in *The Animal Lore of Shakespeare's Time Including Quadrupeds Birds Reptiles and Fishes*, "Although whales, seals, and other marine inhabitants were always included among fish by writers in the Elizabethan period, yet there evidently existed in the minds of some authors a misgiving as to whether this arrangement was correct. Pious Catholics were slow to be persuaded that these aquatic mammalians were blood relations of the bear, and resolved as long as possible to take the benefit of the doubt."[29]

The religious proscription on consuming flesh on Fridays and Lent fueled early modern North Atlantic fisheries, most famously the pursuit of herring and cod for sale in Catholic countries. Marine mammals were a problematic source of nutrition on fast days. Larger "fishes," such as dolphins, porpoises, and walruses, were less systematically exploited but nevertheless part of the expanding European maritime commercial enterprise in the early modern period. Beyond the economic and religious issues arising from human contact with marine mammals, natural historians were puzzled by these animals that seemed to resemble humans in strange ways. Classical, medieval, and early modern natural historians, theologians, painters, and poets were fascinated and mystified by marine mammals as occasional features of the littoral landscape, resources of various kinds (including food and fuel), and as an epistemological challenge. What is the true nature of whales? To what order of being do they belong? Are they monstrous or are they fundamentally similar to humans? Is it possible that we and they belong to the same order of being? In prose descriptions of stranded whales, high tides, storms, and emblematic dolphins, early modern natural history reveals a widespread interest in the relationship between humans and marine mammals.[30]

In the context of this ongoing intellectual preoccupation whales were frequently invoked as a vexing and ontologically strange group of animals characterized by bodily appetites and passions on a huge scale. It is certainly in this sense that Shakespeare invokes whales in *All's Well That Ends Well*, when Paroles protests, "I knew the young Count to be a dangerous and lascivious boy, who is a whale to virginity, and devours up all the fry it finds" (4.3.207–9). The gluttony of the whale here becomes emblematic of sexual desire as a "very ruttish" young count (Roussillon) is likened to a whale and the maids of Florence to the "fry" (small fish) that are his prey (4.3.204, 209). This metaphor turns on a familiarity with the diet of whales, which consists in large part of "fry," or small fish.[31] Small fry and virginity are put on the same plane (linked by innocence), while eating and sexuality are also figured as equivalent manifestations, albeit of appetite. The use of "virginity" in the abstract evokes the *sententiae* of emblem literature: Roussillon, a whale rampant, threatens to consume that which makes a maid "vendible." Shakespeare equates the proverbially immense hunger of whales with other appetites, in this case lust. Noting the association of whales with appetite and abduction, Roger Trienens has argued that "on account of its mythological role, Shakespeare makes the whale a virtual symbol of lust."[32] That certainly seems to be the case here, as it is elsewhere.

Lust, gluttony, and an unchecked physicality are similarly constitutive of Sir John Falstaff, whose attempts to seduce two stolid middle-class wives in *The Merry Wives of Windsor* ultimately make him the butt of ridicule and collective punishment. Falstaff is similarly compared with a stranded whale when Mistress Ford asks, "What tempest, I trow, threw this whale, with so many tuns of oil in his belly ashore at Windsor?" (2.1.57). A tun is a large cask; in the early days of whaling, individual whales were assessed in terms of how many barrels, tuns, or casks of oil they would produce. Famous for his girth and dedication to guzzling sack, overeating, and "venery" in the second tetralogy (*I* and *II Henry IV*), Falstaff returns to the stage as a veritable emblem of embodiment and unregulated appetite, spending his time at Windsor attempting to seduce the eponymous wives. Throughout the play his social status as a member of the hereditary aristocracy differentiates him from the members of the bourgeois Windsor social order; as a knight and a gentleman, he exists—according to the sociology of the time—on a different ontological plane from the townsfolk. Like Roussillon, then, he is a big fish among small fry. As Mistress Ford implies in comparing him to a beached whale, a knight angling for adulterous affairs with the wives of shopkeepers is a fish out of water in a middle-class English town. There is an Ovidian dimension to the comparison: in the trajectory of the plot of *Merry Wives*, Falstaff moves from being a whale rampant, as would-be sexual predator, to a beleaguered (and nearly confounded) stag wandering near Herne's Oak, pinched and harried by the smallest fry in town.

The symbolic excessiveness of whales extended to a princely appetite for violence. Not surprisingly, in *Troilus and Cressida* the wrathful Hector on the battlefield is compared to a ramping whale:

> There is a thousand Hectors in the field,
> Now here he fights on Galathe his horse,
> And there lacks work; anon he's there afoot,
> And there they fly or die, like scaled schools
> Before the belching whale. Then is he yonder,
> And there the strawy Greeks, ripe for his edge,

> Fall down before him like the mower's swath.
> Here, there, and everywhere he leaves and takes,
> Dexterity so obeying appetite
> That what he will he does, and does so much
> That proof is called impossibility. (5.5.19–29)

This mixed metaphor figures Hector as both a "belching whale" consuming "scaled schools" and a skilled mower felling swaths of grass. The Greeks are equated with fish consumed by a warrior whose enormous bloodlust—huge and unstoppable—renders him whalelike. The metaphor then shifts, and "the strawy Greeks," no longer fishes but blades of grass, "fall down before him." Here the wrath of the prince on the battlefield is clearly linked to sexual desire, as evidenced by the interchangeability of "appetite" and "will," both of which had a conspicuously sexual overtone in early modern English. This connection between lust and bloodlust is especially evident in *Troilus and Cressida*, a play about adultery, war, and the forms of betrayal that cause them.

In these examples we can discern "brutal reasoning," for in each instance the figure of the whale acts as a foil to limn—and construct—the category of the human by emphasizing the beastly potential of an unchecked governing passion. Thus, Roussillon is subject to whalelike lust (according to Paroles), while Falstaff clearly occupies a zone of being where human and animal threaten to overlap. In the example from *Troilus* the human-whale comparison threatens to become more than metaphorical, as Hector's bloodlust on the battlefield outside Troy tends to dehumanize him. Defined by a lethal "dexterity" and driven by an "appetite" for battle, he becomes a juggernaut killing machine with an unstoppable "will." That the meeting of passion and execution in human form is best likened to a "belching whale" suggests, at the very least, that whales occupied a metaphorically charged space in the Shakespeare bestiary. The passions of a warrior-aristocrat, while awe-inspiring in Hector, are risible in the burlesque form of Falstaff, who becomes, by play's end, not hunter but quarry, preyed upon by the women and children he initially sought to exploit.

A similar if more contextually encoded comparison of the human with the cetacean appears in *Pericles*, a play in which marine life is continually, yet ambiguously, linked to human traits. The playwright stages a voyeuristic commentary on marine metaphors for human behavior. Overhearing a conversation among fishermen in which human behavior is compared—no surprise here—with whales consuming small fish, Pericles himself comments on the tendency to analogize humans as sea creatures. The "Third Fisherman" opines to his boss, "Master, I marvel how the fishes live in the sea," to which his boss replies, "Why, as men do a-land—the great ones eat up the little ones. I can compare our rich misers to nothing so fitly as to a whale: a plays and tumbles, driving the poor fry before him, and at last devours them all at a mouthful. Such whales have I heard on o'th'land, who never leave gaping till they swallowed the whole parish: church, steeple, bells, and all" (Scene 5, 66–73). Using a metaphor that is still current today, the fisherman compares the great and powerful to big fish, while the lowly are "poor fry"—the small fry or poor folk. The fisherman describes a complex set of early modern socioeconomic relations. The metaphor pertains to the major historical transformation in early modern land use in Britain, the enclosure of land for profit in the transition from feudalism to capitalism.[33] Agrarian capitalists are compared to feeding whales because both were proverbial gluttons.[34] The force of the fisherman's metaphor derives from the comparison of wealthy humans to whales "o'th'land," hungry monsters "who never leave gaping till they have swallowed the whole parish." The metaphor gestures toward economic predation as cannibalism: in their "engrossing" of the land, the wealthy become enormous predatory animals, and in this they resemble the inhabitants of the sea best known for their consumption of others. Clearly, the forensic issues about property and consumption evoked by the discussion of marine animals in *Pericles* do more than reflect the ongoing Tudor-Stuart-era debate over the relationship between regal claims to the foreshore; they mediate widespread cultural anxieties about the relationship between human appetites and power. In crafting a persistent pattern of association linking human with cetacean traits, Shakespeare alludes to a longstanding commonplace linking whales and dolphins with human characteristics.

In the first nine editions of the *Systema Naturae*, Linnaeus categorized humans in the class *Quadrupedia*, thereby acknowledging a kinship between humans and other four-limbed animals. In the tenth edition he created the category of *Mammalia*, thereby radically altering the grouping to include the largest creatures of the sea, four limbs now less significant than lactation, viviparous birth, and warm-bloodedness. In systematizing the human kinship with marine mammals, Linnaeus contributed to the displacement of an anthropocentric cosmology. Thenceforth we were kin to whales (*cetacea*) as well as to seals and sea lions (*phocae*) and manatees and dugongs (*sirenia*). Our transformation from four-footed beasts to the close relatives of sea creatures was, in Wayne Hanley's words, "the result of [Linnaeus's] pondering the problem of what to do with the whale."[35] The growing awareness of our species similarity with sea creatures challenged centuries of thinking about humanity's unique place in the universe. As Hanley quips, "to accommodate the whale, Linnaeus changed man and his hairy cousins into mammals."[36] Hanley gives Linnaeus too much credit. The special relationship between whales and royalty has a strikingly long and developed history, from Aristotle, Pliny, and Oppian to the present day. Long before Linnaeus, Aristotle noted, in the *History of Animals*, that whales were not fish: "The dolphin, the whale and all the rest of the cetacea, all, that is to say, that are provided with a blowhole instead of gills, are viviparous . . . just as in the case of mankind and the viviparous quadrupeds."[37] The comparison to humans is explicit: cetaceans are born live, not hatched from an egg, and breathe air, "just as in the case of mankind."

Influenced by Aristotelian natural history and by a developing proto-empiricism that would produce Francis Bacon, late Renaissance artists and intellectuals reflecting on the rapidly expanding human understanding of the biosphere found the problem of what to do with the whale, or, more precisely, of how to represent the human relationship to marine animals, a peculiarly seductive challenge to their powers. One of the great conceptual challenges for early modern natural historians was the establishment of taxonomic system for terrestrial and aquatic mammals.

Early cetological inquiries emphasize the intellectual challenge of taking the measure of an animal that seemed to epitomize the strangeness and immensity of the sea.[38] Oppian's description of affectionate marine mammals is echoed in the work of Olaus Magnus, the sixteenth-century Swedish churchman whose 1535 *Map of the Northern Regions* and 1555 *Description of the Northern Peoples* provided influential (and largely fanciful) descriptions of whales and whaling practices often echoed in the works of later writers.[39] Although the *Description* is laden with sensationalist claims, derived from mythology, about whales, it is also shot through with relatively accurate descriptions of natural phenomena.[40] After giving a lurid account of various "sea monsters" and their enmity toward sailors, the author describes "the wonderful affection of whales for their young":

Royal Fish

When those [sea creatures] which discharge their young alive have given birth, they may suspect that something is planning to ambush or terrorize their offspring. In that case, to protect them or ally with maternal love the anxieties natural to their tender age, the parent opens its mouth and holds its young between its teeth without harming them, and even takes them back into its body, so it is said, by concealing them inside its womb. Thus it gives them life, in a sense, a second time with the warmth of its body heat and sustains them by its own breathing, so that the two are living in one frame until it brings them to safety, or by setting its body as a barrier, defends its brood at its own peril.[41]

Never mind, for a moment, the inaccuracy of this account; what matters here (for my purposes) is the detailed case being made for the special status of "those which discharge their young alive." Fact is mixed with fantasy, but there is more of the former than we tend to believe. Magnus demonstrates some awareness of the mammalian physiology of whales in the same description: "Since whales have no gills, they breathe through tubes, a feature to be found in few animals. When their young are weak or frail, they carry them, and when they are small they hold them in their mouths. . . . She still accompanies them for a long time after they attain maturity for, although they grow quickly, they reach full size only after ten years." As the fabulist-cum-natural historian then asks his readers, "What human tenderness could match the parental devotion of fishes? See how Nature preserves in them what is seldom discerned in mankind."[42] The "mamas" of viviparous sea creatures deliberately protect their young and keep them warm.

Emblem literature, too, highly popular in the late sixteenth century, employed the work of natural historians to moralize about human life in allegorical images with captions. The well-known emblems of Joachim Camerarius, in his multivolume *Symbola et Emblemata* (Nurnberg 1590–1604), contains a group of allegorical depictions of whales and dolphins that resonates powerfully with Shakespeare's cetacean metaphors. These emblems are highly allusive and intertextual: the opinions of Oppian about dolphins—the smallest of the *cetacea*—were familiar enough in the sixteenth century that Camerarius cites him explicitly. Several of Camerarius's emblems graphically illustrate the human qualities of dolphins, particularly their sociofamilial nature. The twelfth emblem in his collection of emblems of the sea, which bears the title *Haec Cura Parentum* (This is parental care), depicts a small

FIGURE 4. Joachim Camerarius, Emblem XII, sig. D1r, fol. 13 (dolphins). (Folger Shakespeare Library)

fishing boat in which two fishermen are harpooning dolphins (figure 4).[43] Inside the boat is a fresh haul of dolphins; in the water adjacent to the boat are two small dolphins followed by a larger one about to fall victim to human hunters. The caption reads, *Mirus amor sobolis: mater quod comprobat ecce Delphini, captae quae soboli immoritur* (Love for offspring is wondrous: behold the mother of the dolphin proves this, dying with her captured offspring). In his textual commentary on the emblem, Camerarius cites Oppian on dolphins.[44] The ekphrastic display of human-animal kinship in this emblem is an instance of explicitly "brutal reasoning" in its erasure of the line between motherhood and marine mammals. The explicit anthropomorphization of a well-known and—in the symbology of late Renaissance cultural and political life—highly significant marine mammal is offered as a wonder of a somewhat conventional variety.

Another of the emblems of Camerarius, *Metuenda Procella* (The storm should be feared), depicts two dolphins at play on the open sea while, in the background, a threatening sky—dark clouds and rain—looms over a bold coast (figure 5). The caption reads, *Contrahe vela, licet ludant Delphines in alto, / Nam tunc tempestas non procul esse solet* (Draw in your sails, let the dolphins play in the deep, / For then a storm is usually not far), ascribing a harbinger status to dolphins ("a storm is usually not far"). This is precisely

Royal Fish

the sentiment of the fisherman in *Pericles* who tells his fellow worker, apropos of porpoises (in the same family as dolphins), "Nay, master, said not I as much when I saw the porpoise how he bounced and tumbled? They say they're half fish, half flesh. A plague on them, they ne'er come but I look to be washed" (5.63–66). The porpoise implicates the fisherman in a marine ontology: at one level, the claim that he "look[s] to be washed" when he sees one indicates the proverbial harbinger of a squall; at another level this formulation suggests the mirroring function of a sea creature, the company of a marine mammal erasing the boundary between terrestrial and aquatic life. The hint of shared identity in this passage is only reinforced by the lines that follow, in which another fisherman develops the proverbial topos of the cannibalism of marine life as an analogy for human behavior.

The emblems of Camerarius reflect the Renaissance discourse of natural history. In the sixteenth century natural historians such as the Swiss Conrad Gesner entertained the idea of a human kinship with marine mammals; Gesner does this in the fourth volume of his exquisitely illustrated compendium of illustrations and prose description of all known animals, the *Icones Animalium* (1551–58). Gesner discusses and graphically illustrates the fact that all genera of marine mammals, whales (by which he means toothed whales), "*Balenae*" (baleen whales), dolphins, and the "*Phocaena*"

FIGURE 5. Joachim Camerarius, Emblem VII, sig. B4r, fol. 8 (storm with two dolphins). (Folger Shakespeare Library)

(seals) breathe air, give birth to live young, and lactate.[45] In this he follows Aristotle. As if to confirm that Gesner had glimpsed the possibility of a human kinship with marine animals, he includes in his chapter on dolphins and whales an image of a highly anthropomorphic sea monster purported to have been discovered in the Mediterranean. Continental naturalists such as Camerarius and Gesner entertained the idea of humanity's kinship with whales and even based a substantial amount of their life's work on such comparisons.

In *The Description of England*, the Elizabethan William Harrison categorized the *cetacea* as the "round fishes" in his narrative map of the nation's natural resources. For Harrison marine mammals were fundamentally similar in kind to fish, differing only in size and shape. Several decades later the more intellectually curious essayist Thomas Browne would devote a chapter to demystifying the nature of spermaceti in his *Pseudodoxia Epidemica*. Browne understands a natural phenomenon as a conceptual challenge, musing, "What spermacetti is, men might justly doubt, since the learned Hofmannus in his work of thirty years, saith plainly, *Nescio quid sit.*"[46] That Browne would devote a chapter to the nature of spermaceti in this treatise on common intellectual errors about nature (first edition, 1646) confirms the slippery epistemological status of whales in the late Renaissance.[47] For Browne, fascinated by the intellectual foreignness of marine phenomena, the immensity of the sea and its inhabitants was enough to grant marine life a special status in the natural world—at least the equal of terrestrial creatures—which Shakespeare, too, entertained consistently. Whether Shakespeare knew the work of the natural historians who were his contemporaries, he shares with many of them the habit of deriving moral *sententiae* about the symbolic significance of dolphins in human life.

The depiction of whale strandings and the interpretation of their soteriological, national-historical, and moral significance was a widespread preoccupation in Dutch art and English prose tracts at the turn of the seventeenth century. Whale strandings have been described by writers from antiquity to the present, but rarely with such intensity of focus as in the Dutch Netherlands in the final decades of the sixteenth century. The phenomenon of whales accidentally or deliberately getting caught in the shallows and perishing is a common phenomenon in coastal waters around the globe.[48] Aristotle commented on the phenomenon in the *History of Animals*: "It is not known for what reason they run themselves aground on dry land; at all events it is said that they do so at times, and for no obvious reason."[49] "It is not known": here lies the crux. Europeans produced very little knowledge about whales between Aristotle and the sixteenth century. In beached whales they found portentous and disturbing signs of the divine will that evoked the biblical Flood.[50]

The coastal Netherlands was a particularly common region for whales to go fatally astray. In his study of early Dutch national history, Simon Schama notes, "Between 1531 and the end of the seventeenth century there were at least forty occasions when whales landed up on the dune coasts of the Netherlands along a line from the Flemish shore east of Antwerp to Beverwijk just north of Haarlem."[51] Occurring at a time when the entire Netherlands was embroiled with Spain in a religious and political agon of epic proportions, these strandings were seen as momentous events. As Ellis observes, "Most of [these strandings] seem to have been sperm whales, and with its huge head, its mouthful of ivory teeth, and—in what appear to be a majority of the cases—its male genitalia prominently exposed, the dead whale must have been a wonder of wonders to the Dutchmen who came to view these monsters."[52] The spectacle of dying whales on the beach was viewed as a portentous drama of national-political and soteriological significance. As Schama has argued, these episodes became central to the iconography of the young Dutch nation-state: "The North Sea coastline . . . was as treacherous a passage to outsize marine animals as it was to unpiloted ships. The providential geography that guarded the Fatherland from vengeful galleons also fatally bewildered the migrating bachelor bull whales."[53] Religious history as much as natural history shaped the aesthetic representation of whale strandings. Beached whale disaster allegories (in paint and prose) became a major factor in the creation of a distinctly nationalist discourse of the relationship between history, nature, religion, and the emerging nation-state.

Graphic depictions of stranded whales were common enough in the late sixteenth and early seventeenth centuries for Camerarius to have imitated the drawings and engravings that I shall discuss here. Figure 6, for example, depicts what can only be a beached sperm whale, yet it does so in a conspicuously more naturalistic mode than any of his other emblems of whales. What I wish to consider here is a body of work by Dutch artists who found the spectacle of whale strandings to be of theological and political significance. For instance, the 1577 engraving by Johan Wierix in figure 7 dramatically

Shakespeare's Ocean

FIGURE 6. Joachim Camerarius, Emblem V, sig. B2r, fol 6 (whale). (Folger Shakespeare Library)

depicts a pod of sperm whales massed like an armada at the edge of the shore. Three whales are already high and dry, while the rest are headed in that direction. These are not quite the medieval sea monsters with snouts and fangs conventionally depicted in sixteenth-century cartography; with their bulbous heads and torpedo-shaped bodies, they are anatomically somewhat accurate (although their blowholes and pectoral fins are notably inaccurate). The naturalistic dimension of this painting is less prominent than its allegorical elements, which are portentous: in the face of what looks like a naval invasion by a fleet of sea monsters, the human figures on the beach flee toward higher ground. Produced at a tense historical conjuncture when the Dutch were engaged in much soul-searching while casting off the Spanish yoke, this engraving suggests that in spectacular natural phenomena the nation was being reminded by a higher power of its threatened and beleaguered condition. The whales are emblems of threat, tribulation, and divine wrath.

The national-political significance of a single stranded whale plays a major role in the composition of what is perhaps the most famous beached-whale illustration, a drawing by the Haarlem master Hendrik Goltzius from 1598, engraved by the artist's nephew, Jakob Matham, and copied by another artist, Willem van de Gouwen (figure 8). The print dramatically portrays the

Royal Fish

FIGURE 7. Johan Wierix, *Three Beached Whales*, 1577. (Courtesy MIT Museum)

fascination excited among a crowd of Dutch onlookers by a huge male sperm whale lying dead on the beach. The recumbent corpse of the enormous sea creature in the center is crowded by smaller figures. For here the whale is naturalized into the littoral landscape as a curiosity and a resource, something to which the humans are naturally drawn and inevitably engaged in examining, measuring, and describing. What is perhaps most striking about this illustration is the representation of human efforts to "fathom" or measure the immense whale carcass in familiar terms.[54] The human figures are actively engaged in taking measurements, making offerings of bits of the whale to social superiors, climbing on the carcass itself, and intensely contemplating the beast from nearby vantage points. The animal's penis is being carefully measured by one figure while another uses it as a stepstool. The emphasis on conceptually domesticating the immensity of a leviathan in one's own backyard is explicit. For Schama, the difference between the Wierix and Goltzius illustrations is a move from the wondrous to the quotidian: "It is the absorption of the extraordinary into the ordinary that is

FIGURE 8. Willem van der Gouwen, *Beached Whale*, 1598. (Courtesy MIT Museum)

so striking."⁵⁵ The emphasis on the grotesque has been superseded in the later image by an atmosphere of calm interest, the human figures going about the business of business by cutting into the corpse with an axe, filling wooden casks with effluvia from the dead beast.

The increasing verisimilitude of these depictions of sperm whales becomes, by the early seventeenth century, quite striking. The compositional emphasis on human efforts to measure the monstrous whale corpses and thereby find or produce meaning from a nearly shapeless and inevitably rotting carcass become the basis for the allegorical *parerga* in what is perhaps the most magnificent portrait of a beached whale, the 1602 engraving of Jan Saenredam, *Beached Whale near Beverwijk* (figure 9). Saenredam's exquisite illustration is more anatomically accurate than the earlier ones, especially in the placement of the pectoral fin; it is also laden with cartouches, rebuses, and textual apothegms in Latin and Dutch that trumpet various *sententiae* —morals to be drawn about the significance of the event. In the upper left

Royal Fish

frame the Maid of Amsterdam is falling from the heavens, having been shot by the Angel of Death. In the central upper portion, a miniature drawing of Amsterdam reveals a subterranean cutaway showing wheels and the caption *terra motium* (moving land). Everywhere the emphasis is on the unnatural, the cataclysmic—and the portentous.

While Dutch artists produced the most magnificent representations staging wonder at the phenomenon of whale strandings, the subject was of widespread interest in the late Renaissance. In England the representation of whales cast upon the beach caused a horrified fascination with the strange and unnatural spectacle of "that which drew from out the boundless deep" (as Tennyson put it over two centuries later). Prose pamphlets from the seventeenth century emphasize the unnatural in their accounts of beached whales. The title of a 1617 theologico-political rant masquerading as news is suggestive: *A true report and exact description of a mighty sea-monster or whale, cast vpon Langar-shore ouer against Harwich in Essex, this present moneth of Februarie 1617. With a briefe touch of some other strange precedent and present occurents.*[56] The accompanying illustration is a rather poorly executed and unacknowledged copy of the Goltzius/Matham illustration. Equally

FIGURE 9. Jan Saenredam, *Beached Whale near Beverwijk, 1601.* (Rijksmuseum, Amsterdam)

dramatic is the language of the title. This beached whale is a thing half supernatural: not only is it a "mighty sea-monster" but its demise is framed in terms of a discourse of the "strange." Indeed, for the anonymous millenarian writer of this pamphlet, the whale functions as a sign of the unnaturalness of natural phenomena "in these strange times." Among the other natural signs of divine displeasure the pamphleteer discerns, the confusion of waters and lands causes the most alarm: "What grievous deluges outragous Inundations, and unresistable overflowings of Waters, not historie nor man recording the like (since the generall Deluge) whereby many hundreds of Acres of pasture serviceable land have but in a little space turned (as it were) into a Maine-Ocean, that the fishes floating in their new made regiments, have fed on the drowned carkaises of men, women, children, and beasts."[57] Land and sea monstrously overlap. The discourse of the monstrous becomes vivid: human bodies are eaten by fish, "serviceable land" becomes "Maine-Ocean," and divine wrath becomes manifest in the "overflowings of waters" that threaten to erase the crucial religious boundary between the land and the deep.

The final wonder that the pamphlet relates is that "the Maine-Ocean disgorged herself of a mightie Sea-monster or whale, I know not whether to term it." Poised on the border of the natural and the supernatural, the huge beast beggars the descriptive powers of language itself. The pamphleteer wisely concludes by musing, "Now whether this Monster of the Sea bee ominous or not, I had rather leave to the wise and learned than myselfe to determine."[58] Notable about this text is the central place of the whale in illustrating the unnatural recent events that manifest divine wrath. The pamphleteer takes it as self-evident that a whale, a monstrous inhabitant of the "Maine-Ocean," should never be found on land, and in this unnatural displacement there is a religious lesson to be learned. The pamphleteer is merely a ham-fisted follower of the Dutch artists; his sermon follows the contours of conventional disaster allegories. Let this be a lesson for you, the story goes, for by reading the book of nature you can see the hand of God.

Whether Shakespeare was aware of the Dutch seascapes being produced at the height of his own career (and it hardly seems possible that he was not, given the widespread currency of the Dutch material), his references to beached whales share the emphasis on efforts to exert conceptual mastery over the monstrous embodiment of the sea. Yet far from emulating his continental contemporaries in ascribing soteriological, national-political, and cosmological significance to whale strandings, Shakespeare consistently deflates their portentousness. In *II Henry IV* and *The Merry Wives of Windsor* whales act as foils for the very human traits of princes. The comparison of Prince Hal with a stranded whale puts the prince on an even footing with his symbolic kin. Yet while Shakespeare hearkens the sermonizing pamphleteers who found divine portents in the monstrous presence of animals out of their element, he is concerned not with the theological but the psychological significance of these episodes. Whales are for him emblems of human passions, motives, and behavior.

This tendency aligns the playwright with what the intellectual historian Brian Ogilvie describes as "the early modern European cult of the fact."[59] The rise of natural history in the sixteenth century began to transform the prevailing notion of the sea as a dangerous void into a realm of strange life not entirely foreign to the human. The developing late Renaissance cult, or culture, of the fact was transforming the cultural prism through which Europeans viewed the world ocean through a largely supernatural lens to an increasingly empirical and protoscientific one.[60]

How much Shakespeare owes to contemporary depictions of marine animals by artists and natural historians is an open question. What is certain, however, is that whales, princes, passions, and national politics for him shared a strange kinship, and this kinship was a significant feature of protoscientific, forensic, and artistic depiction of marine mammals being produced in the British Isles and on the European Continent throughout the playwright's lifetime. That Shakespeare would refer to stranded whales more than once suggests a remarkable degree of familiarity with marine phenomena. It is tantalizing to speculate about Shakespeare's actual knowledge of cetacean behavior, particularly since the playwright grew up on a tributary of the Severn River, with an estuary that provides a vital marine ecosystem that has supported marine mammals—including cetaceans—for millennia.[61] Noting that "Shakespeare mentions the whale several times," Phipson speculated that "it is quite possible he may have seen a stranded specimen."[62] Yet the temptation to locate knowledge of the natural world in the playwright's biography obscures a different and more likely basis for the beached whale metaphors: a burgeoning cultural production—from natural histories to Dutch art to emblem literature—in which the behavior and significance of whales became a special topos for reflecting on the human relationship to the marine environment.

Modern environmentalism evokes the biblical account of whales' proximity to the divine by defining them as one of the foremost emblems of environmental ethics. In recent years whales have become emblematic of the human ability to incorporate the radical alterity of the sea into familiar definitions of the environment—in short, to find ourselves in the space of the Other. In 1980, the year the International Whaling Commission (IWC) voted for a moratorium on commercial whaling, the exhortation to "Save the Whales" often shared a bumper with "No Nukes." The IWC moratorium was the result of a dramatic rise in environmental activism spurred by a boom in cetological inquiry. Scientists studying whale "songs" had demonstrated that many of the larger cetaceans can communicate across vast distances—tens, hundreds, possibly even thousands of miles—at sea. Trainers at aquaria had learned to communicate with dolphins, beluga whales, and orcas, putting on public display behaviors that vividly demonstrated the extraordinary intelligence of the smaller toothed whales. Volunteers for Sea Shepherd Foundation regularly risked their lives in their efforts to rescue whales from commercial harvesting by Japanese, Icelandic, and Norwegian whalers, often motivated by a powerful sense of kinship with marine mammals.[63] The terrible death of Dawn Brancheau, which I discussed at the start of this chapter, produced a counternarrative to the dominant cultural narrative of whales that had recently been given new power by the documentary film *The Cove* and by the television series *Whale Wars*, both of which appeal to a sense of human kinship with marine mammals.[64]

In the same year that commercial whaling was officially proscribed and the "Save the Whales" movement reached its height, Raffi Cavoukian recorded "Baby Beluga" (which no parent of the past three decades can have ignored), a melodic evocation of the idea of shared mammalian identity. This children's song encapsulates the major themes of the Western cultural history of whales, not least of which is a theologically inflected articulation of the idea of a shared mammalian identity linking humans with marine mammals: a "baby" Beluga whale is addressed as if it were a human child. "Heaven above and the sea below," the scenario evokes Psalm 107, with the playful whale frolicking under the eye of an approving deity. "Is your mama home?" asks the songwriter, putting a whale on the same ontological plane as a human child: frolicking in a warm sea under the sign of a beneficent "heaven above," the eponymous "baby" is a thoroughly anthropomorphic creature, a human baby imagined as "wild" and "free." Lest the audience miss the tenor of the song's conceit (whale equals human child) the "mama" in the chorus reminds us that fellow-feeling for another mammal is what is at stake.

Psalm 107 evokes a similarly frolicsome whale: "There go the ships: there is that leviathan, / Whom thou has made to play therein."[65] The little whale is an emblem of human harmony with the environment. By questioning that harmony, Raffi asks us to reconsider our own relationship with the natural world. Raffi, who styles himself an "eco-troubadour," was not the first to articulate the idea of a human-cetacean kinship, as we have seen, but the specific form of his articulation hit an international nerve.[66] As Simon Schama puts it, "the moral indignation generated over the commercial slaughter of whales is of a different order from concern for other endangered species like the osprey or the tiger. Its bulky innocence—power without guile—seems to act as a prophetic reproof against the capacity of humanity to court hubris."[67] Writing about a very different historical conjuncture than late twentieth-century environmentalism, Schama, like Raffi, nevertheless offers an insightful assessment of the cultural status of whales as emblems of innocence and foils for human nature. In killing them, we kill something of ourselves.

6

Shakespeare among the Fishmongers

> We being little fishes, as Jesus Christ is our great Fish, begin our life in the water and only when we abide in the water are we safe and sound.
>
> TERTULLIAN, *De Baptismo*

The story of Britain's terrestrial commons has often been told in literary scholarship, yet one of the most dramatic chapters in the early modern "tragedy of the commons" is an oceanic one.[1] The mutual impact of a global ocean on an explosive European bourgeoisie took place not merely in the imagination but also on an ecological level. The first global fish market emerged in Europe between the eighth and tenth centuries as a response to increasing demand for cold flesh among the ecclesiastical community and thence gained momentum during the early modern period.[2] In the England of the Tudors and the Stuarts, fish was a staple food, a religious symbol, and a ubiquitous feature of everyday street life in London and most English towns. Seafood was also a commodity of such quotidian familiarity as to be nearly beneath notice: humans consumed crabs and oysters at the open-air theaters; cats fed on fish offal in the ill-drained London streets; and fishing fleets landed enormous hauls (by today's diminished standards) in London, Yarmouth, Brixham, and Hull. From the salmon that spawned in the Thames to the herring, pilchard, and cod that sustained the English populace during the many fasting periods of the year, the fruits of the sea were commonplace in Shakespeare's England. Seafood also provided fodder for another kind of commonplace, literary topoi employed by poets and playwrights to articulate the nature of the human animal.

The sheer quantity of piscatory imagery in the Shakespeare corpus makes it all the more surprising that scholarship has neglected to account for the massive cultural and nutritional debt owed by Britons to the sea, and for England's role as a pioneer of fisheries. While it might seem absurd to look to Shakespeare for commentary on the historical development of European fisheries, his writings display a highly developed metaphorics of marine life, hitherto unremarked, that not only bespeaks a nuanced awareness of the particular qualities of commercially viable species and their social impact but vividly contributes to a distinctly late-Renaissance discourse of human-animal relations.

In this chapter I argue that Shakespeare's plays and poems mediate the cultural effects and human implications of the modern global fish market, at an early stage of its development, in a metaphorics of fish that imparts a notably salty flavor to plays that would at first seem unlikely. Even in a play set entirely on land, such as *Romeo and Juliet*, fish do crucial figurative work, as they do in plays with recognizably maritime settings—*Twelfth Night*, *Pericles*, and *The Tempest*. Shakespeare was not "our contemporary,"[3] but he did inhabit a culture saturated by fish—much more so than ours (if by "ours" we mean a world in which the majority of food comes from grocery stores selling delocalized food commodities), and his plays evoke a world in which human social and somatic space were to a significant degree constituted by fish. Shakespeare contributed to a cultural poetics of fish in metaphors and imagery that link human ontology—desire, hunger, mortality, and the fact of embodiment—with the bodies of marine animals gathered from the depths of the global ocean and sold in the street. In coded metaphors and allusions that too often go overlooked, Shakespeare transmuted the reeking remains of the herring, pilchard, eels, whiting, cod, and sprat that he knew so well into a dramatic world that owes some of its pungency to its maritime nature.

This chapter explores the nature of that piscatory transmutation throughout Shakespeare's works. I examine the cultural poetics of fish and fish markets in late Renaissance England to decode Shakespeare's complex figurative association between humans and marine animals. I argue that, far more than just an allusion to the ubiquity and threat of an ever-expanding placeless market, the metaphorics of fish are an index of the constitutive role of the sea in the production of social institutions and human bodies. Food is both metaphorical and resoundingly literal in Shakespeare; he everywhere emphasizes the materiality of the food products of the early modern global ocean. Shakespeare never seems to lose sight of the fact that seafood played a constitutive role in the body social and the body private. Unlike an earlier generation of scholars who insisted that Shakespeare's notably accurate depictions of the sea were evidence of his personal experience with it, I doubt if Shakespeare ever knew the thrill of a fish on the line, the glee of a full boatload, or the despair of working depleted fishing grounds.[4] He certainly never knew the mortification, as we do today, of being told that the salmon special of the day—brought to table after a brief life of antibiotics and dyed a "natural" shade of pink by petroleum byproducts—was "organic farm-raised Atlantic salmon."[5] But Shakespeare demonstrably associated the verbal trickery of "turning" words by troping on fish (itself on occasion "turning" —rotting or going rank) with fishmongers, and with his own craft.

Shakespeare may or may not have known a hawk from a handsaw, but he certainly knew a herring from a pilchard. While bantering with the disguised Viola in *Twelfth Night*, Feste employs a simile turning on the distinction between the two kinds of fish. When "Cesario" asks the melancholy fool, "Are you the Lady's Fool, sir?" the latter responds with a verbal dissimulation: "No, indeed, sir; the Lady Olivia has no folly: she will keep no fool, sir, till she be married; and fools are as like husbands as pilchards are to herrings: the husband's the bigger. I am indeed not her fool, but her corrupter of words" (3.1.27–31). The wit in Feste's simile hinges on the audience's awareness that herrings and pilchards are nearly indistinguishable in appearance but differ slightly in size. By gesturing to them in a simile that turns on visual familiarity with their physical qualities, Feste foregrounds the thematics of disguise, misrecognition, and twinning that drive Shakespeare's comedies. For by claiming that he is not what he is (a fool) and that the lady's future husband will be the bigger fool in any case, Feste renders himself a fishy character, a "corrupter of words" who turns meaning as quickly as fish turns on a hot day. The simile evokes an ontological continuum between and within animal species. Just as there is little apparent difference between a pilchard and a herring, so, too, do a fool and a husband resemble one another: the former is merely a smaller version of the latter. Thus, two nearly identical species of fish become figures for the fool's commentary on the interconnections between corruption, language, and sexuality.

In Feste's simile human nature is refracted through a saltwater lens to amusing and unsettling effect. Identity, figured in terms of two nearly indistinguishable kinds of fish, becomes a matter of exchangeability. At the moment Feste hints to the disguised Viola that human beings can uncannily duplicate one another, she is herself dissimulating her gender and taking part in a sexual game that links her—like a seafood commodity washed up on the beach—to the entire social order of Illyria. Feste's figure of speech is situationally apt, for separating the identity of Viola from that of Cesario is merely a thin veneer of clothing and a minor adjustment of affect—a difference as small as that between herrings and pilchards. Dramatic irony emerges from the suggestion of replication: Shakespeare's characteristic metatheatrical humor flashes forth in a wink at the audience, which is expected to be able to distinguish between herring and pilchards, while Olivia (and the other Illyrians) consistently fail to see the difference between the twins Viola and Sebastian (presumably different in size as well).[6]

To compare a human with a herring was in fact to reference one of the largest markets in late Renaissance Europe. The global fishing bonanza that has led to empty nets around the world and a comparatively empty global ocean began in late medieval Europe and accelerated in the early modern period as North Atlantic fisheries boomed to keep pace with rising demand.[7] Closely related to several species of small, silvery fish commonly found in European waters, including sardines, anchovies, sprat, and herring, pilchard are members of the genus *Clupea* (family *Clupeidae*). Fish of this kind were popular staples in various European diets. Salted, smoked, or fresh, herring and pilchard were ubiquitous sources of food in Shakespeare's England.[8] The great seventeenth-century English naturalist John Ray remarked on the similarities in physical appearance among the various *Clupeidae* on a visit to Italy in 1694: "I remember very well I took Notice of the *Sardina* and *Sardone* at Rome, calling them always at dinner *Pilchard* and *Herring*. All the *English* were of my Opinion. . . . I cannot think of any Difference, only (that which you intimate) Magnitude."[9] Sometimes, size matters: "magnitude" seems to have been the only differentiating feature in distinguishing among the herring-like fishes, even for an extraordinarily perceptive observer such as Ray. As he goes on to observe, "*Sprats* I know to be nothing else but the young fry of *Herrings* and *Pilchards*; both which Fishes come to their full growth in a Years time or less, and then breed."[10] Ray had good reason to invoke the opinions of his fellow English diners, for pilchards and herring are abundant in the cold northern waters around the British Isles, their annual migratory pattern making them available to fishermen from the north of Scotland to the south of England in the fishing season (summer and fall).[11]

That such marine species were familiar to the likes of Shakespeare and

Ray—writing at either end of the same century—undoubtedly owes more to the early modern fish market than to either man's seafaring experience. The enormous growth of this market throughout Western Europe made herring an extremely lucrative—and common—staple and a key feature of several national cuisines, and the English were major players in the North Sea herring fishery. Between the beginning of the seventeenth century and the middle of the nineteenth, notes the Danish environmental historian Bo Poulsen, "salted herring was one of the principal bulk commodities to be traded in the North Sea and Baltic area, and was the most important type of food transported between the two seas in the early modern period with the exception of grain."[12] The significance of the herring market in shaping early modern European tastes, sensibilities, and urban spaces has recently been demonstrated by economic, environmental, and cultural historians who argue that the rapidly expanding world picture of late fifteenth- through seventeenth-century Europeans reeked of fish.[13]

In his study of the development of North Atlantic fisheries to supply the rising demand for cold flesh on religious fast days, the historian Brian Fagan argues that the international herring fishery that developed in the late middle ages motivated the voyages of early modern European navigators more than any concern for "discovering" a New World. Investors and mariners strove to develop the fisheries that were so lucrative in European markets because of the proscription on eating land-borne "hot flesh" on fast days.[14] For religious reasons, then, salted and smoked herring were nothing new in late Tudor England. The scope of the medieval herring fishery had expanded enormously between the eleventh and fourteenth centuries to keep pace with burgeoning monastic demand, a churchly appetite that expanded over time owing to the development of new methods of preserving fish. The late medieval explosion in fish markets had several results: by the fourteenth century, herring had become the premier seafood in Europe (in terms of its widespread availability, not its appeal to refined palates), fish stocks in onshore waters were being depleted, fishermen were making longer and longer voyages, the Scarborough and Yarmouth fairs—primarily herring markets —were major institutions, and we can be confident that nearly any Briton would have been familiar with the shape and smell of several forms of herring preparation.[15]

Another result was the development of new fisheries as herring stocks fluctuated. The pilchard fishery rose to prominence in Shakespeare's lifetime. With competition for herring rising, demand for the pilchard also grew rapidly in the fifteenth century as West Country fishermen increased their activity on the Irish Sea (which abounded in the species):

> Pilchard became a major commodity somewhat later [than herring]; the first export references to it come from the 1460s. It was a regular export by the 1490s but not a large-scale one until the late sixteenth century. New processing methods preserved it for transport. The curers salted the catch for a month, then washed it and packed it in barrels before pressing it with heavy weights to drain off the oil. The result, called fumadoe pilchard, became popular in hot Mediterranean lands, because it lasted longer than North Sea herring and required less salt to cure.[16]

Feste's simile, then, evokes the extraordinary development of the first multinational European fish market (herring), associated with East Anglian ports such as Great Yarmouth, and the growth of a relatively new domestic fishery in the West Country (pilchard), a region intimately tied to England's rise as a maritime power. In economic terms herring and pilchards were commodities supplied by fisherfolk of Northwest European nations for a multinational market across Western Europe. In cultural terms these members of the family *Clupeia* were a literary commonplace so familiar that the playwright could use them as a metaphorically available yet polysemous emblem of the street, the space of circulating bodies and commodities where appetite, sexuality, and cheapness converged.[17]

By Shakespeare's era herring and pilchard were commonly available in London and, for that matter, the rest of the kingdom, to the point where they had become synonymous with the satisfaction of Lenten appetites. When in *King Lear* Edgar, disguised as Tom O'Bedlam, complains of being hungry while out of doors on the heath, he specifically craves a meal of herring: "Hopdance cries in Tom's belly for two white herring" (3.6.28). Edgar's craving threatens to give away his identity, for he names a delicacy more familiar to the first sons of aristocrats than to sturdy beggars: "white" herring referred to the fresh fish, not the more common salted and smoked variety known in England as "red herring," and was associated with the Scottish fishery.[18] Because of their oily flesh—laden with the Omega 3 fatty acids so well marketed today, among their other desirable nutrients—herring are difficult to preserve, which presented a real challenge in a time before refrigeration, flash freezing, vacuum sealing, and next-day shipping.[19] Whereas before the development of curing processes that preserved fish for more than a few hours, seafood—and particularly herring and pilchards—moved through coastal markets to be consumed locally, by the late Renaissance they were available in population centers all over Europe, some of which were located well inland (but nearly all on rivers or deltas). In England most herring were preserved by a laborious process of pickling and smoking that turned skin and flesh a vivid shade of red. White herring was less commonly available. By the early seventeenth century, the lowly herring—unlike larger species of fish such as turbot and tuna, which appealed to patrician tastes—was common fare for all, even to the point of losing their appeal: "Heavily salted medieval herring were disliked by the poor and the sailors and soldiers who received them as rations. The fish were dry, sticklike, and if poorly preserved could be either tasteless or rancid, very like a poor form of modern-day jerky."[20] The same quality that makes herring a highly nutritious food also makes them ephemeral; herein lies the metaphorical appeal for a playwright enamored of metamorphosis. The oily flesh "corrupts" quite rapidly—just as Feste turns words.

The herring is synonymous with corruption, in the fleshly form of libido and in the discursive transformations of a character such as Feste.[21] The quality of rank transience undergirds the tenor and the vehicle of Feste's simile: different species of fish can be nearly indistinguishable, while a single fish itself can transform from food to offal in short order. Later in the same scene, scarcely a hundred lines after Feste's simile links fools with pilchards and husbands with herrings, Viola herself takes up this linkage of social identity and foolery as a fishy matter. Olivia's nascent desire for Viola/Cesario, who is apparently a potential herring-husband but in fact closer to a pilchard-fool, produces a crisis of identity that puts into question the status of erotic and embodied selves. When (s)he tells Olivia, "I am not what I am," the Lady replies, amorously, "I would you were as I would have you be." Viola responds, "Would it be better, madam, than I am? I wish it might, for now I am your fool" (3.1.132, 135). Or her pilchard. In its limited resistance to decay and its protean ability to permeate and restructure the social fabric, salt fish blurs the line between nature and culture. This flirtatious exchange evokes the idea of a continuum between being a small fish in the game of love ("Now I am your fool"—recall Feste's simile) and the possibility of becoming a bigger one, a herring-husband, at the moment when Olivia becomes aware of her own attraction to the mercurial Cesario.

In *Twelfth Night* Shakespeare persistently suggests an ontological connection between humans and the sea: he seems to delight in constantly reminding his audience of the seaside setting of the action, and that Viola and Sebastian—who cause so many realignments and transformations by landing in the social order of Illyria—are themselves human salvage, recently redeemed from the surf, who become objects of sexual appetite as they circulate in Illyrian society. My maritime reading might at this point begin to seem a bit Malvolian ("Let me crush this a little") if the lines that follow did not explicitly evoke a maritime context. For Olivia attempts to dismiss Cesario by saying "There lies your way, due west," to which the disgruntled go-between replies, "Then westward ho!" echoing the way Thames watermen advertised transport upriver (3.1.126–27). This formulation evokes for the audience a transitional space, the watery boundary and preeminent maritime superhighway of the Thames.[22] She is neither here nor there, fish nor fowl, master nor man. The coast of Illyria is not merely a vehicle for putting in motion an essentially terrestrial plot based on misrecognition and providential reclamation; it is simply the most visible feature of a thematic "marine ecology"—the idea that humans resemble sea creatures—that the playwright subtly develops throughout the play. Feste's fishy simile, then, tellingly comments on Viola's (and Sebastian's) existential condition: they are strange fish redeemed from the sea, and they are both in the process of "turning." Even if human lives transpire on land, nothing about them truly stands on solid ground.

This crisis of identity, located on the liminal seashore of an uncertain coast, suggests an aquatic dimension of human identity. Shakespeare does something similar in *The Comedy of Errors*, when Antipholus of Syracuse ponders the problem of identity with the telling line "But if that I am I," asking Lucia, "Are you a god? Would you create me new?" (3.2.41, 39–40). He then enjoins her to metamorphose him: "Transform me, then, and to your power I yield," calling her a "sweet mermaid" (3.2.40, 45). The dramatic irony here lies in the audience's awareness that Antipholus and his twin have indeed been transformed already by the cosmic agency of the sea; he is himself something of a merman. In this he resembles Iago, another dissembling character associated with a maritime context. Iago and Viola both insist, "I am not what I am."

Commenting on Viola's temporary condition as a "beachcomber" in search of her brother, Mentz argues that "Viola's 'not,' her self-negation and radical distance from herself, underlie her beachcomber's identity. . . . The destabilizing force of the seashore, the place in which she can't tell Illyria from Elysium, undergirds Viola's crisis of identity."[23] Mentz's assessment of Viola's oceanic instability is insightful: the sea is a powerfully disruptive force throughout the play, and the twins operate at its edge, on the margins of the social order of Illyria and the structures of gender that suture it. I would add to this notion of an oceanic crisis of identity that the disruptive power of the sea is carefully laid out in terms of fish and "fools" as embodied selves caught in a net of discursive play. Finding a future spouse is contingent on Olivia's own willingness to put herself into circulation on the marriage market, which she has resisted doing because of her demonstrative love for her dead brother.[24] The fact that Olivia falls in love with Viola in the latter's masculine guise and ultimately pairs off with her twin Sebastian develops the notion, latent in Feste's fishy simile, of human identities circulating like exchangeable commodities. A simple misrecognition of one type of body for another nearly identical one powerfully affects the social structure of Illyria, and order is only restored once accounts are reckoned—accounts that reckon human identity and human flesh in terms of the marriage market. Shakespeare thus offers a coded commentary on the foolishness of humans as vendible (marriageable) creatures by depicting characters as commodities circulating in analogous markets. There is something fishy about such a complex human transaction in gendered bodies: by entering the marriage market we become, like fish, commodities circulating within social space. In our social lives we are closer to fish than we know.

For Shakespeare, who regularly depicts marriage as a market in which lovers are both merchants and merchandise, peddling and peddled, to mention herring is to invoke a market in cold flesh, putting into question the distinction between human flesh and salt fish, desire and commodification, disguise and the early modern subject. Human bodies in Shakespeare circulate in spaces much like the herrings and pilchards to which Feste likens their condition; somatic space is interarticulated with commercial space. At the same time, audiences and readers are often reminded in reading or

Shakespeare among the Fishmongers

watching the plays that humans are nourished by the preserved flesh of radically deracinated (as it were) dead animals imported from distant seas. Throughout the corpus, Shakespeare's humans have a profound and complex ontological connection to the sea based not only in religious history (as the epigraph to this chapter makes clear) but also in the material nature of the body. At once desirable and potentially abject, the dead bodies of preserved fish perform a peculiar kind of figurative work in the writings of Shakespeare, which I call *figurative fishmongering*—the comparison of human flesh to fish and human communities to fish markets.[25]

Figurative fishmongering is not unique to *Twelfth Night*. Elsewhere in the corpus can be found a similar tendency to link humans and fish by way of hinting at a shared corporeal marketability. Meat—whether cold or hot—inevitably carries sexual overtones in the early modern imagination, and we know from *Hamlet* that the line between panderer and purveyor of fish was a thin one. Polonius is twice called a fishmonger.[26] The meddling old courtier gets at least something right when he links the charge with pandering: "Still harping on my daughter. Yet he knew me not at first—a said I was a fishmonger. 'A is far gone, far gone, and truly, in my youth I suffered much extremity for love, very near this" (*Hamlet*, 2.2.187–91). Polonius misreads Hamlet's motives, but he is right—in a metatheatrical fashion—to connect eros with the fish market.

In *Romeo and Juliet* Mercutio, that rhetorical protean, describes Romeo with the unique descriptor "fishified," a participle that occurs nowhere else in Shakespeare, notwithstanding numerous other references to fishes of many kinds. In the second act Benvolio announces, "Here comes Romeo, here comes Romeo!" to which Mercutio adds, "Without his roe, like a dried herring. O flesh, flesh, how art thou fishified!" The line is heavily laden with puns. Romeo without his "R-o" becomes a lover's solipsistic lament, "Me, O" (2.3.32–34). Unaccompanied by his lover, conventionally figured in love poetry as a female roe deer, Romeo is a hart who at the moment "lack[s] a hind," as another fool puts it in a different play.[27] The additional simile, "like a dried herring," then complicates the animal imagery by comparing Romeo not to a male deer but to a fish that has lost its roe (eggs) in the process of curing.[28] A dead fish is a limp thing, and Romeo's lovesickness has, in Mercutio's view, weakened and feminized him, rendering him a poor substitute for the piece of man-flesh he once was. The lover is a dried herring.

The fish that Mercutio uses so familiarly as a simile for his friend's condition was in the playwright's lifetime an everyday object and a cheap meal—a quick fix, as it were, for Lenten appetites, hence nothing special.[29] Just as it does in all the comedies, desire here produces insecurity and instability regarding the construction of gender. The linked notions that excessive Petrarchan posturing rendered one self-involved, too much dedication to female company emasculated men, and that fish was a less nourishing substitute for "hot" flesh (appropriate for feast days because "cold")—all this is relatively obvious seen through the lens of early modern cultural history.

Less clear is what Mercutio means by "fishified" flesh. Beyond the obvious sexual imputation of Romeo's having become a limp man, his friend implies that the young lover is no longer truly himself. Latent in Mercutio's use of the term *fishified* is the implication that Romeo has prostituted himself, dissimulating his true nature and thereby demeaning himself. When he thus rails at the lover's self-induced commodification for a market in human bodies, Mercutio resembles that other wise fool, Feste; both of these mercurial skeptics associate dissimulation with the corruption of the flesh. This link between fishiness and abasement becomes more apparent in the next several lines of the scene, where literary lovers of yore lose their luster in comparison to Romeo's new desire: "Now is he for the numbers that Petrarch flowed in. Laura to his lady was a kitchen wench—marry, she had a better love to berhyme her—Dido a dowdy, Cleopatra a gypsy, Helen and Hero hildings and harlots, Thisbe a grey eye or so, but not to the purpose" (2.3.32–38). Classical female love objects are cheapened by comparison to Rosaline, not only because they fail to measure up to her in Romeo's estimation but because, in Mercutio's construction, they are, like the dried herring that describes him, common, cheap literary devices with which Romeo can indulge himself in pseudo-Petrarchan posturing. These lovers are also very much in evidence on the street, served up as cheap discursive commodities. So is Romeo's love. Thus Mercutio implies that Romeo is his own fishmonger: in pimping himself out to a cheap and derivative style of love, Romeo figuratively becomes both merchant and commodity. The lengthy exchange between Mercutio and Romeo that follows the latter's arrival on the scene is laden with sexual puns and colorfully lays out a panoply of meanings for "fishified flesh." The readiness with which Mercutio's criticisms turn to good-natured banter also suggests that, for Shakespeare, the market in human flesh, like the herring market, was a quotidian feature of life in a late

Renaissance city such as London or Verona and at the same time a pungent material challenge to emergent notions of self-fashioning, the conspicuous display of mastery over symbolic and semiotic codes.[30]

In these examples humans are composed not of the neoplatonic essences imagined by Petrarchan lovers but of the oceanic commodities they eat and strangely resemble. There is a literal as well as a metaphorical dimension to the insight that we are *of* the fish we eat, nourished by matter transported from the sea: at one level we are reminded of the material fact that early modern human bodies were materially constituted by the consumption of fish; at another level, dramatic art—like urban space—in the late Renaissance was to some extent constructed as a mosaic of consumable objects imported from afar. The result is something of a *verfremdungseffekt*, a denaturalization of familiar objects (human faces and bodies), emotions (love, desire), institutions (marriage), and discourses (gender) made pungent by the evocation of fishes—those rank oceanic bodies always on the verge of "turning." Shakespeare's figurative fishmongering renders characters, such as Viola and Romeo, not subjects so much as figures of embodied desire caught in the social networks of signification that surround them.

Herring enjoyed a widespread currency elsewhere in the literature of the time, inciting Thomas Nashe to sing its praises and made infamous as the last meal of Robert Greene. That literary culture—not only theater—was affected by the herring market is attested by the prose of Greene's fellow Cambridge alumnus Nashe, in *Lenten Stuffe*, his sprawling prose narrative of Pierce Pennilesse of Yarmouth—for centuries England's premier herring port. Nashe writes copiously of herring. Pierce, a youth who "(almost) goes to sea," discovers a utopia of herring.[31] In a text that incorporates and parodies chorography, chronicle history, and encomium, Nashe inaccurately but confidently boasts, "I am the first that euer set quill to papers in prayse of any fish or fisherman." He goes on to praise

> the puissant red herring, the golden Hesperides red herring, the Meonian red herring, the red herring of Red Herringes Hall, every pregnant particular of whose resplendent laud and honor to delineate and adumbrate to the ample life were a work that would drink dry fourscore and eighteen Castalian fountains of eloquence, consume another Athens of fecundity, and abate the haughtiest poetical fury twixt this and the burning zone and the tropic of Cancer.[32]

Nashe's paean to the fish commodity derives its humor from the incommensurate. Comparing the grandeur of classical culture (the Islands of the Hesperides) with the quotidian street food does more than induce laughter: "The herring's metaphoric thrust opens outward to a brave new watery world," one where fishermen and the herring they catch are exalted and Great Yarmouth is crowned England's Mecca of fish.[33] Even the landscape of the port of Yarmouth, a sandy locale, is a fluid one, formed by shifting sands over the years.

Nashe renders the red herring a figure for the commodity and market relations and in so doing represents the body in similar fashion as a commodity in the erotic markets of *Twelfth Night* and *Romeo and Juliet*. To write about herring in Tudor-Stuart England was to meditate on the material substance of the nation-state as well as of the body. English red herring, "salted but not gutted and left to rest for two or three days before being smoked over a slow-burning fire in special smokehouses, smoked and aged," was considered a poorer product than the fresher, firmer flesh of Scottish white herring.[34] Thus, not only does Nashe's encomium exalt a humble object, it also builds a nationalist narrative around its emblematically English —and distinctively ranker—method of preparation. In light of the fact that "the Dutch high seas herring fishery, *De Grote Visserij*, was the largest and most organized fishery in pre-modern Europe," competing for the same herring stocks as the English fleet sailing out of Yarmouth, we should take Nashe's claims with a dash of salt.[35] Yet by aping the rhetoric of scholarly inquiry Nashe offers something substantial: buried in the verbal barrages is a ludic epistemological inquiry into the nature of matter and form.

In his discussion of "the epistemology of the commodity" in *Lenten Stuffe*, Henry Turner calls attention to "the flourishing interest in the physical substance of everyday life that characterized early modern England": "Although the red herring appears at first as merely the immediate occasion for Nashe's bravura rhetorical performance, it soon emerges as a trope for any object of knowledge whatsoever and sets in motion a series of competing epistemologies of the object that together provide both the form and the content of Nashe's text."[36]

Nashe's overheated style masks a serious conceptual dimension that connects the narrative with the work of early modern natural historians:

Shakespeare among the Fishmongers

> Beneath the patina of neologisms and nonsense phrasing that lends to *Lenten Stuffe* its air of deliberate inscrutability, Nashe's treatment of his red herring in fact corresponds closely to Aristotle's conceptualization of change as motion, and I suggest that the encomiastic sections of *Lenten Stuffe* reflect the basic principles of hylomorphism, in which a particular substance might be decomposed into its constitutive *forma*, its properties, qualities, or attributes.[37]

For all his unsystematic verbiage, Nashe looked deeply into the physical substance of persons, places, and things—and what he saw was market relations refracted through the red and silver scales. As Turner argues, by making familiar objects strange in a frantic prose that apes various learned discourses, particularly chorography and natural history, Nashe employs and critiques "the hylomorphism, or matter-form theory, of neo-Aristotelian philosophy."[38] The hylomorphism that Turner locates in *Lenten Stuffe* offers a critical purchase on early modern thinking about the boundary between the human and the animal as well as the line between nature and culture.

As I discussed in the previous chapter, recent studies of human-animal relations in early modern literature have analyzed the discursive construction of the human as an unstable ontological category in religious and protoscientific discourse. The work of Erika Fudge, Bruce Boehrer, and others has challenged and complicated our understanding of "the limits of the human"; these scholars have illuminated the logic of Shakespeare's figurative use of animals to negotiate the status of human characters.[39] Humans live in constant danger of falling back (or down, in the *scala naturae*) into an animal nature that constitutes our fleshly, fallen nature and gives a somatic vestiture to our "animal" appetites. The discourse of the human-animal boundary is, ultimately, hylomorphic if the status of the human—the very humanity of human beings—is fundamentally unstable, constructed in iterative comparisons with what "we" are not.[40] What Turner identifies as a discourse of the commodity in *Lenten Stuffe* I locate in Shakespeare as a critical discourse of the marine environment in constituting the human. The Shakespearean metaphorics of fish suggests that the instability of the rational human animal derives not only from the threat of slippage "downward" toward the bestial but, more viscerally, from our physical connection to the materiality of the commodities that nourish us. The idea that human beings are essentially composed of fungible qualities, subject to being "fishified" (rendered self-alien) at every turn, is a peculiar instance of human-animal hylomorphism. For the metamorphic (and metaphoric) qualities of herring put the status of "the human," and the categories that define it (gender, social station), radically into question. Other kinds of fish have a similar metaphorical significance, as I will argue later.

The market forces that made fish—in a "dry, stick-like" form—a daily feature of life in early modern England exerted a cryptic (and before Darwin, cryptogenic) agency over human lives. Put simply, we are what we eat, in our somatic condition and our social lives, and we also *resemble* fish in peculiar ways that lend themselves especially well to metaphor. Thus, fish evoke mutability, an originary liquidity that slips under the radar of Aristotelian hylomorphism in the protean undermining of the distinction between form and matter, land-borne beings and sea creatures, human bodies and fishified flesh.

This insight is remarkably consistent with the insights of the environmental writer Wendell Berry, who argues, "'Environment' means that which surrounds or encircles us; it means a world separate from ourselves, outside us. The real state of things, of course, is far more complex and intimate and interesting than that. The world that environs us, that is around us, is also within us. We are made of it; we eat, drink, and breathe it; it is bone of our bone and flesh of our flesh."[41] Berry's point of view is, of course, historically quite removed from that of Shakespeare and Nashe, but the way Shakespeare writes about the natural world aligns him with these claims. For fish is not *merely* a metaphorical presence in the writings of Shakespeare; it is a floating signifier for materiality. Far from producing the kind of oneness with place, landscape, and creation that Berry and many ecocritics pursue, the insight that the human body is materially *of* this world (including the sea in all its strangeness) and not hovering above destabilizes traditional conceptions of nature and human nature. The effect of this insight is certainly unsettling for such characters as Feste and Mercutio, whose laughter is tinged with melancholy and bitter railing against mortality. If we are what we eat, then we do not truly know ourselves, or, to modify Viola's protestation to Olivia, if we truly are marketable bodies (like fish), then perhaps "[We] are not what [we are]."[42]

The use of fish as metaphors for human qualities and appetites tends to denaturalize human motives, bodies, and the institutions within which

Shakespeare among the Fishmongers

Shakespeare's characters circulate. As Karen Raber writes of recent studies of human-animal relations, "The more early modern discourses about human identity attempt to establish a clear division of human from beast, the less stable that division becomes,"[43] precisely because the human animal comes to be seen as *constituted* by what it putatively is not: a discursive and material assemblage of parts derived from other bodies (by eating) and distant places (by means of the market). For not only is food (particularly meat) metaphorically and symbolically charged (as in all cultures), it also connects the body with markets in potentially self-alienating ways. This is especially true of herring, as Turner emphasizes in his reading of *Lenten Stuffe*:

> The red herring exceeds all other commodities and renders them superfluous through its prodigious generative power. But even in its very "materiality" the red herring is perpetually transforming and evolving, an object that is never self-identical at any given instant and one that remains, finally, too particular, too heterogeneous in and of itself to submit to any given form of equation or quantification—exactly the operations that define the commodity form and that are necessary for the generation or appearance of value."[44]

Aristotle's distinction between form (*morphe*) and matter (*hyle*) elevated the idea of lumber (Nashe's "stuffe") to a metaphysical status (*materia*, matter).

As gender theorists such as Judith Butler have observed, this distinction also encodes a traditional binary between an active male principle of form (*schema*) and a passive female matter (*materia*). In Butler's analysis, "The matrix is an originating and formative principle which inaugurates a development of some organism or object. . . . In reproduction, women are said to contribute the matter; men, the form."[45] This association between gender, "sex," and substance was not lost on Shakespeare, whose fishy metaphors in *Twelfth Night* and *Romeo and Juliet* exploit that binary in a festive interrogation of the mutability and materiality of persons. What if the form of an object—its schema—is indeterminate and mutable, as in the case of herrings and pilchards? The inevitable result is to put the stability of matter into question.

This, I submit, is the figurative function of herring in Shakespeare. Olivia's relationship to her own sexuality and Viola's status in the marriage market of Illyria are depicted figuratively in terms of a relationship between appearance (Viola's masculine form) and hidden substance (her feminine "matter") which the dramatic action reveals to be illusory or, at least, a product of dissimulation (and discourse). Similarly, Romeo's amorous posturing threatens to erode the distinction between masculine and feminine—as Mercutio notes in likening him to a female herring cheaply (and effeminately) doting on love-objects who are themselves defined by a shopworn Petrarchism. Just such a metaphorical exposure of the instability of language and the mutability of flesh haunts Falstaff's protestations of valor in *I Henry IV*: "If manhood, good manhood, be not forgot upon the face of the earth, then am I a shotten herring" (2.5.116–17). A "shotten herring" is a lean fish because it has "shot" or spawned its roe (eggs); it is, thus, an inapt figure for the fat Sir John (more apt for Romeo).[46] Even funnier than the juxtaposition of a corpulent human with a slim fish in this figure is the audience's awareness that the "manhood" Falstaff claims to embody is a joke. Linking his own (nonexistent) valor to his rotund shape, Falstaff gestures to a dramatic irony: we know him to be a coward, no more the embodiment of martial *virtu* than a dead fish. His manhood, like his valor, is cheap and evanescent.

This erosion of boundaries goes beyond the construction of gender by revealing the fungibility of social spaces as well. Noting that "animals cross lines we usually draw imaginatively between wild or rural places and towns or cities," Raber argues that the figurative boundaries between human and animal are not only vexed and porous, but "they are also transgressive of physical environmental boundaries."[47] In examining the role of parasites, Raber follows "animals' transgressive trace" in *Romeo and Juliet* and *Hamlet*, plays that are saturated with the language of parasites and vermin. Cats—those persecutors of mammalian vermin—loom large as well in the former play and are particularly significant in the construction of characters such as Tybalt ("thou prince of cats"), while rats play a major figurative and spatial role in the latter. While human-animal metaphors threaten as much to denaturalize—to make something strange by exposing its constitutive parts—as to construct the category of the human, foregrounding vermin and parasites offers a commentary on the social body, which, far from being inimical to the parasitic, is constituted by the illicit species it polices but nevertheless requires. Social structure is as much a product of the organization of interspecies interaction as it is a matter of policing the boundaries of licit and illicit species. This is especially true of marine animals, as evidenced by the pervasiveness of fish as a vehicle for mediating gender, desire, and matter in Shakespearean drama. Fish, an abundant commodity that permeates both bodily orders, the somatic and the social, exposes the facticity of norms just as other animal metaphors reveal humanity to be a construct. Comparing people with fish differs significantly from comparisons with apes, dogs, cats, or asses, in part because of the greater extremity in the degree of difference between the two sides of the simile.

By Shakespeare's lifetime herring found stiff competition from cod as the foremost cheap seafood commodity. Cod and its commercially viable relations comprise the *gadoids* (*Gadiformes*), a group of midsized predator fish that includes haddock, pollock, hake, cusk, and whiting. The most commercially viable of the *gadoids* are commonly known to fishermen as "groundfish" because of their tendency to feed at the bottom of the water column, "on the ground," in the cold waters above relatively shallow banks (or shoals).[48] These banks have long been known as fishing grounds, and those of the North Atlantic—east and west—have historically been among the most fertile in the world. Commercially viable fish species (particularly cod) were massively abundant in many regions of the North Atlantic until quite recently, and in the sixteenth and seventeenth centuries they became a supremely important source of protein and food culture all over northern, western, and southern Europe.[49] Harvested for centuries in Norway, the Faeroe Islands, and Iceland, codfish became the basis for a European fish market that would become, by the nineteenth century, truly global in scope.

Because of its extremely high levels of protein and low levels of fat, the flesh of the cod was a far superior candidate for preservation and transshipment in a world without refrigeration than herring, pilchard, or any of the *Clupeidae*. The Norse had been fishing cod and preserving it by drying the fillets on shore for centuries before it became an international food commodity. The Dutch word for dried cod, *stikvis*, from which the English "stockfish" derives, literally means "stickfish."[50] The board-like product could be transported and stored with relative ease because laborers were able to stack it like cordwood. Indeed, a piece of stockfish so resembled a plank of wood that the aquatic prankster John Taylor (1578–1653), a Thames waterman who dubbed himself "the water poet," once rowed a paper boat, with oars made of stockfish tied to canes, down the Thames from London to the island of Sheppey in the Thames estuary (where the makeshift rowboat finally fell apart).⁵¹ This exploit is celebrated in his poem "The Hemp-seed," which enjoyed a certain vogue when it was first published. Fish as lumber: stockfish oar blades. Fish as timber: "stickfish" stacked high like cordwood. It is as easy to overlook the material histories of early modernity as to miss the cultural connotations of matter in all its diverse permutations.

As Butler argues, matter itself is a discursive product and not merely the inert real that lies somehow outside of discourse: "The Greek *hyle* is wood that already has been cut from trees, instrumentalized and instrumentalizable, artifactual, on the way to being put to use. *Materia* in Latin denotes the stuff out of which things are made, not only the timber for houses and ships but whatever serves as nourishment for infants: nutrients that act as extensions of the mother's body."⁵² The implications of Butler's discussion for my own turn on the gender politics of fish as commodities, which I believe function to emblematize the fundamental instability and mutability of matter, particularly of human flesh in its gendered (dis)guises. One implication of Shakespeare's metaphoric insistence that humans are like fishes (a cultural commonplace that I will examine later) is that flesh itself is radically mutable, always in a state of becoming, ontologically ungrounded, and subject to "turn" or transform. In its longstanding association with maternality, the womb, and productivity, the sea (Sp. *la mar*, Fr. *le mer*) evokes a primal materiality differentiated from the land or firmament by its lack of a schema, or legible form. Just as the timber (hyle) provides the material for the edifices of civilization, fish commodities provide the material nourishment for the bodies that circulate within those structures.

Somatic matter and socio-spatial matter are physically interconnected: both are products of discourse, and of the market. As Butler goes on to observe, "Matter seems in these cases to be invested with a certain capacity to originate." The fruits of the sea, present to the senses as matter always in a state of transformation, synecdochically represent the sea itself. Shakespeare's metaphors of fishified flesh not only expose some of the constitutive ingredients of the human bodies that make up European civilization, they make those bodies doubly strange by suggesting a profoundly mutable basis for matter (thus the body) itself. Bodies that circulate in the marketplace, such as Viola's and Mercutio's, bespeak an originary liquidity—a metamorphic essence that cannot be stilled. A metaphorics of stockfish would thus provide a superb instance of the hylomorphism that Turner articulates in his discussion of *Lenten Stuffe*, for the material qualities of the substance, and its etymology, remind us of the materiality and the mortality of flesh. Stockfish was a bit like beef jerky—even more so than herring—and so offered an efficient source of protein that was easily transported and extremely durable. It was also proverbially dry, which virtually ensured that it would also be figuratively associated with sexual aridity.

Shakespeare exploits the figurative association between stockfish, hardness, and dryness in *Measure for Measure* when Lucio describes the puritanical hypocrite (or hypocritical puritan) Angelo in memorable fashion: "Some report a sea-maid spawned him; some that he was begot between two stockfishes. But it is certain that when he makes water his urine is congealed ice" (3.2.16–18). The symbolism is well worth unpacking. First, Angelo's coldness, literal and sexual, associates him with a "sea-maid," a supernatural being, half woman, half fish, long thought to lure seamen to their deaths. The joke about his frozen urine reinforces the association of the sea and Angelo's "unnatural" (asexual) generation. Angelo is a cold fish below the belt; he was not born but "spawned." His sexual prudishness makes him not only cold but also dry; thus, it is symbolically appropriate to imagine him, alternatively, as the offspring of "two stock-fishes," emblematic of aridity. Comparing him to dead fish also implies that he can "turn" with ill effects, which proves prophetic, as Angelo indeed turns out to be spectacularly subject to the same vices that he polices and scorns. Eventually he is exposed as a creature as rank as the lowest criminal in the dungeon—appropriately enough, the pirate Ragozine.

Shakespeare was drawn to the figurative possibilities of stockfish on more than one occasion. In *1 Henry IV*, Falstaff exploits the association of stockfish with dry flesh in the litany of insults that he levels at Prince Hal: "'Sblood, you starveling, you elf-skin, you dried neat's tongue, you gull's pizzle, you stock-fish! O for breath to utter what is like thee! You tailor's yard, you sheath, you bowcase; you vile standing-tuck" (2.5.226–29). From insults directed at Hal's relatively abstemious physique, "you starveling," to sexual insults linking phallic objects with malnourishment, "you tailor's yard," Falstaff's derisive ladder builds on the central figure of the stick-like dried codfish. This catalogue of long, dry, hard objects foregrounds an etymological connection between food, sex, and phallic objects, for "cod" in the early modern idiom not only signified a particular species of fish, it also had sexual connotations, with codpieces most prominently and also, more broadly, with the body and its appetites. In Old English a "cod" was a bag or bag-shaped object.⁵³ The "cod-end" of a fishing net, where the netted fish collect, is not, as one might expect, named after a specific species of fish that would end up there; rather, it is so named because "cod" denotes anything resembling a bag or sack. The end of the net, where the fish collect, is shaped like a sack. Many a codfish has met its end in the cod end of a fishing net.⁵⁴

When in *The Tempest* Stephano the tippling butler forges a drunken alliance with the strange fish Caliban and begins to plot an insurrection against Prospero's regime, he warns his fellow servant, "Trinculo, run into no further danger: interrupt the monster one word further, and, by this hand, I'll turn my mercy out o'doors and make a stock-fish of thee" (3.2.66–68). Stockfish was traditionally beaten before being cooked, in hopes of tenderizing the flesh, so Stephano is threatening his fellow servant with a beating.⁵⁵ Yet the suggestion of killing and dismemberment animates the threat as well, for stockfish were dried fillets (beheaded and gutted). This threat takes place in a scene where human life overlaps with marine life: Trinculo calls Caliban "thou debauched fish," referring to the fact that Caliban, like the two marooned servants themselves, is quite drunk. Trinculo then describes Caliban as "being but half a fish and half a monster" (3.2. 24, 26–27). In a brief part of one scene, then, both the familiarity and the foreignness of the global ocean are emphasized.⁵⁶ Stockfish, a common item in Shakespeare's world, and an alien creature "half a fish and half a monster"—both can be found on England's shores.

In addition to drying, the main method of preserving the flesh of *gadoids* was by curing them in salt. Drying and salting took place ashore on drying racks known as "fish flakes" until the nineteenth century, when larger vessels effectively became factory-processors with the capacity to catch and cure fish. In some coastal regions fish are still cured on the beach. Salt cod came in several grades; one of the lowest of these grades, generally from the Newfoundland cod fishery and common enough in England, was known as poor-john.⁵⁷ Nashe mentions this substance as the quotidian nutrition of Yarmouth fishermen when he makes a case for the importance of the herring fishery in producing English mariners:

> And lightly not a slop of a rope-hauler they send forth to the Queen's ships but he is first broken to the sea in the herring-man's skiff or cockboat, where having learned to brook all waters and drink as he can out of a tarry can, and eat poor John out of sooty platters, when he may get it, without butter

or mustard, there is no hold with him, but once heartened thus, he will needs be a man of war, a tobacco-taker, and wear a silver whistle.

Here a herring fisherman is described in detail, and it transpires that the food he eats is not herring but cod. Only the toughest of tars could consume unaccommodated poor-john "without butter or mustard," and from "sooty platters" at that.[58]

In contrast to stockfish, poor-john was "green" (fresh) and not thoroughly dried before salting; it was also not as rigid a substance as stockfish, and it inevitably carried a riper aroma. Its limpness, not surprisingly, made it an easy target for Shakespeare's salacious wit. In *Romeo and Juliet*, Gregory tells Samson, "'Tis well thou art not fish. If thou hadst, thou hadst been poor-john" (1.1.27–28). The insult concludes their game of bantering about their own sexual prowess. Because it was cheap, limp—compared to the drier stockfish—and somewhat shriveled, poor-john makes a fine insult to belittle Samson's boasts. It is this fishy substance that Trinculo invokes to describe Caliban's bodily presence on the beach in *The Tempest*. Caliban's initial impression to the European beachcombers as a "strange fish" is developed in language that refers to the global cod fishery—and possibly to herring fisheries as well. When he sings "No more dams I'll make for fish" (2.2.171), he is referring to fish weirs, nets attached to poles for trapping anadromous fish such as alewives—a New World cousin of herring and pilchards. Caliban's physical presence bespeaks an ontological hybridity that encompasses man and fish.[59] When Trinculo asks, "What have we here, a man or a fish?" he answers his own question with a striking description: "A fish, he smells like a fish; a very ancient and fish-like smell; a kind of not-of-the-newest poor-John. A strange fish!" (2.2.25–26). The jester's first impression of the islander appeals to smell, the most visceral of the senses. Poor-john was the lowest grade of dried salt cod available in the European market; many months and miles away from its origins in the cold waters of the Northwest Atlantic, it inevitably stunk.[60] The Grand Banks cod fishery, which by Shakespeare's day had overtaken the herring fishery as the premier source of Lenten protein, is only one basis for the jester's expostulation on "strange fish."

Caliban's status as a "monster"—the most common term used to describe him—connects him to sea creatures, particularly those of unusual appearance that were treated as marvels during the Tudor-Stuart vogue of exhibiting strange fish for public entertainment. The Victorian Edward F. Rimbault commented in 1859 on the use of the phrase "strange fish" to describe a marvel or oddity: "To call a person, distinguished by odd ways or quaint conceits, a 'strange fish,' is not uncommon in our own days; but it took its origin in times long since past, when strange monsters in fish and flesh were among the daily amusements of the sight-seeing gazers of the old metropolis. . . . The exhibition of strange fishes appears to have been at its height in the age of Elizabeth."[61] Rimbault's philological inquiries turned up some literary references to strange fish in broadsides, plays, and chronicles. In the Stationers' registers of 1595 he found an entry for a "strange report of a monstrous fish that appeared in the form of a woman from her waist upward, seene in the sea," and a "licence to Francis Sherret to show a straunge fish for a yeare, from the tenth of March, 1635."[62] An interest in sea monsters featured prominently in the writings of sixteenth-century natural historians as well. The line between samples of marine life and marvels was not a strong one (as is the case today). Conrad Gesner's well-known illustration of a humanoid sea monster, for example, depicts a fanciful beast belonging more to the mythical than the empirical world.

These examples provide ample evidence for the currency of the strange in describing the creatures of the sea. Antonio calls Caliban "a plain fish, and no doubt marketable"; Prospero then refers to him as "this misshapen knave" and "this thing of darkness" (5.1.269, 278). Since he has just described Sycorax as "a witch, and one so strong / That could control the moon, make flows and ebbs, / And deal in her command without her power," it requires no great leap of the imagination to see Caliban's ontological "darkness" in terms of a connection to the salty depths.

These fishy moments in Shakespeare bespeak a fascination with the sea as a present absence exerting a powerful effect on literary discourse. English national fisheries were very much on the public mind as the sixteenth century drew to a close. Writing as Shakespeare's career, too, reached its finale, John Smith opined of the Dutch, "Herring, Cod, and Ling, is that triplicities that mekes their wealth & shipping multiplicities."[63] The young poet who grew up on a tributary of the Severn would unquestionably have recognized a pilchard, perhaps even by its smell. As a mature member of a playing company located near the south bank of the Thames, he would also, inevitably, have been familiar with the most common kind of urban street food, dried salt herring, the smell of which surrounded him.[64] Fish markets were a central and ubiquitous feature of urban space in late Elizabethan London. When the Lord Chamberlain's Men moved from Shoreditch to Southwark, they crossed a river that was a major fisheries conduit. The Globe was erected with recycled timbers transported across the Thames in a commercial district dedicated to hawking the seemingly incommensurate commodities of plays and fish.

Steven Mullaney's discussion of the significance of place in shaping late Elizabethan and Jacobean theatrical production is instructive: the nature of the district was commercial, and market relations inflected all features of the urban landscape.[65] Southwark was a space structured by the production, distribution, and consumption of commodities—licit and illicit—used to feed appetites of various kinds, including the spectacles put on at the outdoor theaters, where the baiting of large captive mammals was seen as entertainment comparable with going to the Globe to see a play.[66] The open-air theaters were of course commercial structures built to display embodied stories (plays) and the active dismembering of animals. Nearly half of Yarmouth's herring was transshipped to fishmongers in London.[67] Other forms of bodily entertainment were available close at hand. Urban "stews," like the open-air theaters, offered a commodity associated in popular culture with captive animals, albeit of a rather different order of being than bears and bulls. The fact that the word *stew* could mean either a bordello or a fishpond is highly suggestive in this context, raising the longstanding association of human genitals (and sexual intercourse) with fish. Shakespeare makes this connection explicitly in *The Winter's Tale* when he compares adultery to the unlicensed fishing of a private pond: "He doth suspect that another has fished his pond."[68] Fish ponds were a serious topic among Shakespeare's enterprising contemporaries, such as Gervase Markham and John Taverner, whose husbandry consisted (at least in part) of growing fish.

It makes spatial sense that when Shakespeare considers human sexual behavior in terms of the market, the commodity that seems to come most readily to mind is herring. The unlading and selling of fish took place in the middle of the city, on either side of the bridge that any theatergoer from London would have taken to see a show at the Globe. Just across the river from Southwark, on either side of London Bridge, were Fishmonger's Hall and the Billingsgate Fishmarket, important institutions controlled by the

Worshipful Company of Fishmongers, one of the twelve livery companies of the City of London. First chartered in 1172 and again, combining with the salt fishmongers, in 1537, the Fishmongers were an important institution in the city, their coat of arms a shield, flanked by a mermaid and a merman, displaying crossed herrings. These depict not live herrings, active and swimming in the sea, but herrings as commodities, stiff, dried, and salted, ready for the local market. The urban space of the playhouses was structured—and saturated—by the logic of the commodity in an urban system of interlinked markets where plays and fish mingled promiscuously. The Blackfriars Theater, located across the Thames from the Southwark Bankside where the open-air theaters held sway, had its own wharf where boats landed and anglers fished.

After a particularly harrowing misadventure at sea, Pericles overhears a fisherman waxing philosophical at the shore and comments, "How from the finny subject of the sea / These fishers tell th'infirmities of men, / And from their wat'ry empire recollect / All that may men approve or men detect!" (*Pericles*, 5, 85–88). The "finny subject" evokes a proverbial commonplace, the analogy of human social behavior to fish-eating fish was fodder for numerous early modern artists reflecting on human nature. Shakespeare was not alone in imagining, at the end of the sixteenth century, the implications of the fishiness of human flesh nourished by seafood gathered hundreds or even thousands of miles away from its point of consumption.[69] By the time *Pericles* was written there existed a highly developed literature on this topic.[70] While Shakespeare does not draw explicitly on this literature, it is worth considering his contribution to the representation of marine life in terms of a widespread intellectual and aesthetic preoccupation.

Brueghel's drawing *Big Fish Eat Little Fish* (1557) is a spectacular realization of the proverbial cannibalism of the sea and certainly one that Shakespeare might have had in mind when he wrote *Pericles* (figure 10).[71] In Brueghel's drawing is depicted the dismemberment of various sizes and kinds of fish by several fishermen on a seashore where human existence and marine life overlap in visually horrifying ways. The largest sea creature depicted is an enormous fish lying on the beach and stuffed to the gills with smaller fish, which are being exposed as several human figures eviscerate the larger animal. It has eaten an entire food chain, from mollusks to smaller fish of every variety. A grotesque cornucopia, the body of the dead fish contains a microcosm of the entire sea. Typical of Brueghel's work is the moralistic

Shakespeare among the Fishmongers

FIGURE 10. Pieter van der Heyden, after Pieter Brueghel the Elder, *Big Fish Eat Little Fish*, 1557. (Metropolitan Museum of Art, Harris Brisbane Dick Fund, 1917, 17.3.859)

allegory about humanity this drawing offers. The allegory inheres in the compositional relationship between the humans and fishes that share the coastal scene.

In the foreground is a small boat with three human figures: the man in the stern guts a fish inside of which is a smaller fish, while a man in the bow gestures towards the gutting going on forward to a boy who watches. The small human figure juxtaposed with the larger human figure eerily mirrors the parallel juxtaposition of large and small fish. But this is not the only compositional feature that strongly suggests an ontological similarity—even an identity—between fish and humanity, for a peculiar animal walks on the beach behind the enormous stranded fish, a biped with the body of a fish and the legs of a human. This fish-man is in the act of—no surprise here— eating a small fish. Another bipedal fish-man climbs a nearby ladder leaning against a tree; "he" is an executioner in the act of hanging several small fish. The entire drawing disconcertingly suggests that human beings and fishes share a good deal in common: our bodies and our behaviors overlap, for both kinds of animal are constituted by the consumption of fish. In our appetites we resemble fish, and in this resemblance we see the lineaments of a human nature that partakes disconcertingly of "the hungry ocean."[72]

This mirroring has preoccupied artists for centuries, as Melville's chapter "Brit," in *Moby-Dick*, attests: "Consider, once more, the universal cannibalism of the sea; all whose creatures prey upon each other, . . . and then turn to this green, gentle, and most docile earth; consider them both, the sea and the land; and do you not find a strange analogy to something in yourself?"[73] Melville, an avid reader of Shakespeare, gave us in this novel one of the greatest instances of the idea of humanity's implication in the ocean's hunger.

For Shakespeare as for Melville the nature of this hunger is ambiguous: if the ocean is hungry, it is so because we see in it a mirror of our hungry selves. So did the Milanese painter Giuseppe Arcimboldo. Like Brueghel before and northward of him, Arcimboldo painted extraordinary portraits of humanoid figures; his are composed of natural objects (vegetables, flowers) arranged as faces and busts. His work, commissioned by Hapsburg royalty, was much admired in his day by scholars and aristocrats. In what is to my eye the most arresting of these paintings, *The Water* (1563–64), Arcimboldo depicts a man's profile as a grotesque bodily aggregate composed of diverse marine animals (figure 11). This is fishified flesh made vividly apparent: an entire marine food web forms the human head, with mollusks and crustaceans near the base of the skull and larger finfish (various kinds of edible fish, a seal, and a whale) near the top. The vertical arrangement of creatures suggests the *scala naturae*, but the effect of the entire composition is the opposite, as the placement of scallops and skates on what resembles a human cranium seems to mock the very idea of a hierarchic order of being. The visual effect is at once grotesque and uncanny, a recognizably human figure, not the least bit unitary, as a microcosmic marine ecosystem. The denaturalization of the human face implies a constitutive ontological relationship between the human and the aquatic. Human flesh is replaced or constituted by sea creatures. We are large; we contain multitudes—of fish.

In his ecocritical reading of *A Midsummer Night's Dream*, Robert Watson makes a powerful case for what he construes as an early modern deconstruction of the autonomous subject enacted by artists working on the eve of the subject's inception in European intellectual and aesthetic history. Running counter to the discursive construction of the subject are texts and

Shakespeare among the Fishmongers

FIGURE 11. Giuseppe Arcimboldo, *Water*, 1566. (Kunsthistorisches Museum, Vienna, Austria. Photo Credit: Erich Lessing/ Art Resource, NY)

paintings that expose the facticity of a discursive-somatic entity associated with the unified human subject. Watson points to Arcimboldo's paintings as examples of human figures that are not sutured somatic totalities but composite constructions of smaller entities. When these smaller entities are sea creatures, the implication is that the self becomes as figuratively farfetched as these animals are literally so: native to different geographic regions as well as different marine ecosystems, seals and scallops jockey for space in a human construct (the painting) as they would in a fish market. Arcimboldo implies that we are what we seek to know of nature as much as what we eat, while Shakespeare reveals that we are products of structures, fish market and marriage market, and entities, aquatic life, working through us that determine our actions in strange, unpredictable, and defamiliarizing ways. The body's material being partakes of a market that threatens all kinds of "unnatural" combinations and equivalences. In Arcimboldo as in Shakespeare, the sea and its fruits function not so much as a mirror of human ontology as an anamorphosis of the strange materiality of the flesh—at once self and other—that lies between skin and bone.

When Shakespeare invokes the human relationship to the sea and the creatures that inhabit it he does so in a manner that reminds us of our own ontological condition of partial belonging in the world. The sea is not our home, and the strange presence of fish among us is a reminder that our bodies and social structures are constituted by a hodgepodge of substances and circuits of exchange that blurs the line between the natural and the unnatural. Perhaps that obscurity goes some way toward explaining the currency of fish in Christian symbology. As the epigraph I have chosen for this chapter indicates, the invocation of the divine fills the explanatory vacuum of how on Earth we might be connected to a global ocean that has such creatures in it. Herring are not ultimately reducible to mere emblems of anxiety about markets and the spread of the money form of the commodity (although they are all of that); they also emblematize mortality (as corrupting flesh), transubstantiation (as material instances of the IXTHEUS), and metamorphic gender (cold flesh reheated). Perhaps it is because of the oceans' ubiquitous presence in English culture and society in the form of cheap, salty commodities that Shakespeare persistently associates the depths with mortality.

Shakespeare's contribution to the cultural history of the global fish market exposes the discursive constructions that make bodies—human, animal, and social—socially legible and economically valued and valuable entities, emblematizing with salt fish a market economy in which human bodies and appetites are sustained by resources extracted from distant seas. As Hamlet puts it, "A man may fish with the worm that hath eat of a king, / and eat of the fish that hath fed of that worm" (4.3.27–28). In the end we have our being in a fishy world, impelled toward a condition in which the cloak of flesh that constitutes us will become, as it is in the sea, food for worms or other fish. Fish—the protean protein of early modern Europe for Shakespeare—bespeaks a verminous liquidity: like vermin, the commodity is transgressive, crossing boundaries and undermining categorical distinctions between objects, orders of being, and selves. The presence of fish in the social body is uncanny, evoking a universal plasticity of matter that bears a whiff of death. The odor of the fish market imparts an oceanic strangeness to apparently quotidian characters and scenes; it makes "something rich and strange" of everyday human affairs. All is vendible; all is corruptible; mortality is a theater of fish. Seen in this context, Hamlet's "inky cloak" can be read as an allusion to the esoteric tradition—popular at Cambridge in Shakespeare's lifetime—of portraying Aristotle as a cuttlefish.[74] Appearances hide, not a unique inwardness, but the fishy corruptibility of "this too, too solid [or sullied] flesh," which will inevitably "thaw, melt and resolve into a dew" and possibly "go a progress through the guts of a beggar." Kings no less than beggars are composed of fishified flesh, as Shakespeare emphasizes with glee. The human connection to the creatures of the sea makes nature strange and the self (a) stranger. Faced with "ingratitude . . . More hideous . . . than the sea-monster," Lear asks his Fool, "Who is it that can tell me who I am?" (1.4.236–8, 205). Feste and Viola, both given to dissimulation, savor the same question on the coast of Illyria.

7

Prospero's Maps

> Our planet is invested with two great oceans; one visible, the other invisible; one underfoot, the other overhead; one entirely envelopes it, the other covers about two thirds of its surface. All the water of the one weighs about four times as much as all the air of the other.
>
> MATTHEW FONTAINE MAURY

In his articulation of human life as a condition deeply but obscurely connected to the marine environment Shakespeare seems to delight in reminding us of the blue-green immensity of the globe and the near impossibility of fathoming its fluid vastness.[1] Are we truly at home on this blue globe? Do we even know what the nature of *here* really is? The very concept of place, rooted in culture, agriculture, the hearth, and the social order, belongs to the land. For centuries the vast watery plain that began at the edge of the shore could only be conceived as a space—a void to be crossed at considerable danger to self and community. To venture upon the sea (physically or conceptually) is to embark on a metaphysical quest—"a wild dedication of yourselves / To unpathed waters, undreamed shores," the goal of which is, in large part, self-discovery (*The Winter's Tale*, 4.4.554–55). Shakespeare's ocean is a wild space, undomesticated and protean yet also familiar enough to be employed with exquisite nuance and detailed description. Even if anthropogenic transformation of the ocean's blue-green immensity could scarcely have been imagined by early moderns, Shakespeare could (and did) imagine a Creator God, in whose image he and his fellow humans were said to have been made, exercising complete (or near complete) control over the global "flood," which, it was thought, could rise again. He also created at least one character, Prospero in *The Tempest*, who exercises similar powers over the biophysical environment, and several others (Lear, Hotspur, Macbeth) who wish to do so. Shakespeare's oceanic imagination can be labeled

Prospero's Maps

ecological, then, in that it investigates the idea of the *oikos* as a matter of global positioning. Our being at home in the world hangs on our ability to come to terms with a fluid element—water—that was traditionally figured as hostile and incomprehensible.

In *The Tempest* the playwright depicts this challenge as a problem of orientation and location. Locating the island setting of *The Tempest* has long been a scholarly preoccupation, and with good reason. To demarcate a literal territory for Shakespeare's insular plot would solve many interpretive problems: Caliban's identity would then become somewhat less overdetermined; Prospero would become a conquistador (or not); the eponymous storm would, or would not, be the Bard's imaginative rendition of that quintessentially New World phenomenon, the hurricane. But if the precise geographic location of the play's action has been one of the most persistently debated features of *The Tempest*, it has also been one of the least stable. The island's imagery evokes archipelagoes such as Bermuda and the Bahamas even as its most obvious geographical coordinates remain squarely within the bounds of the Mediterranean. This disruption of conventional notions of place has vexed scholars for generations. The introduction to the most recent Arden edition of the play, for instance, offers this account:

> If plotted literally, it must have been within a hundred or so miles from a line between Naples and Tunis. Although its precise location is unspecified —"an un-inhabited Island" says the Folio—several nineteenth-century literary critics debated the most likely Mediterranean isle, based on the imaginary intersection point of a drifting "rotten carcass of a butt" (1.2.146) from the coast near Milan and, twelve years later, of a tempest-tossed ship en route from Tunis to Naples.[2]

The phrase "must have been" here strangely suggests actual historical events, yet there is, historically speaking, no such island. Clearly, the positivistic calculations of nineteenth-century readers wishing to assign a strict geographical location to the action of the play still haunt modern scholarship, for whom locating the island is something of an empirical matter.

The scholarly impetus to locate the play, historically, geographically, and culturally, has obscured Shakespeare's own thematic emphasis on dislocation and disorientation. For what seems to take place in this play is largely illusory. It is a conspicuous feature of the plot that none of the characters knows where he or she is (except perhaps Prospero), and this dislocation drives the various forms of insurrection that constitute the plot. Moreover, the island setting of *The Tempest* conforms to the geography of romance, based on poetic and theatrical requirements of place. Acts of placing (and of plotting, which is both a spatial and a political exercise)—all quite vain—are already at work and always uncertain in *The Tempest*, pursued by a number of characters wishing to make sense of their novel circumstances, as when Stephano and Trinculo try to identify Caliban and can only describe him as a monster half-fish, half "Indian." *The Tempest* teaches us that the issue of social standing, or "place" in the early modern idiom, is deeply attached to the question of geographic location, while location itself is determined by acts of force.

Nineteenth-century attempts to locate Prospero's island echo in the ongoing effort by what we might call literary-critical strict constructionists to deny the significance of the New World in the play. If we can only fix the island somewhere between Italy and Tunis, they thought, then we can ignore the difficult political questions raised by the allusions to the Americas. Such attempts have been entirely unsuccessful, and there is now a consensus that New World imagery permeates the play—but it has taken more than a generation of scholarship to achieve it. After a number of groundbreaking studies in the 1980s and 1990s demonstrated the significance of the New World context on the imagery and plot of *The Tempest*, scholarship in the twenty-first century has shown a marked turn to the Mediterranean. Jonathan Goldberg claims that "an emphasis on the Mediterranean and the Old World Tempest now all but ignores such [new historicist and cultural materialist] readings when it does not seem to deny them."[3] While the play clearly alludes to the Bermudas, Caribs, hurricanes, and Native American deities, it is more concerned with *staging representations* of the New World than with representing the New World itself; it is, in short, a contribution to utopian fiction.

If the theatrical context of Gonzalo's famous speech echoing Montaigne's "Des Cannibales," "Had I the plantation of this isle, my lord . . . I would by contraries / Execute all things" (2.1.141), invites the audience to laugh at the excesses and hypocrisies of utopian rhetoric in the face of its manifest contradictions, the rest of the play nonetheless offers a utopian vision of political reform (of sorts) at the site of *nowhere*. Jeffrey Knapp argues that *The Tempest* offers "an antimaterialism holding that the best way to win

America is to raise the minds of one's insular nation above the low thoughts of mere earthly possession."[4] "Nowhere" has a thoroughly cartographic history, as the topos of terra incognita and as the *ou-topia* that licenses utopian fictions by removing political critique from Europe proper. Utopian discourse complicates the plot of *The Tempest* on multiple levels. Arguably the product of such discourse (inevitably echoing the *Essaies*), Caliban himself is not so much a representation of an American indigene as a complex aggregate portrait of such representations, one that solicits a notoriously mixed set of responses from audiences. Attempts to deal with the problem of location have unearthed several possible sources for Caliban's name, for the cultural roots of his Algerian mother Sycorax, and for the religious history of his Patagonian god Setebos (which features in the written accounts of Magellan's voyage).[5]

The mixed American and Mediterranean sources of these names are one reason for the scholarly shift in focus in the past several decades from the Old World to the New and back again. Caliban's ontological proximity to the island (in the words of Julia Reinhard Lupton, he is "at one with the island") adds a dimension to our understanding of the setting. As Lupton argues in her discussion of Caliban's "creatureliness," the "indeterminacy of Caliban's being also sets him adrift between the cosmos in its vast totality—the brave new world of primal Creation—and the particular worlds defined by culture and nation: Bermuda, Algiers, Milan, Naples."[6] So, too, with the island, whose poetic geography also encompasses those disparate coordinates. Caliban is a notoriously unreliable guide, however, for the wealth of cultural and geographical options that he offers sends us down a metonymic and homophonic journey into a never-never land of competing readings.[7] Should we understand his name as an anagram for "canibal," or as a gypsy word meaning "dark one"? Is he a Carib lost somewhere off the coast of Italy or an African lost in the Caribbean? Such questions are rich in contextual significance but ultimately irresolvable. While Caliban helps us to understand how *The Tempest* refracts differing early modern conceptions of exoticism, it is the geographical mise-en-scène that offers the richest possibilities for a reading of the play's complex poetics of space and place.

This intertextual structure of reference foregrounds the problem of disorientation and associates Prospero's thaumaturgy—employed in the service of a plot to return to Italy—with the arts of geography and cartography.[8] As John Gillies has argued of Shakespearean drama generally, "Something rather more than a conventional notion of geography is involved. The geography of these plays is much more than a literal quantity and much more than a backdrop. It is a complex and dynamic imaginative quantity, with a characterological and symbolic agenda."[9] Gillies offers as an alternative to positivistic geography the notion of "poetic geography," derived from Vico, according to which the assignation of geographic form has as much to do with the imperative of producing meaning as it does with schematically representing space. Previous attempts to decode the complex mythopoetic representation of place and space according to positivistic criteria have largely overlooked the cartographic codes that permeate *The Tempest*—its poetic geography.[10] This is not a question of sources but of models for the depiction of space, place, and direction:

> "Poetic geography" is . . . defined as "the property of human nature that 'in describing unknown or distant things, in respect of which they . . . have not had the true idea themselves . . . men make use of the semblances of things known or near at hand.'" What is interesting for our purposes is less Vico's methods—an unashamed mythology of origins supported by an elaborate skein of inferences drawn from fanciful etymologies—than his vision: boldly deconstructing the Enlightenment assumption that the Greeks invented "geography" essentially in order to understand their world rather than to project it in their own parochial image.[11]

Poetic geography, then, is the projection of familiar ways of seeing onto the unknown in order to give alterity recognizable shape and meaning. Giving form to terra incognita necessarily involves projecting the familiar in the space of the strange. *The Tempest* does precisely that, and in doing so employs and alludes to cartographic conventions. Not only does the play offer a visualization of what might take place at terra incognita, it playfully mixes bits and pieces of information from far-flung regions in a manner that vividly evokes the works of sixteenth and early seventeenth-century European cartographers.

My wish to dislocate the prevalent scholarly debate between those who advocate situating the play in a New World context and those who insist on keeping the play in the Mediterranean begins with the play itself, which ludically refuses to submit to placement within strict geographic coordinates. A playwright who can set a scene on the coast of Bohemia can certainly transport a ship from the Mediterranean to the western Atlantic between the scenes, imbuing his art with more than a whiff of both regions. The eponymous squall with which the play begins creates confusion, dislocation within the social hierarchy, and disorientation both diegetically and metadiegetically. Moreover, the squall and the island are both magical phenomena, as Dryden recognized when he subtitled his revision of the play *The Enchanted Island*. Alonso's ship, like the rotten dinghy in which Prospero and Miranda were set adrift twelve years before, has been whisked off like Dorothy and Toto to an Oz-like elsewhere, a fantasy island where what takes place is a staging of Renaissance modes of placing, mapping, and projecting. The pervasiveness of magic marks the island as the space of ideological fantasy, a utopian projection of the islands that lay beyond the reach of Western eyes; this magic, however, closely approximates the arts of the cartographer, geographer, and cosmographer.

Indeterminacy, disorientation, and disarray characterize the scholarly response to the play as well as the characters' responses to the island. It is precisely this indeterminacy that interests me. I will argue that such fluidity of location lies at the thematic heart of the play. Prospero's island (or Caliban's, depending on one's reading of the politics of the play), has remained unmappable, but this unmappability has a figurative genealogy extending back to 1516, with the publication of Thomas More's *Utopia*. The persistent thematization of disorientation and dislocation to describe the European experience of the island—it is a space of wonder characterized by illusion, magic, and "strange noises"—accords with the predominant figurative strategy of utopian literature. Utopian literature from More's mock travel narrative of 1516 to Montaigne's celebration of the Other in "Of Cannibals" relies on a figural mode of negation or paradox in which the description of the other world—mythical, real, or blazing—acts as a sort of counterexample to European states. Utopian fictions, we might say, are a form of poetic geography that function as a counterdiscourse to the positivistic geography based on measurement and the diagrammatic assembly of data.

Shakespeare continually ironizes the issue of location by projecting European phantasms of political domination and reconciliation onto terra incognita, the cartographic topos for nowhere. The ludic undermining of attempts to locate and fix, discursively and geographically, an island that is both nowhere and a lot like England was nothing new in 1610. This figurative strategy of disorientation, which *Utopia* deploys in the rhetorical figures of paradox, *ironia*, and litotes, engages with the "cartographic impulse" of the sixteenth century as European attempts to map the world.[12] More's pervasive use of such rhetorical strategies forms a pattern that Shakespeare adapts to the stage as dislocation, the undermining of any strict sense of place or space. Disorientation functions as a kind of theatrical *ironia* in *The Tempest*, a staging of the utopian figurative strategy of simultaneous affirmation and denial that interrogates acts of placement and mapping. As a contribution to the literature of utopia, *The Tempest* depends on a figuration of place that baffles and dislocates conventional codes of geographic placement. As with previous Renaissance utopias, the island setting is a special kind of nowhere, an *ou-topia* dominated by a master of illusion dedicated to executing all things "by contraries" (2.1.147), where the European political problems of authoritarianism and masterlessness, kingly neglect, and criminality are magically negotiated and resolved by a statecraft that is stagecraft.

It is a critical commonplace that *The Tempest* is the most musical of Shakespeare's plays; less obvious is the fact that it is also one of the windiest.[13] Even before the action begins, the title suggests that the plot will be driven by a meteorological disturbance. What is a tempest but an overabundance of wind? By placing weather at the forefront of the play—no other title in the Shakespeare corpus does so—the playwright seems to suggest that powerful natural forces are integral to plot, character, and theme. The action begins in the middle of a storm and ends with a plea for the "gentle breath" of the audience and the promise of "auspicious gales" (5.1.314). In his 1954 introduction to the Arden edition, Frank Kermode noted that "Prospero's Art controls Nature; Ariel's music performs his master's art."[14] In a similar vein, John P. Cutts argued that "the whole play is conceived as taking part on an island that resounds continually to music in the air, which is, I believe, equivalent to music of the spheres."[15] Auden argued that "Ariel is neither a singer, that is to say, a human being whose vocal gifts provide him with a social function, nor a nonmusical person who in certain moods feels like singing. Ariel is song; when he is truly himself, he sings."[16] The clamorous first scene exemplifies and complicates the title: the sea is "at war" with the winds, which is echoed in the insubordination of mariners who talk back to their social superiors. When the play ends with Prospero telling the audience that we are not merely passive bystanders but actors in his drama of exile and return—"gentle breath of yours my sails / Must fill, or else my project fails" (Epilogue, 329–30)—he comes full circle from the opening scene, in which roaring voices and howling winds disrupt a sea voyage and threaten utter ruin. A thematics of winds, airs, and breath frame a story about the contingencies of early modern navigation.

The opening scene carefully lays out a panoply of winds which, together, form a meteorological antimasque.[17] Shakespeare conjures the frightening scenario of a ship encountering a sudden squall at precisely the moment an unknown island is spied to leeward.[18] The Boatswain's call to reduce sail, "take in the topsail," indicates that the wind has strengthened, while the shipmaster's worry that "we run ourselves aground" signals the presence of a navigational hazard—in this case the dreaded lee shore of sailors.[19]

> *Boatswain:* Hey, my hearts! Cheerly, cheerly, my hearts! Yare, yare! Take in the topsail. Tend to the master's whistle. (*To the storm*)—Blow till thou burst thy wind, if room enough (1.1.1–8).

In a scene full of howling, shouting, blowing, and roaring, the Boatswain becomes identified with the unruly elements. When Alonso enters the scene with the enjoinder, "Good Boatswain, have care. Where's the master? Play the men," his words are met with a churlish reply: "do you not hear him [the master]? You mar our labor. Keep your cabins: you do assist the storm. / What cares these roarers [waves] for the name of King?" (1.1.8–9, 12–14). The "roarers" in question are conventionally understood to mean the waves, but the Boatswain also implies that the elements form a disordered and potentially rebellious crowd. Generally glossed with the stage direction "(*To the storm*)," the Boatswain's apostrophe to the elements personifies natural forces in such a way as to suggest an ontological proximity between the winds and the mariners.[20]

In the midst of this crisis the Boatswain's command to "tend to the Master's whistle" evokes breath as a force with which to combat the storm. His challenge to the storm, to "blow till thou burst thy wind, if room enough," reflects the traditional preference of sailors for "sea room" between the ship and any coastline. Unlike the disparate and anarchic forces of wind and waves, the Master's whistle represents a containment of breath that performs a precise function, the call of all hands. When the Boatswain speaks to the storm, we are reminded that the Master has just commanded him to "speak to th'mariners" (1.1.3). The social hierarchy is challenged by unruly elements that roar, such that the Boatswain's initial churlishness to his aristocratic passengers echoes throughout the play as various subordinates challenge their social superiors.

The combination of meteorological catastrophe and shouting sailors in the first scene creates a momentary threat to political authority—a threat associated with the sea and the storm. Aristocrats are ordered below by a mere sailor as the elements apparently threaten the control of the ship and the governance of its human freight; thus, the work of navigation, figured as a kind of communication with wind and sea, threatens the court-based social hierarchy.[21] Not only does the action create a momentary world-turned-upside-down, the surly Boatswain temporarily becomes a revolutionary voice when he articulates a meteorological basis for his own primacy in the gale when he challenges Gonzalo to command the winds: "You are a councillor: if you can command these elements to silence and work the peace of the present, we will not hand a rope more; use your authority. If you cannot, give thanks you have lived so long, and make yourself ready in your cabin for the mischance of the hour, if it so hap (1.1.19–24). Here the Boatswain suggests that royal authority is valueless in the face of a natural disaster.

The association of roaring with rebellion is not limited to the opening scene. The roaring elements are invoked again in the next scene, when Miranda asks her father, "If by your art, my dearest father, you have / Put the wild waters in this roar, allay them" (1.2.1–2). Here it is the sea that roars—"the wild waters" worked up by the squall—much like the anarchic, roaring Boatswain and mariners. Soon thereafter Prospero reminisces on "th'sea that roared to us" (1.2.149). The dramatic irony in the Boatswain's challenge to Gonzalo lies in the fact that Prospero, not Alonso, can indeed "command these elements to silence" with the help of his "airy sprite" Ariel. Prospero will eventually pacify the winds and the forces of political contention by the end of the play, for the storm that the audience and the shipwrecked crew imagine we have just witnessed turns out to be entirely illusory, a magically orchestrated trompe l'oeil brought about by the invisible Ariel working at the behest of Prospero.

Ariel's magic is constituted by a magic of "sounds and sweet airs" (3.2.136). Not only does Ariel do the work of producing order and harmony by dint of magical songs, he is himself—the First Folio informs us—"an airy sprite." Like the island itself, he is also difficult if not impossible to locate without

Prospero's Maps

the assistance of Prospero's occult knowledge. Upon hearing Ariel's song "Full Fathom Five," Ferdinand asks, "where should this music be? I'th'air, or th'earth" (1.2.388). Later Ariel will refer to "the loud winds," while much later Prospero refers to "the mutinous winds"; both instances personify the elements (3.3.63; 5.1.42). Again, much later, Prospero describes his stage-managed gale as a bout between wind and sea; he has "'twixt the green sea and the azured vault / Set roaring war" (5.1.43–44).[22] The animated elements clearly share an affinity with mutineers of all stripes: with Caliban, who is consistently associated with nature as wildness; with the rebellion of the courtiers Antonio and Sebastian; and with the mutinous subordinates Trinculo and Stephano, who enlist Caliban's help. Antonio describes the noise that providentially awakens the sleeping Alonso as "the roar / Of a whole herd of lions" (2.1.310). Later Prospero exclaims of the revolting Caliban, Stephano, and Trinculo, "I will vex them / Even to roaring" (4.1.192–93). Something of an acoustic pattern takes shape, whereby the roaring of wind and seas becomes associated with revolt, while Prospero's controlled rhetoric and Ariel's artful songs enact the providential ability to "allay" such violence. In the words of Marjorie Garber, "What we have interpreted as storm and chaos is actually a function of order and art."[23] The meteorological antimasque of the opening scene becomes more than a motif: it is instead the basis for most of the episodic plot structure of the play, which is organized as a series of conflicts resolved by Prospero and his agents through magical music.[24]

The winds have a deep significance in early modern cartographic history. The post-ptolemaic *mappae mundi* of the sixteenth century constitute a cartographic imaginary that permeates the play in ways that have remained largely invisible to scholarship. To make this argument it will be necessary to excavate an early modern poetic geography of the winds. The representation of the winds was part of the early modern cartographer's arts.[25] There is more to what the Boatswain later calls "these elements" than a spell of rough weather. The acoustic pattern I have outlined can be understood as a symphonically complex structure of imagery that invokes early modern cartographic conventions (within this structure, roaring forms merely what we might call the percussion section). The interaction of sea and waves produces a kind of wildness that will undergo numerous transformations throughout the play. Characters proximate to the anarchic forces are consistently associated with nature: Caliban's lust and physicality; Ferdinand's desire for Miranda (and vice versa); the political overreaching of brothers, rivals, and subordinates all shape the landscape of the island. Wind performs a crucial graphic function in sixteenth- and early seventeenth-century maps of several genres—nautical charts as well as world maps—establishing direction and the relative locations of territories. That the Boatswain should personify the gale so readily is an indication that the playwright imagined the scene in cartographic terms. The stage direction "(*To the storm*)" apparently grounds our understanding of the "thou" whom the Boatswain addresses, but it is imprecise. Vaughan and Vaughan claim that the Boatswain's challenge in line seven "is a defiant challenge to the storm to blow until it is out of wind, or, perhaps, a challenge to the clouds to blow until their cheeks burst. Also possible is the scatalogical notion of the storm blowing until it loses force by breaking wind. In a similar situation in *Pericles* a sailor cries to the storm, 'blow, and split thyself' (3.1.44)."[26] The field of meaning here can be significantly reduced in the context of early modern cartographic conventions. To begin a play on the deck of a ship, and one having a great deal of trouble with the wind, is to paint the stage as the space of navigation; it is also to invoke cartography, which was preoccupied with the depiction of wind as the driving force of navigation and, hence, the basis for geographic knowledge.

Even after the opening storm scene gives way to the relative calm of the island in the next scene, the Boatswain's ornery challenge to authority haunts the action. As Paul Brown points out in his essay on *The Tempest* and the discourse of imperialism,

> This initial "tempest" becomes retroactively a kind of antimasque or disorderly prelude to the assertion of that courtly authority which was supposedly in jeopardy. From Prospero's first appearance it becomes clear that disruption was produced to create a series of problems precisely in order to effect their resolution. The dramatic conflict of the opening of the play is to be reordered to declare the mastery of Prospero in being able to initiate and control such dislocation and dispersal.[27]

Throughout the play Prospero engages the winds to assist him. In the fifth act his ability to control the winds is proof of his power. What Brown calls "the dislocation and dispersal" of the antimasque are figured in terms of the invisible force of wind and "airs": Prospero orchestrates the storm and stage-

Prospero's Maps

manages natural forces, while the marooned Italian aristocrats are persistently baffled by the same forces.

While Brown's reading is concerned with the way in which the political forces in the Jacobean court inform the representation of Prospero's domination of the island, what interests me are the meteorological forces that blow through the play. For the winds in *The Tempest* constitute a cartographic imaginary, a persistent allusion to numerous early modern attempts to represent an invisible, locomotive force of nature. Prospero is not only a thaumaturge, but his particular form of thaumaturgy derives from the arts of cartography. From the opening storm to the elaborate wedding masque, Prospero's arts are figured as the mastery of natural forces and of space. His various conflicts of power, with Caliban, Antonio, Alonso, Ariel, and the deposed ghost of a bygone social order, Sycorax, are all organized as dramatic engagements between a centrally located, Western, autocratic subject and a peripheral but threatening Other. Martin Procházka observes that "Prospero exercises control over each character precisely because of his visual mastery of space. In each carefully orchestrated conflict, Prospero consolidates his position at the center of social space, as its (spatially) legitimate subject—what Catherine Belsey calls 'the Absolute Subject (God, the king, the boss, Man, conscience).'"[28] Each recounting of their history buttresses Prospero's agenda. As Prospero recalls the story of their exile to Miranda: "There they hoist us / To cry to th'sea that roared to us, to sigh / To th'winds, whose pity, sighing back again, / Did us but loving wrong" (1.2.148–51). This breathy exchange between the castaways and the elements evokes a beneficent audience of winds who hear the cries of the exiled duo and blow back pity. Again the winds are personified: Prospero suggests an early intimacy with the elements that he will later turn to his advantage. By recalling the winds in this manner, he also adumbrates a relationship between theater and cartography that will form the basis for the Epilogue. The winds are an audience, "sighing back again." It is Prospero's ability to conjure both the natural and supernatural forces of the island—both directly and indirectly, by means of Ariel—that sustains his authority. Prospero's plot of land (the island) is an integral part of his plot (or itinerary) to recover his dukedom and recapitulates the spatial narratives inscribed on the globe by sixteenth- and seventeenth-century cartographers.

In renouncing his magic at the end of the play, Prospero will boast, "I have bedimmed / The noontide sun, called forth the mutinous winds, / And 'twixt the green sea and the azured vault / Set roaring war" (5.1.41–44). These winds are "mutinous" because they can kick up a gale and because it is through them that Prospero undermines the political authority of his fellow aristocrats and eventually reconstructs his own political legitimacy. Paradoxically, Prospero harnesses the most chaotic and destructive of winds, a storm at sea, which becomes domesticated as a figurative mode of locomotion. When, in his last lines before the Epilogue, Prospero promises Alonso, and the other aristocrats in his entourage, "I'll deliver all; / And promise you calm seas, auspicious gales, / And sail so expeditious that [you] shall catch / Your royal fleet far off," the promises of the magus echo the mapmaker, whose creations offer the world as a spectacle to the royal and aristocratic patrons of his art (5.1. 313–16).

I am arguing, then, that Prospero enforces his own geographical hegemony over his political opponents by a stagecraft that is a form of navigation, intervening in the nautical journey of the Neapolitan and Milanese heads of state in a spectacular attempt to reclaim political power—not directly, but rather by representing his own political legitimacy by displaying his total mastery over space. Prospero repeatedly parenthesizes his listeners so they will acknowledge him as the bearer of history and the legitimate ruler of the island. First he interrogates Miranda about their first arrival on the island with "Doest thou attend me?" "Thou attend'st not," "I pray thee mark me," and "Doest thou hear?" and then continues in interrogatory mode with Ariel (1.2.78, 87, 89, 106). In an ascending order of intensity and antagonism, Prospero oversees three separate but linked historical narratives that situate him squarely on the throne of island sovereignty.[29] A manifestation of spatial mastery, Prospero's language—hot air—inscribes his authority as the landlord of the island; his commands constitute his power.[30] If, as Christian Jacob theorizes, "Nomination is a mode of symbolic appropriation that furnishes virgin territories with a memory, with a gridding that dispossesses space of its alterity and produces an object of discovery subjected to the constraints of linguistic reference, that intends that at every identifiable site there correspond a name,"[31] then Prospero's orchestration of his and Miranda's narrative of arrival can be seen as a mode of territorial appropriation. Prospero maps a strategic history—his version—onto the island by naming his Others: Ariel, Caliban, and Miranda (1.2.318–19). His relationships with each of these characters, and with the Italian aristocrats he causes

Prospero's Maps

to wreck on an island under his almost complete control, are mediated by a magic that entails the command over natural forces, the wind and the waves in particular, associated with navigation.

Prospero is a navigator, then, but paradoxically one who controls the mise-en-scène in which navigation takes place. He is, in a sense, a cartographer whose materials are not parchment and ink but the elements themselves. The plot is a visual and acoustic demonstration of Prospero's scheme to map his own trajectory back into power, legitimacy, and, ultimately, a dignified death. The power to create the magical opening storm permits him to enforce his authority and regain his dukedom. Like the unruly elements, the cheeky Boatswain is instrumental in Prospero's project of teaching the marooned Italian aristocracy a lesson in the (spatial) arts of power. Geographical alterity becomes increasingly connected to issues of political authority, as Prospero's absolute rule over the island becomes a rehearsal for his return to Milan; the magus is a cartographer whose project is to inscribe a political itinerary of exile and return at the site of terra incognita.

As the initial storm is put into perspective in the second scene, Miranda exclaims of the storm, "the sky, it seems, would pour down stinking pitch, / But that the sea, mounting to the welkin's cheek, / Dashes the fire out" (1.2.3–5). Miranda's description of natural forces notably personifies "the welkin," or heavens. But why "cheek"? Why not "head," or "nose," or "top"? Why not simply "mounting to the welkin?" At least part of the answer to this question lies in one of the probable sources for *The Tempest*, Strachey's "True Reportery," which describes the heavy weather off Bermuda in similar terms:

> And this I did still observe, that whereas upon the land, when a storm hath poured itself forth once in drifts of rain, the winds as beaten down and vanquished therewith not long after endureth, here the glut of water, as if throttling the wind erewhile, was no sooner a little emptied and qualified but instantly *the winds, as having gotten their mouths now free and at liberty, spake more loud and grew more tumultuous and malignant*. What shall I say? Winds and seas were as mad as fury and rage could make them.[32]

Particularly striking is the specific imagery with which Strachey personifies "winds and seas" ("roarers" both). For the winds are imagined as having mouths, "free and at liberty," that both "spake" and "grew . . . malignant." Surely the Boatswain's apostrophe to the "roarers" in the first scene, as well as his own persona, owes a debt to this particular account.

Shakespeare's debt to Strachey's description of the wreck of the *Sea Venture* has long been the subject of scholarly discussion.[33] What has not been noted before, however, is that images of "the winds" as faces with puffed cheeks were commonplace on early modern maps and charts. A look at any number of early modern world maps shows us that "the welkin" (heavens, firmament, sky) has cheeks because of its conventional association with cartographic wind blowers. These iconic illustrations were generally situated at the perimeter of the cartographic tableau to illustrate north, south, east, west, and finer gradations between. It is on these icons of the winds that I would like to stake my cartographic reading of *The Tempest*. For Miranda's strikingly visual account of the opening storm evokes the Boatswain's earlier challenge to the storm, to "blow till *thou* burst *thy* wind" (emphasis added); both personifications reference a specifically cartographic personification of the winds. Shakespeare gives "cheeks" to the winds in *King Lear*, too: "Blow, winds, and crack your cheeks! Rage! Blow!" (3.2.1). Here, too, the winds are plural and personified; crucially, they are envisioned with cheeks. In *The Tempest*, as in *Lear*, the playwright surrounds the stage with the cheeky wind blowers of sixteenth- and seventeenth-century world maps.[34]

The topsy-turvy opening scene stages the widespread Renaissance fascination with wind. Invisible in its own right but visible by its effects, wind was an aesthetic challenge for early modern artists. Because of their traditional association with the seasons and particular climatic states (the heat of the Scirocco, the cold of the Mistral), Mediterranean winds are named. They are also personified on early modern maps and paintings.[35] Botticelli's personification of Zephyrus in *The Birth of Venus* is a particularly magnificent example of the iconography of wind in the period: a wide-chopped Zephyrus, cheeks distended, blows the flowers of spring across the canvas, while the goddess herself arises from the sea as if she were spontaneously produced by the interaction of the wind and the waves. Forces that harmonize, the elements of sea and wind produce the goddess of love and desire. In viewing such a painting, one is reminded of the creative and anarchic power of passion in Ovid's stories, which transforms men and gods into beasts, trees, pools, and flowers. Shakespeare's debt to Golding's translation of the *Metamorphoses*, particularly in *The Tempest*, is well known; less obvious is the pervasiveness of an Ovidian interplay between humanity and nature that begins in the first scene of the play.[36]

Leonardo studied the winds rigorously and systematically in his *Notebooks*, where the description that follows the entry "How to Represent a Tempest" paints a particularly dramatic verbal picture:

> If you wish to represent a tempest consider and arrange its effects when the wind blowing over the face of the sea and of the land lifts and carries with it everything that is not fixed firmly in the general mass.... Let the sea be wild and tempestuous, and full of foam whirled between the big waves, and the wind should carry the finer spray through the stormy air resembling a dense and all-enveloping mist. Of the ships that are there, some should be shown with sails rent and the shreds fluttering in the air in company with the broken ropes and some of the masts split and fallen, and the vessel itself lying disabled and broken by the fury of the waves, with the men shrieking and clinging to the fragments of the wreck (186).

This word picture strikingly resembles the illusion of destruction produced in the opening scene of *The Tempest*, with its own ship apparently about to "split" and its shouting characters leaping into the sea (1.1.62). Even the tattered clothing of the figures in Leonardo's written sketch are invoked negatively when Gonzalo remarks, "Methinks our garments are now as fresh as when we put them on first in Africa, at the marriage of the King's fair daughter Claribel and the King of Tunis" (2.1.70–72). Too much wind presents a paradox, at once an overabundance of the means of propulsion and the threat of destruction. Representing the effects of wind was, clearly, a particular aesthetic challenge.[37]

While painters represented the winds allegorically and pioneers of science studied it systematically, it was in the realm of cartography that Renaissance representations of wind achieved their most sophisticated results. The *portolano* (or *portulan*) chart is the inevitable cartographic genre to consider in thinking about a play that takes place in a nautical setting.[38] *Portolani* began as written descriptions of coasts and harbors that the mariner used for advice; in their earliest form they were simply lists describing the geographical features of a given coastline, such as hills, cliffs, reefs, and safe harbors.

Portolani were eminently practical tools as well as ornamental objects, used by mariners to find to safe harbors and anchorages where they could put in for the night. One historian refers to the *portolano* as "the harbor-finding chart," highlighting their practical function.[39] Until the end of the fifteenth century these charts remained a predominantly Mediterranean genre. Their representational conventions, particularly the careful outlining and labeling of coastal topographical features, were adapted to world maps as the Americas were mapped out and terra incognita was gradually replaced with the shapes and contours of the New World. As Italian, Iberian, and later Flemish and French cartographers adapted their own practices to New World coastlines, Mediterranean cartographic conventions went global. In the world maps of the sixteenth century we find a highly developed iconography of wind.

To invoke wind is to reference the primary means of indicating direction and location at sea in early modern Europe.[40] Until the widespread acceptance of the compass in the fifteenth century, sailors navigated largely by following the winds:

> [The cartographer] designated the principal winds, the half-winds and the quarter-winds with different colors. For example, on Italian charts of the fifteenth century the principal winds were done in gold, the half-winds in green and the quarter-winds in red. Moreover, these three colors were carried out in the rhumbs or loxodromes radiating from the central compass rose across the chart, which made it easier for the navigator to follow a given line from the compass rose to some other point on the chart.[41]

Out of the medieval *portolan* developed a mode of projection based on a grid system of lines connecting the wind roses. Such rhumb lines still are occasionally used by modern sailors, albeit with different diagrammatic conventions (see figure 12).

To navigate in the Mediterranean meant catching the right wind at the right time and riding it to a destination (this is precisely what the Neapolitan flagship is prevented from doing by Prospero). Meteorological conditions of Mediterranean navigation lend themselves to the association of wind with direction. "Winds blow across the Mediterranean with a constancy as dependable (according to the season) as the sunrise, and places were located by wind direction," writes one cartographic historian; thus, "eventually the horizon was divided into thirty-two directions, all called,

Prospero's Maps

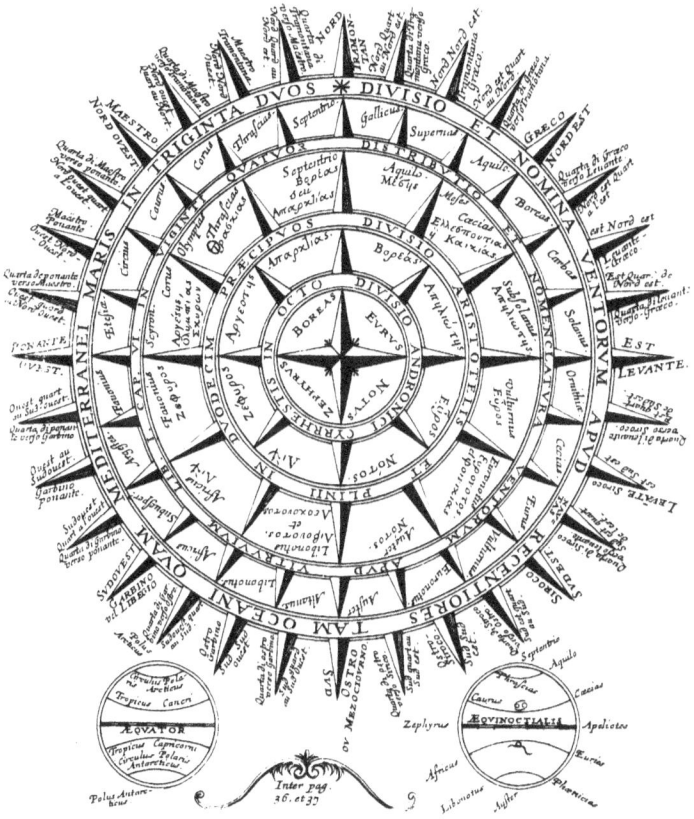

FIGURE 12. Wind Rose, seventeenth century. (From Lloyd A. Brown, *The Story of Maps*)

in the classic manner, 'winds.'"[42] Because of their predictability and constancy, winds in the Mediterranean were (and still are) known by name. Each of the winds—now called the cardinal points of the compass—were named: Zephyr (west wind), Eurus (east wind), Notus (south wind), and Boreas (north wind), like the Mistral and the Scirocco, were understood as cosmic forces with their own personalities and as vectors of possibility. Thus, the representations of wind on nautical charts acted as road signs for mariners, cues to plotting direction and establishing location. Accordingly,

Shakespeare's Ocean

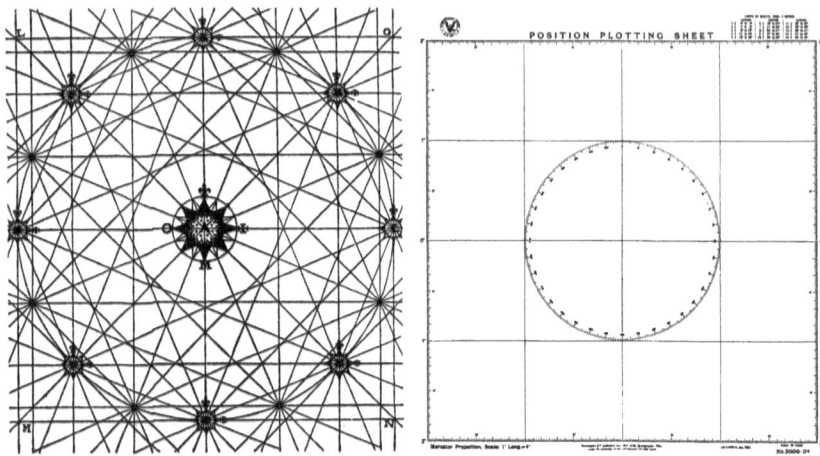

FIGURE 13. Sea chart designed by Oronce Finé, 1532, and the same kind of chart 400 years later. (From Lloyd A. Brown, *The Story of Maps*)

the iconic life of wind in Renaissance world maps and nautical charts is a rich one (see figure 13).

It is this developed aesthetic and diagrammatic tradition that lies behind the extraordinary richness of Shakespeare's thematic use of wind in *The Tempest*. When Ariel informs Prospero,

> Safely in harbor
> Is the king's ship, in the deep nook where once
> Thou called'st me up at midnight to fetch dew
> From the still-vexed Bermoothes, there she's hid;
> The mariners all under hatches stowed, (1.2.226–30)

not only is the New World invoked, but so is the telos of Old World cartography, a safe harbor. Instead of a watery grave, the sailors aboard Alonso's flagship find a snug anchorage and sleep. Whether we understand this moment as an explicit cartographic allusion or would prefer to see it as Shakespeare casually imagining an island topography for the sake of moving the plot forward, the mention of a specific harbor ("the deep nook") connects Prospero's magic, in the form of Ariel, with the practical function of late medieval and early modern harbor-finding charts.

Prospero's Maps

While the winds figure prominently in *The Tempest*, and in a multiplicity of ways, as "airs" or songs, as howling spirits in trees, and as roaring storms, less obvious is the fact that winds are also mentioned in terms of their directional specificity. Prospero accuses Ariel of ingratitude by accusing the latter, "Think'st it much to tread the ooze of the salt deep, / To run upon the sharp wind of the north" (1.2.252–54). This mention of the north wind, Boreas, as it was conventionally labeled by early modern cartographers, is followed by a reference to a specific place, Algiers, the home port of Sycorax. Soon thereafter, when Caliban is introduced in the scene, a different wind is mentioned quite specifically. Caliban grumbles to Prospero, "A south-west blow on ye / And blister you all o'er" (1.2.323–24). That a southwest wind would be hot and unhealthy is consistent with the Mediterranean context of Algiers and Naples, but it also suggests that the magic Prospero wields is in some sense a property of the island and, thus, contested by Caliban as part of his birthright. Later, in the third act, Caliban informs his fellow rebels that they should be "not afeard, the isle is full of noises, / Sounds, and sweet airs, that give delight and hurt not" (3.2.133–34). Shakespeare takes pains, thus, to weave together a thematic tapestry of winds and airs that connect conventional cartographic topoi—the north and southwest winds—with the illusory and baffling meteorology of an island that cannot be precisely located.

In the fifteenth and sixteenth centuries, Catalan and Italian *portolan* charts developed into elaborately decorative works of graphic art. The illustrations of wind would become more sophisticated as the European seagoing nations competed to decipher terra incognita. What we would now consider decorative illustrations served a specific navigational purpose: finding direction. The entire composition of any nautical chart is an elaborate means of representing the relationality of the winds, as a series of potential vectors for navigation. It is at this level that Shakespeare engages with sixteenth- and seventeenth-century cartography: wind and the island as terra incognita allude to cartographic codes that scholarship has hitherto explained only in terms of the visual and aural culture of the court (the masque). Yet the *mappae mundi* of the period contain a dramatic parergonal depiction of the winds.

Ptolemy's *Geographia* (ca. 150 AD) began to exert an enormous influence over humanists beginning with its rediscovery in Florence in 1400 and continuing with its republication in Venice in 1475 and in Bologna in 1477 (figure 14). The world is framed by wind blowers around the margins of the

Shakespeare's Ocean

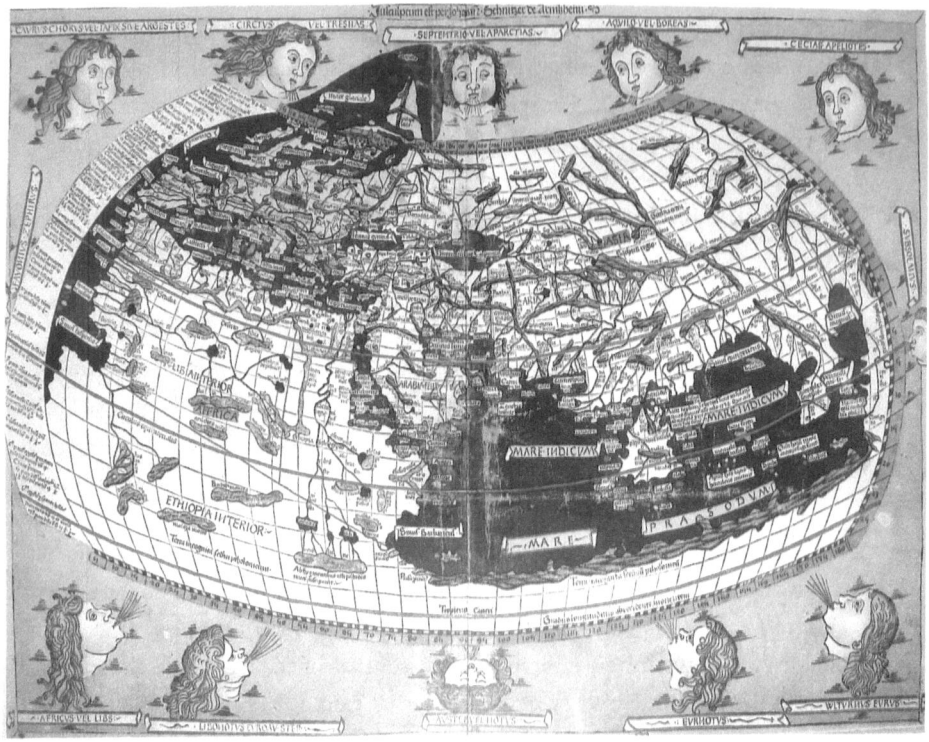

FIGURE 14. Ptolemaic world map, sixteenth century. (Courtesy World Imaging)

map, all of them labeled. The image of the world takes form in the space between them. The faces emit diverging lines to indicate the winds associated with them. "Favonius Zephirus" and "Subsolanus," at the west and the east, respectively, blow winds at each other along a thick red line, the equator, labeled "circulus equinoctialus." Wind-blowers are a crucial framing device in this instance, but they are more than that as well: the winds seem to give form to a theatricalized globe.

The prominence of the wind blowers in the Ptolemaic world map becomes more striking still in the subsequent world maps, particularly those drawn by Martin Waldseemüller. In his world map of 1508 Waldseemüller, who should be credited with making the vastness of the global ocean visible for the first time in graphic form, incorporates the wind-blowers into the frame of his planispheric image (see figure 15). The very form of the globe seems to be emitted from the mouth of a wind-blower: the meridians emerge from the lines of force representing the exhalation of breath. Similarly, in figure 16, the Dürer-Stabius map of the eastern hemisphere (1515), the relationship between cartographic form and the wind blowers is more significant than has been heretofore acknowledged. The wind blowers here are grotesques, heads with wings and peacock feathers that float upon the clouds. The somewhat threatening expressions on the faces of the wind blowers suggest an adversarial relationship between the heavens and the earth.

The Waldseemüller world map takes Ptolemy's image of the world and adds the Americas. This *mappa mundi* also places images of Ptolemy and Vespucci at the top of the tableau, outside the framing margin that borders the image of the world. The two men, whose work—as Waldseemüller suggests—transformed the *imago mundi*, stand outside of the tableau looking down on the world from the heavens; they are flanked by two wind blowers, Aquilo and Circius.[43] The proximity of the great classical geographer and the famed early modern navigator to these faces suggests the close association in the period between the winds and knowledge of the globe. And neither Ptolemy nor Vespucci holds the perspectival center of the tableau. This place is reserved for another wind blower, Septentrio, the North Wind, situated between the two smaller hemispheres that separate Ptolemy's image from that of Vespucci. It is this figure that draws the gaze, for it not only operates as a symbolic feature of the map, it has an active role in creating geographical form: Septentrio blows the meridians into being, the breath lines emitted from the mouth becoming meridians in the map below. It is as if the cartographic image of the world were constituted by the breath of the north wind, the world a distorted balloon being inflated by the wide-chopped wind blowers that surround it.

The role of the framing winds is more sophisticated, for the winds actually blow lines of ink that become the rhumb lines connecting the compass roses. Cartographic form is, in this case, identical to navigational itineraries, for the world is depicted as a tableau of winds whose directional vectors showed the navigator where to sail. When European navigators began the systematic conquest of the world's oceans with the eastward voyages of Diaz and Da Gama and the westward voyages of Columbus, Cabot, and Vespucci, they did so by learning the prevailing directions of winds and currents. Columbus learned that it was not terribly difficult to reach "the Indies," albeit the wrong ones, by sailing due west with the northeast trades. But the key to a successful voyage was the return home, which became much

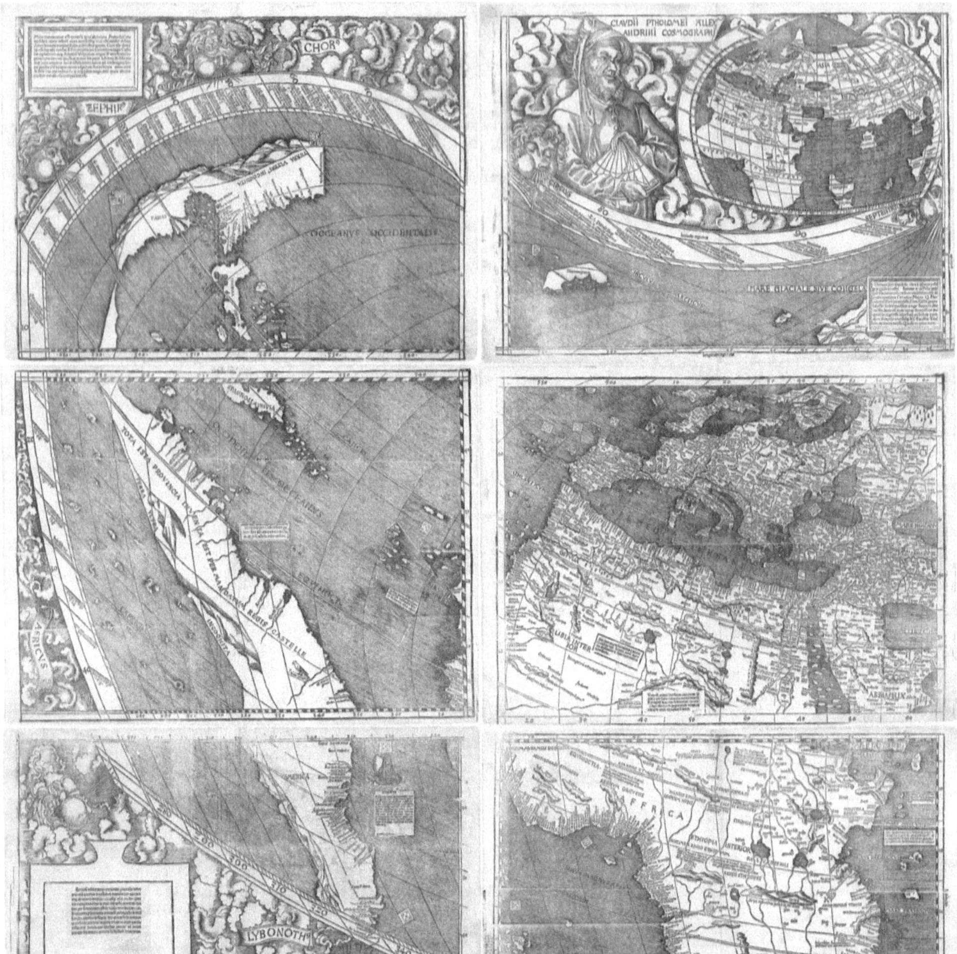

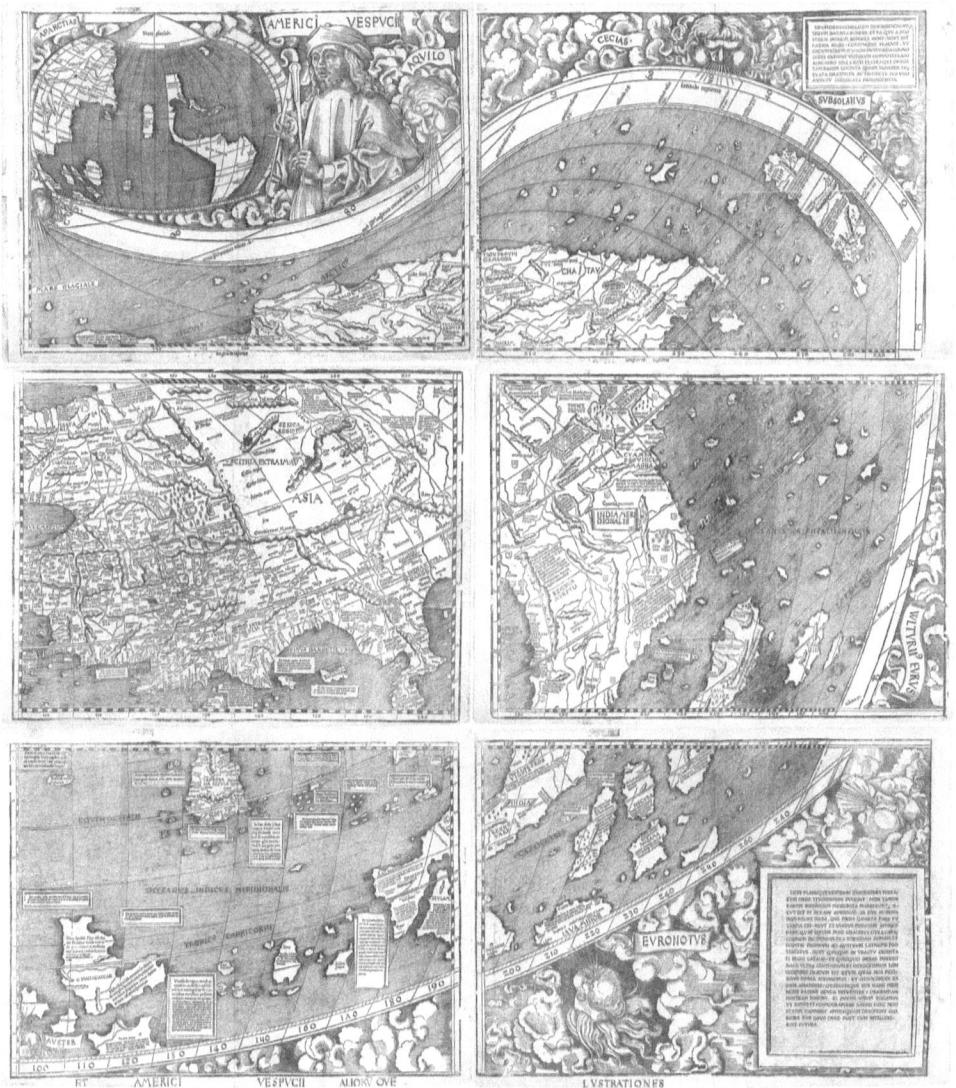

FIGURE 15. Martin Waldseemüller, World Map, 1508. Details show wind blowers in upper-middle panels. (Library of Congress, Geography and Map Division, G3200 1508.W3)

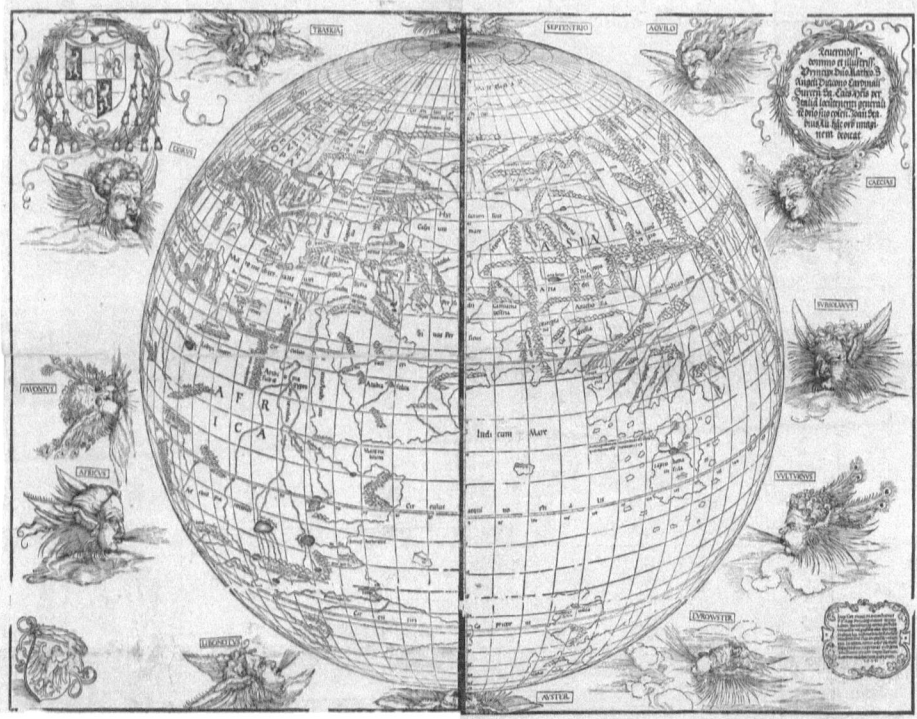

FIGURE 16. Albrecht Dürer, Terrestrial Map (The Eastern Hemisphere), 1515. (Photograph © 2012 Museum of Fine Arts, Boston)

easier with the knowledge of the clockwise pattern of prevailing winds in the Atlantic, a pattern that eventually allowed for predictable routes of departure and return.[44]

The implications for a reading of *The Tempest* are clear: apparently only a leitmotif, wind and breath—invoked so frequently in the play—in fact constitute a complex and highly allusive engagement with the diagrammatic conventions of sixteenth-century European cartography. The wind blowers resemble the Boatswain, whom Antonio calls an "insolent noisemaker" (1.1.43).[45] These grotesques also suggest a visual tradition of cartographic illustration with which to contextualize Ariel, whose airy essence has been so variously interpreted. When we add to this complex cultural poetics of wind and breath the historical fascination of Europeans with two kinds of wind associated with the new world, the Trades (or *las brisas*, as they were known to the Spanish who earlier made use of them), and a new kind of cyclonic storm that only develops in the heat of tropical and subtropical seas, the plot thickens yet again.

As Peter Hulme has argued, a particular kind of storm fascinated Europeans throughout the early modern period: the hurricane. Variously named "furacane," "vracan," "haurachana," "hyrricano," or "hurricano," the hurricane was a previously unknown meteorological phenomenon that fascinated Europeans in the sixteenth and seventeenth centuries. The word is a Spanish approximation of an indigenous Arawak term. Not the name only, but the phenomenon itself was a New World wonder: tropical cyclones do not occur in Europe. "Arguably no phenomenon—not even the natives themselves—characterized so well the novelty of the New World for Europeans; and as a result no natural phenomenon was more open to the interpretative skills of the age."[46] Hulme is right in pointing to the hurricane as an interpretive challenge, a force of nature so immense that it baffled early modern European modes of representing space and place. More than a distant terror or exotic wonder, hurricanes were the apotheosis of wind and, thus, the limit-experience of European navigation.[47] The hurricane signifies a radical inversion of the dominant European conception of wind: it is a wind from nowhere, a natural force that defies representation by dint of its sheer excess and then-unknown origins.

In arguing that the eponymous tempest references a specifically New World meteorological phenomenon, Hulme and others pursue context as far as the Caribbean. But *The Tempest* pursues cartography to the extreme boundaries of the early modern map of the world by placing a microcosmic version of terra incognita in the Mediterranean. To understand the thematic interconnection of voice, breath, wind, and (dis)location in the play, it is necessary to see the movement of air as a central topos in the entire cartographic oeuvre of the early modern period. If we do so, it is abundantly evident that to personify the winds is to invoke early modern cartographic codes of direction and location.

The coastlines of the *portolan*-inspired world maps of the sixteenth century, in which the Pacific rim and *terra australis* appear as amorphous masses, depict the globe as an incomplete visual tableau; frequently, the realm of the unknown is filled with text or fanciful illustrations. It is here, at the site where mythology usurps the claims of diagrammatic representation, that *The Tempest* directs our view by foregrounding the mythopoetic codes of cartography. From the first act, European modes of giving form to the unknown reaches of the New World are invoked and denied at the same time that they are employed to provide the imagery and plot. This very ambivalence, however, has a thoroughly cartographic basis, the representation of terra incognita as a diagrammatic procedure in its own right. The unknown land forms a major early modern cultural and cartographic topos; it was a conventional site on Renaissance *mappae mundi* and *portolani* in the sixteenth and seventeenth centuries, not merely a principle of geographical negativity or empty space, but a topos upon which European fantasies could be projected.[48] What Shakespeare thematizes with such subtlety in *The Tempest* is the graphic interplay of wind as an index of direction and terra incognita as the space of ideological fantasy. For it is at the intersection of these two cartographic topoi that Shakespeare playfully "locates" his drama of European autocracy in terms of a series of sea voyages that cross at a magical island. Paradoxically, and tellingly, he does so by refusing to specify a fixed geographic location, instead forcing the reader to come to terms with the disorientation brought about by multiple airs and winds.

The Tempest is as much a play about the navigational arts as it is an aesthetic investigation into the relationship between art and power. Shakespeare seems intent on foregrounding early modern discursive codes, geographic, political, and social, of place. In *The Tempest* we witness the *staging* of Renaissance modes of placing, mapping, and projecting. The question of what takes place, of who takes over the place, and, indeed, whether in fact anything is taking place at all, animates the plot and finds vivid expression in the thematics of wind. Shakespeare's awareness of the arts of navigation and the world maps produced by the likes of Ptolemy, Waldseemüller, and Edward Wright that transformed the early modern world map from a terrestrial to a maritime picture registers vividly in the playwright's late-career works. What distinguishes Shakespeare's incorporation of wind and waves into his own art from that of a Leonardo or a Thomas More is his skepticism about the value of such knowledge. Throughout the corpus the sea functions to interrogate characters' ability to know themselves and their world and to poke holes in their plans; the sea in Shakespeare is that part of nature which we can never fully know. As such, it is a constant epistemological challenge and source of powerful aesthetic effects, encoding a complex poetics of space that readers have tended to oversimplify by locating the island within strict geographic, cultural, or textual parameters. What makes *The Tempest* particularly challenging to read in terms of poetic geography, however, is that it subverts and conceals the cartographic codes that it employs. The play's setting and plot consistently undermine any attempts at orientation.

The Tempest is, then, the ideological fantasy of a territory whose phenomenological being (its *nature*) is almost entirely under the control of a European cartographer-autocrat. The experience of the island—its location, appearance, layout, and effects on those who find it—is strategic, not essential. It is a strategic space. The island where the Boatswain and his shipmates seem to wreck is the materialization of Prospero's version of history, the projection of a particular story of Milanese political usurpation; it is a cartographic *itinerario*. Prospero inhabits this space as a magus who can conjure the possibility of European domination over a space not his own because he has visual mastery afforded by his "art."

By play's end the cartographic themes of wind, navigation, and location have been assimilated to the stage, while the stage has been thoroughly figured as the site of various forms of projection. In the Epilogue, the successful thaumaturge, guaranteed of his return to the Dukedom of Milan, abdicates his magical powers as he prepares to leave the island where he exercised them:

> Now my charms are all o'erthrown,
> And what strength I have's mine own,
> Which is most faint. Now 'tis true
> I must be here confined by you,
> Or sent to Naples. Let me not,
> Since I have my dukedom got
> And pardoned the deceiver, dwell
> In this bare island by your spell;
> But release me from my bands
> With the help of your good hands.
> Gentle breath of yours my sails
> Must fill, or else my project fails. (1–13)

The mention of "your good hands" appeals to the audience for applause, while the plea for "gentle breath" calls for bravos rather than hisses. The powerful wind summoned by Prospero in the first act has given way to a milder one as the audience is rhetorically positioned as a group of wind blowers surrounding the stage.

Prospero's appeal to the audience in the Epilogue—we may now find this obvious—invokes cartography. If it is the "gentle breath" of the audience that will fill the sails of Prospero, the audience becomes a grouping of winds, a congregation of puffed cheeks surrounding the stage and shouting approval of Prospero's imminent departure (which is also a return). The Epilogue thus offers an analogy between the stage and the map of the world. Prospero is a cartographic subject, a Magellan returning from an undiscovered country by means of the winds that provide orientation in the theater of the world. Like the breath of the wind blowers becoming the rhumb lines that make navigation possible in Waldseemüller's remarkable *mappa mundi* of 1516, the breath of the audience at the Globe (or Blackfriars) is represented as the condition of possibility for the navigator's return and the actor's release from the space of the stage. In an era when "theater" meant "map" as well as the space of dramatic performance, this foregrounding of theatricality must have been particularly suggestive for its audience.[49]

The Tempest, thus, not only enters into a dialogue with early modern cartography but playfully examines the notion—derived from utopian fiction—that literature itself can be a form of mapping. As Steven Mullaney has noted, "a map in the modern sense of the term is a guide to the present: a graphic index to the location of things in space, a traveler's aid which makes the passage from here to there less difficult, the mastery of a given topography available to newcomer and native alike."[50] Just as a map represents space instrumentally for a viewing subject, the spatial order of *The Tempest* conforms almost entirely to Prospero's view of his own predicament in the space of exile, one stage of a voyage geographical, political, and familial. Hence the setting of the play mirrors the representational regime of the early modern map, which traces circuits of possibility for a cartographic subject by inscribing the navigator's data—coastlines, islands, rhumb lines. The island domesticates the world's blank spaces by illustrating terra incognita as the product of projection—a European *plot* (as story, locus, and itinerary). The island, thus, represents the limit-experience of the European ability to mediate and contain alterity (not just the island, but Caliban and Ariel as well).

By linking the uncertain location of the island with the problematic status of Prospero's rule, Shakespeare creates a second-order poetic cartography, a representation of place that stages cartographic modes of representing place. This spatial metapoetics also characterizes Renaissance cartography generally, as the historian Michel De Certeau has argued:

> Transformed first by Euclidean geometry and then by descriptive geometry, constituted as a formal ensemble of abstract places, [the map] is a "theater" (as one used to call atlases) in which the same system of projection nevertheless juxtaposes two very different elements: the data furnished by a tradition (Ptolemy's *Geography*, for instance) and those that came from navigators (portulans, for example). The map thus collates on the same plane heterogeneous places, some received from a tradition and others produced by observation. But the important thing here is the erasure of the itineraries which, presupposing the first category of places and conditioning the second, makes it possible to move from one to the other. The map, a totalizing stage on which elements of diverse origin are brought together to form the tableau of a "state" of geographical knowledge, pushes away into its prehistory or into its posterity, as if into the wings, the operations of which it is the result or the necessary condition.[51]

De Certeau is interested in the way the "data furnished by a tradition," what we would now consider the mythopoetic dimensions of medieval and Renaissance maps (heraldic icons, wind roses, wind blowers, and other forms of illustration), become gradually replaced by the diagrammatic features of "the map itself." Over time, the "narrative figures" on maps disappear, as the ships that inscribe European itineraries upon terra incognita and the puffed faces that blow the winds across the globe no longer occupy the tableau. Today's maps—the "totalizing stage" or "tableau" of De Certeau—retain precious few traces of the visual narratives that Renaissance maps and charts so richly depict. De Certeau's observations help to explain why modern readers have remained unaware of the cartographic codes that structure *The Tempest*. We, the heirs of the post-Enlightenment rationalization and reduction of the geographic text to empirical data and mathematical coordinates, overlook the antic wind blowers that surround and animate Shakespeare's island and his stage. In so doing we have swallowed Prospero's bait, like the marooned courtiers, by seeking orientation in the space of illusion.

Coda

Toward a Terraqueous Ecocriticism

> *Ocean*, n. A body of water occupying about two-thirds
> of a world made for man—who has no gills.
> AMBROSE BIERCE, *The Devil's Dictionary*

The irony of Ambrose Bierce's wry observation that humans have no gills gestures humorously (and skeptically) to the biblical notion of human dominion over the Earth. Bierce's tongue-in-cheek definition of the noun *ocean* undercuts the idea, articulated in Genesis, of Adam (and his offspring) having "dominion over the fish of the sea, and over the fowl of the air, and over the cattle, and over all the earth, and over every creeping thing that creepeth upon the earth" by implying that human experience is limited to the land.[1] While Bierce was prescient in pointing out the insufficiency of the biblical accounts of humanity's relationship to this terraqueous planet, he was wrong about our lack of gills.

We begin our lives as aquatic animals, and our bodies reflect our evolutionary forebears as well as the oceanic cousins with whom we share mammalian traits. In addition to our vestigial (and temporary) gill slits, the salt water that forms the basis of our blood, sweat, and tears has roughly the same concentration of sodium chloride as that of the world's oceans and seas. The human body, thus, retains the biological and chemical traces of a marine ancestry, composed as it is of approximately the same ratio of water (70 percent) as the Earth itself.

Near the end of Shakespeare's career his contemporary Robert Daborne wrote a play about the life of the notorious Tudor-era pirate John Ward called *A Christian Turned Turk* (1609–12). This play, like the romances

Coda

Shakespeare wrote around the same date, contains scenes set at sea. In one of them Ward's sidekick Gismund responds to another ship's demand that they identify themselves by announcing, boldly, "We are of the Sea!"[3] As Claire Jowitt observes, Gismund's reply indicates "that for him the pirate vessel represents an alternate political space, and that his allegiances are free from the claims of orthodox national identity."[4] Yet Gismund's defiant response need not only be read in the context of piracy's vexed relationship to the emergent nation-state. In the larger context of the Renaissance "discovery of the sea," discussed in the introduction to this book, Gismund—whose name says "world" in its second syllable—allies his ship with a fascinating, threatening, and potentially liberating marine environment. To be "of the sea" implied belonging to a marine environment the global scope of which was only just becoming apparent.

We are indeed physically derived from marine animals and in large part chemically constituted by salt water. Daborne could have had no inkling of such a connection (any more than Shakespeare could have), yet his pirate articulates an insight that resonates not only in modern science but in early modern literature and culture. The possibility that human beings could be of the sea—belonging to the global ocean instead of to a monarch or nation-state—ignited the imaginations of artists and writers of the late Renaissance. This strange belonging meant more than simply that pirates were extra-national outlaws; it meant that they partook of a marine environment that rendered them global, not national, subjects and creatures of the sea.

In the preceding chapters I have argued that the writings of William Shakespeare persistently entertain the idea that we are of the sea, not in the limited political or economic sense that piracy implies, but at a more global level. Shakespeare everywhere evinces an awareness of an ontological connection between humanity and the ocean. Forever drawn to water, Shakespeare was acutely aware that humanity and salt water are strangely allied; as Melville would later put it, ours is a "terraqueous globe," and "meditation and water are wedded forever."[5] The aesthetic possibilities of water constitute a sort of metaphorical undertow throughout the plays and poems, drawing our attention to marine phenomena at the most unlikely moments. The mobility and mutability of the surface, the ineffability of the depths, and the vastness of the newly discovered oceans themselves together constituted a motivating challenge for the playwright's powers. Even in scenes set in gardens, woods, a heath, or a palace Shakespeare reminds his audience that this is a watery planet. Everywhere in the plays and poems he turns to the sea, reminding us that the ocean makes its claims on human lives. Shakespeare produced poetry that remapped the globe. Both a hostile boundary for landborne beings and an essential part of human ontology, Shakespeare's ocean interrogates human claims to being at home in the world. In explicating this dimension of his writings I have shown that a serious attention to the human relationship to marine environments is not entirely a modern notion, nor is it limited to marine scientists or environmental historians.

Yet as I have argued, this aspect of his works has been curiously neglected—all the more so in light of the present boom in ecocritical early modern studies. My readings in the preceding chapters have, thus, addressed the significance of depths, tides, coastal environments, whales, fish, and winds. In exploring these topics I have also argued that ecocritical scholarship has heretofore remained peculiarly landlocked in its outlook, disposition, and terminology. Not only is the ecocritical object of inquiry habitually defined in terms of the "green" space (be it pastoral or georgic in mode) of dry land, but the conceptual foundations of ecocriticism are themselves rooted in terminology that represses the very existence of the world ocean. Merely pointing out that this is a watery world and that ecocritics would do well to reconsider its physical parameters, however, is an insufficient remedy. Necessary, too, is some demonstration of the role of the oceanic environment in constituting the cultural imaginary of "nature." The neglect of the ocean and of the marine sciences in current ecocritical scholarship impoverishes our understanding of the full richness of the playwright's engagement with the natural world.

"Shakespeare," in my view, represents an enormously rich and varied cultural text in which can be found an alternative—and decidedly saltier and wetter—model of what constitutes the biophysical environment. In the centuries since he lived and wrote we have narrowed our perspective on what constitutes the environment, and we are impoverished by this narrowing. For Shakespeare, that which environs our experience of being-in-the-world is aquatic (or terraqueous)—a panoply of land-borne and sea-born life, a hauntingly invisible submarine world of shoals, shelves, banks, sands, and tides ruled by occult forces. His marine environment is an entity at once strange and familiar, orienting and disorienting, life giving and life destroying. If this maritime imagination adumbrates contemporary discussions of the impact of humanity on the natural world, it also draws our gaze back in time to the moment when the global ocean itself took form in the early modern European imagination.

If my critique has been driven by the countervalent currents of presentism and historicism, it has also been shaped by my own experience studying different coastal and deep-sea regions in the company of marine scientists for whom the global ocean is quite simply the central fact of the Earth's biophysical environment. In William Shakespeare I have found an unlikely but staunch sailing companion. His remarkable intimacy with marine life offers a model for a terraqueous ecocriticism (or blue cultural studies), but it does so only through the kaleidoscopic lens of a materially oriented historicism joined to an interdisciplinary presentism, which some readers may find anachronistic, incongruous, or a mere hodgepodge of multidisciplinary dabbling (a bit of maritime history thrown in with some marine environmental history, marine biology, art history, and a pinch of legal theory). So be it: our culture—consumerist, "ecophobic," and unsustainable—has turned its back on the sea and in so doing has confined its understanding of nature (and of literature) to a well-mown green monoculture of the mind.[6]

One question that remains is, of course, why the poet remained so preoccupied with the sea throughout his writing life. While I have emphasized the maritime dimensions of early modern English culture, I have tried to avoid speculating about Shakespeare's biography. To argue (with the likes of Falconer and G. B. Harrison) that Shakespeare's knowledge of nautical terms, ship-handling, marine animals, winds, and tides must derive from time spent at sea is to beg the question of how he mastered the terminology and technical features of swordplay, horsemanship, shoemaking, herbology, and the language and manners of the court. While he demonstrably knew a good deal of nautical terminology and an astonishing amount about marine life (as, I hope, the preceding chapters make clear), the insistence on a biographical basis for Shakespeare's nautical credentials is entirely unnecessary and largely unwarranted. As Jonathan Raban notes, "It is not known whether Shakespeare ever went to sea, or even whether he set eyes on it"; moreover, to insist on a biographical basis for specialized knowledge is "seriously to undervalue Shakespeare's ability to imagine the world and make it palpable."[7] The poet's familiarity with the culture of mariners and the moods of the sea no doubt owes far more to the location of the international maritime entrepôt in which he plied his trade and to his unmatched ear for language than it does to any seagoing experience.[8] For Shakespeare to have made something as foreign as the bottom of the sea so vibrantly palpable attests to the playwright's supreme imaginative gifts.

While it is not difficult to imagine the playwright's gaze being caught by the rushing tide as he walked across London Bridge, our biographical understanding of the Bard need not place him at the helm of a ship, such as the *Golden Hind* or the *Sovereign of the Seas*, bawling his belonging to the sea like Gismund in Daborne's play. In much the same way that he absorbed and employed the language of falconry, forestry, jousting, law, and the court, he assimilated the language of mariners and the brush strokes of the marine artist. This we can only imagine he accomplished the same way he learned the idiolects of other trades and pastimes—at the Mermaid Tavern, the book-sellers' stalls, the Billingsgate Fishmarket, and on many a wherry ride on the Thames. Whether Shakespeare went to sea in his so-called lost years is not my concern. What is my concern, as the previous chapters attest, is the extraordinary extent to which the experience of the ocean affected William Shakespeare's creative vision of what we call the environment—that which environs or, in the early modern idiom, "compasses" us. In his imagination, to be human is in some sense to be compassed by the sea.

Those of us who have a longing for what David Abram has called the "more-than-human world" place a great value on going outdoors to encounter a biophysical environment that is not entirely manmade.[9] Other heroes of environmentalism have also led us out of doors, past the last post of our culturally delimited comfort zones. In *Walden* Henry David Thoreau enjoins his readers to "go to grass," like farm animals released from pen and fold to green pastures. The injunction is a plea for fieldwork, which in the humanities tends to mean a walk in the woods or a sabbatical hike to Dove Cottage, Walden Pond, or the Sierras. As I mentioned in the introduction, my own equivalent of fieldwork has been sea time. In many days and nights at sea I have been inspired by the writings of William Shakespeare, a poet who enjoins us to go to water. The readings I have offered are in no way intended to be definitive, nor do I claim to have been comprehensive in my approach. Where there are gaps and inadequacies—I pay too little attention to the gender politics of seafaring, the social history of maritime labor, the history of piracy, and to shipwreck (that ubiquitous trope in early modern religious discourse)—I hope others will go further. Shakespeare is not alone in his love for "the mirror of the sea," that great blue surface in which we can find more than ourselves reflected. Yet he looked more deeply than most into the depths and across the surface, and he found—as we continue to find—in the saltwater realm a magical otherness that turns out to be strangely familiar.

NOTES

Introduction

1. The Russian oceanographer Yuly Mikhailovich Shokalsky (1856–1940) is credited with coining the phrase "global ocean" (or "world ocean"); his *Oceanography* (Petrograd, 1913) was a seminal text in the development of the marine sciences.

2. "For ever may my knees grow to the earth, / My tongue cleave to my roof within my mouth / Unless a pardon ere I rise or speak" (*Richard II*, 5.3.29–31). All Shakespeare quotations in this text will indicate the act, scene, and line number in this format and are from *The Norton Shakespeare*, first edition, except where noted otherwise.

3. Sanders, *Cultural Geography of Early Modern Drama*, p. 27.

4. Wedgwood, *King's Peace, 1637–1641*, p. 24.

5. Mentz, *At the Bottom*, p. 56.

6. I return to this image, and discuss it further, in chapter 3.

7. Paintings of shipwrecks, such as Pieter Brueghel the Elder's *Landscape with the Fall of Icarus* (ca. 1558), and the anonymous *Wreck of the Amsterdam* (ca. 1630), were particularly popular in the late Renaissance.

8. As the title of Parry's *The Discovery of the Sea* suggests.

9. *Ecological Imperialism*, pp. 104–31. More recently, the topic has been addressed by Fernández-Armesto, *Pathfinders*. For a further discussion of the winds, see the final chapter of the present book.

10. Wallerstein, *The Modern World-System*.

11. Shakespeare, *The Tempest* (1.2.405).

12. In *The Norton Shakespeare* eighteen lines from the Second Quarto but not present in the Folio (including the phrase "Neptune's empire") are delineated as 106.1–106.18.

13. Studies in "the new thalassology" include Horden and Purcell, *Corrupting Sea*; Peters, "*Quid nobis cum pelago?*"; and Corbin, *Territoire du vide*, translated by Jocelyn Phelps as *The Lure of the Sea*. See also Rediker, *Between the Devil and the Deep Blue Sea* and *Villains of All Nations*.

14. As I have argued elsewhere: Brayton, 2009, p. 241. See also Henderson, *Collaborations with the Past*; and McLuskie, "The Future in an Instant."

15. Bartolovich, for example, argues, "'Shakespeare's Globe' cannot be extricated fully from colonial connotations . . . especially since 'Shakespeare' has been called upon to

play a role in 'colonizing the minds' of subject peoples in the past" ("Shakespeare's Globe?" p. 179).

16. See Porter, *Flesh in the Age of Reason*.

17. In this I join a growing number of literature scholars working on "oceanic studies," as attested to by a recent themed issue of the *Publications of the Modern Language Association* 125, no. 3 (May 2010).

18. Latour, *Politics of Nature*, p. 58. Bill McKibben made the same argument twenty years earlier, in *The End of Nature*.

19. In their article on Robert Frost's poem "Spring Pools," for example, John Elder and Glenn Adelson have analyzed the poet's figurative use of the water cycle to evoke a precise cyclicality—and a note of hope—overlooked by most readers ("Robert Frost's Ecosystem of Meanings in 'Spring Pools'").

20. Heise, *Sense of Place*, p. 506. Heise's book curiously omits any mention of the global ocean. It is puzzling that the "sense of planet" she celebrates in representations of "the global" ignores the ocean that covers most of this planet.

21. Greenblatt, *Shakespearean Negotiations*, p. 5.

22. While cultural materialism has long been a major feature of early modern literary scholarship, I am particularly interested in the discourse of things as evidenced by Brown's discussion of literary "object matter" in *A Sense of Things*.

23. I recycle this chiasmus from an earlier project, *Ecocritical Shakespeare*, p. 7.

24. Louv, *Last Child in the Woods: Saving Our Children from Nature-Deficit Disorder*.

25. "Ecocriticism" was coined by William Rueckert in 1978 in "Literature and Ecology: An Experiment in Ecocriticism" (reprinted in Glotfelty and Fromm, *The Ecocriticism Reader*).

26. Patton, *Sea Can Wash Away*, pp. 2–3.

27. Cramer, *Great Waters*, p. 8.

28. Yaeger, "Editor's Column," p. 524.

29. Wolf, "Environmental Ethics and Marine Ecosystems," p. 29.

30. *Antony*, 2.6.1221; *Caesar*, 1.3.424; Sonnet 64, line 5; *Gentlemen*, 2.7.999; *Henry V*, 2.1.1092; *Macbeth*, 5.4.2537.

31. See Jackson et al., "Historical Overfishing," which argues that the human removal of biomass (marine life) over time has drastically transformed marine ecosystems all over the world. Also see Pauly, "Fishing Down Marine Foodwebs"; Pauly et al., "The Future for Fisheries"; and Rosenberg et al., "History of Ocean Resources."

32. Tsunamis, for example, such as the one that in 2007 devastated countries around the Indian Ocean and the 2011 disaster in Japan, change entire coastlines and the civilizations that inhabit them. Coastal development diminishes the buffer zones of swamps and marshes. Similarly, runoff of fertilizers from Midwest agro-industry helps create a summer "dead zone" in the Gulf of Mexico the size of New Jersey by causing algal blooms that decompose aerobically, robbing seawater of oxygen.

33. McKibben, *End of Nature*, pp. 8–9.

34. Moore, "Trashed." See also Patricia Yaeger's excellent discussion of the Eastern Garbage Patch in "Editor's Note," pp. 523–45.

Notes to Pages 10–16

35. Ebbesmeyer and Scigliano, *Flotsametrics and the Floating World*.

36. *SSV*, a US Coast Guard classification that stands for *Sailing School Vessel*, is a strictly regulated category that was instituted specifically for Sea Semester's erstwhile sail training vessel *Westward*.

37. In the summer of 2010 scientists at Sea Education Association completed a data-gathering voyage to the southwestern North Atlantic Ocean as part of their grant-funded research into the causes and effects of such "garbage patches"; the data gathered on this voyage have been analyzed by Chief Scientist Kara Lavender Law and others in Lavender Law et al., "Plastic Accumulation."

38. McKibben, *End of Nature*; Latour, *Politics of Nature*, p. 58.

39. The collaborative international Census of Marine Life, an interdisciplinary project to map the marine biosphere, has provided key data and models about the human impact on numerous species, particularly commercially viable ones. For an overview and links, see http://www.coml.org.

40. See Safina, *Song for the Blue Ocean*; Clover, *End of the Line*; Bavington, *Managed Annihilation*. Blue Ocean Institute's website, http://www.blueocean.org, has relevant articles and links.

41. Patton, *Sea Can Wash Away*, p. 12.

42. See Steinberg, *Social Construction of the Ocean*, for an excellent analysis of the Western tendency to define the ocean as a blank space.

43. Raban, *Oxford Book of the Sea*, p. 6.

44. Cohen, "Undiscovered Country," p. 133.

45. Knight, *Shakespearean Tempest*.

46. Falconer, *Shakespeare and the Sea*, p. 2.

47. Mentz has been exceptionally active in promoting early modern thalassalogical scholarship, organizing the seminar "Shakespeare and the Maritime Scene" at the 2005 convention of the Shakespeare Association of America; curating a 2010 exhibition at the Folger Shakespeare Library entitled *Lost at Sea*; and organizing the 2011 "Hungry Ocean" conference at the John Carter Brown Library in Providence, Rhode Island, as well as a seminar at the 2011 convention of the International Shakespeare Association in Prague.

48. For an article-length treatment, see Mentz's "Toward a Blue Cultural Studies."

49. Michael Blackstock has termed the water-centered study of the natural world a "blue ecology" in his article "Blue Ecology." See also Safina, *Song for the Blue Ocean*.

50. By "cultural studies" I mean expanding the scope of scholarship beyond the literary artifact to a multiplicity of contexts.

1. Backs to the Sea?

1. See, for example, Armbruster and Wallace, *Beyond Nature Writing*; Elder and Finch, *Norton Book of Nature Writing*, 2nd ed.

2. That ecocriticism is a metafield is manifest by a glance at the work of postcolonial ecocritics and ecocritical early modernists and medievalists whose works lie within the traditional taxonomy that organizes literary scholarship. Ecocritical historicists have

bridged the gap between subfield and metafield. See Watson, *Back to Nature*; Egan, *Green Shakespeare*; and Hiltner, *Renaissance Ecology*.

3. For an essay that historicizes climate change in the context of seventeenth-century London, see Hiltner, "Renaissance Literature and Our Contemporary Attitude toward Global Warming."

4. "The Waves," line 5, in Raban, *Oxford Book of the Sea*, p. 508.

5. Pastoral and georgic, for instance, not only denote two literary modes; they also imply two very different ways of defining the human relationship to the physical environment.

6. O'Dair, "State of the Green," p. 478.

7. Buell, *Endangered World*, p. 12.

8. Philips, *Truth of Ecology*, p. 44.

9. No doubt I am one. Morton, *Ecology without Nature*.

10. See Garrard, *Ecocriticism*. To his credit, Garrard cites the 1960s television show *Flipper* for raising public awareness about dolphins. The fact that he only mentions marine life in passing is less a fault than a symptom.

11. "Primitive" terms in philosophical discourse are fundamental categories of meaning with which we frame our subject or analysis—the conceptual bedrock of a discipline.

12. Several titles and subtitles of the excellent books in the University of Virginia Press's Under the Sign of Nature series refer to "the land" in this way: see Scott Herring, *Lines on the Land: Writers, Art, and the National Parks*; Michael Bryson, *Visions of the Land: Science Literature, and the Environment from the Era of Exploration to the Age of Ecology*; and Rinda West, *Out of the Shadow: Ecopsychology, Story, and Encounters with the Land*. The title "Voices from the Land" has been used for a film, several books, and at least one journal.

13. Introduction to Glotfelty and Fromm, *Ecocriticism Reader*, p. xix.

14. Leopold, *Sand County Almanac*, p. 243.

15. Meine, *Aldo Leopold*, pp. 370.

16. Quoted in ibid., p. 370.

17. Ibid., p. 239.

18. More recently, the marine scientist Carl Safina has argued for the necessity of a "sea ethic" and has founded the Blue Ocean Institute to promote this movement (http://www.blueocean.org).

19. A recent book by the renowned marine biologist Sylvia Earle bears the title *The World Is Blue!* I shall return to Earle's work in chapter 2.

20. Melville, *Moby-Dick*, p. 65.

21. Cronon, *Changes in the Land*. In a similarly titled (and insightful) book, *Hands on the Land*, Jan Albers demonstrates the degree to which the bucolic landscape of Vermont is itself a product of human activities of many kinds.

22. To his credit, Cronon does mention fish and fisheries, cod and alewives in particular. Marine environmental history did not exist as a discipline when Cronon wrote *Changes in the Land*, and indeed it probably could not have developed so rapidly without his work.

23. Kroeber, *Ecological Literary Criticism*, p. 22. The self-awareness that Kroeber calls for is an indispensible feature of responsible ecocritical scholarship.

24. Love, "Ecocriticism and Science," p. 561.

25. Yaeger, "Editor's Column," p. 538.

26. Balasopoulos, "Suffer a Sea Change," p. 133.

27. Auden, *Enchafèd Flood*, pp. 7–8.

28. Tennyson vividly evokes this narrative in "The Kraken." Part mythological beast and part giant squid (genus *Architeuthis*), the Kraken embodies the occultation—and occult overtones—of the biblical "deep." At the "latter fire" it will arise from the deep and "on the surface die."

29. See Connery, "There Was No More Sea."

30. Genesis 1:2. All bible references throughout will be listed by book, chapter, and verse, and are from *The Bible: Authorized King James Version with Apocrypha*, edited by Robert Carroll and Stephen Prickett (Oxford: Oxford University Press, 1998).

31. Nicolson, *Seamanship*, p. 2.

32. Patton, *Sea Can Wash Away*, p. 50.

33. Samuel Taylor Coleridge, "Rime of the Ancient Mariner," lines 23–24, in Wordsworth and Coleridge, *Lyrical Ballads*, pp. 8–9; John Masefield, "Sea-Fever," line 1, in Raban, *Oxford Book of the Sea*, p. 326.

34. Patton, *Sea Can Wash Away*, p. 57.

35. Ibid., p. 58.

36. Ibid., p. 65. See also Robert Parker, *Miasma: Pollution and Purification in Early Greek Religion*, New York: Oxford University Press, 1990.

37. *Etymologicum magnum*, quoted in Patton, *Sea Can Wash Away*, p. 64.

38. Patton, *Sea Can Wash Away*, p. 53.

39. Quoted in Dening, "Deep Times, Deep Spaces," p. 13.

40. Balasopoulos, "Suffer a Sea Change," p. 131.

41. Steinberg, *Social Construction of the Ocean*, p. 35. This study elucidates the ways the oceans have been defined in Western culture as an incomprehensible space proximate to the supernatural and alien to the human.

42. Conforti, *Saints and Strangers*; Wallerstein, *Modern World-System*.

43. Jowitt, *Culture of Piracy*, p. 7.

44. Quoted in Steinberg, *Social Construction of the Ocean*, p. 91.

45. Quoted in Steinberg, *Social Construction of the Ocean*, p. 92.

46. Quoted in Jowitt, *Culture of Piracy*, p. 5.

47. For example, see Bate, *Romantic Ecology* and *Song of the Earth*.

48. Yaeger, "Editor's Column," p. 538.

49. In Raban, *Oxford Book of the Sea*, p. 179.

50. To those who would claim that the *surface* of the sea looks much the same today as it did a millennium ago I would note the proliferation of algae, largely due to anthropogenic impacts on the biochemistry of salt water, in the past century.

51. Yaeger, "Editor's Column," p. 538.

52. Quoted in Clover, *End of the Line*, p. 102

53. Kolbert, "The Scales Fall," pp. 71, 73.

54. On trawlers, see Clover, *End of the Line*, pp. 48–49, 66–68, 91–92, 98–99.

55. Clover, ibid., p. 67. See also Yaeger's excellent discussion in "Editor's Column," p. 529.

56. See Clover, ibid., pp. 1–2, 66–68; see also Roberts, *Unnatural History*, pp. 185–98, 200–209.

57. For more on the significance of the benthos, or bottom of the sea, see chapter 3 of the present book.

58. The most productive fisheries are located on particular grounds or banks, such as the Grand Banks of Newfoundland, Georges Bank (off Cape Cod), Dogger Bank, in the North Sea (for centuries the most productive ground for the herring fishery), and are hence associated with them.

59. Bolster describes a related instance of "overfishing," whaling: "Killing large numbers of whales in a relatively short time removed their qualitative contribution to ecosystem stability. . . . As long-living large predators, whales embody vast biomass in stable form. Even in a relatively small area like the Gulf of Maine, the pre-harvest whale population concentrated hundreds of thousands of tons of biomass, thus imposing certain constraints on the variability of the system. . . . Colonial hunters' overharvesting of whales freed considerable prey from capture, and may have allowed prey populations to oscillate more dramatically than they had before" ("Opportunities," p. 4).

60. Quoted in Roberts, *Unnatural History*, p. 34

61. Quoted in Bolster, "Opportunities in Marine Environmental History," p. 6.

62. Carson, *Sea around Us*, p. 23.

63. Ibid., p. 15.

64. Quoted in Kolbert, "The Scales Fall," p. 72.

65. The cover of the July 14, 2003, issue of *Newsweek* asked in bold letters, "Are the Oceans Dying?" Kolbert refers to the moment, in the late 1980s (just before the crash of the Newfoundland cod stocks), when the total global catch of seafood reached approximately eighty-five million tons as "peak fish." Total reported catch yields have *apparently* continued to rise since then because of bogus reporting by the Chinese—a case of grotesque distortion.

66. *Facing the Ocean*, p. 1. Cunliffe's lapse into such nonsense is surprising in light of his expertise at analyzing terrestrial landscapes for signs of human history. Not only have underwater archaeologists studied the human history of the seafloor, but the surface of the sea itself is a blank space primarily to those unaccustomed to reading it for signs of life—schools of fish, gusts of wind, currents, and the refraction patterns of waves, all of which signify specific phenomena (the presence of marine predators, for example) that are historically contingent.

67. Bolster, "Opportunities," p. 8.

68. The relatively nascent discipline of marine environmental history has recently made great strides. See Bolster, "Opportunities," pp. 1–32, and Roberts, *Unnatural History*.

69. For an excellent review, see Karen Raber, "Recent Ecostudies in Tudor and Stuart

Literature." See also McColley, *Poetry and Ecology*; Egan, *Green Shakespeare*; Watson, *Back to Nature*; and Hiltner, *Milton and Ecology*.

70. Thomas, *Man and the Natural World*. Bolster notes this weakness as well ("Opportunities," p. 6).

71. Abram, *Spell of the Sensuous*.

72. The Green World of the comedies is but one instance of Shakespeare's peculiar talent for materializing the social order by projecting it onto specific sites. See Berger, *Second World and Green World*; Barber, *Shakespeare's Festive Comedy*.

73. On "waste" lands in early modern England, see Hill, *World Turned Upside Down*, pp. 51–56, and *Liberty Against the Law*, especially pp. 98–99.

74. *Paradise* itself derives from a Persian word signifying an enclosed, private garden, as Giamatti notes in *Earthly Paradise and the Renaissance Epic*.

75. Bruce R. Smith offers some fascinating answers to this question in his recent book *The Key of Green: Passion and Perception in Renaissance Culture*. While it can hardly be called ecocritical, this study brilliantly historicizes the cultural resonances of the color green in the Renaissance.

76. Egan, *Green Shakespeare*, p. 4.

77. See Langewiesche, *Outlaw Sea*.

78. To his credit, Egan does justice to the textual crux of "green fields" in his introduction, "Babbling of Green Fields" (*Green Shakespeare*, pp. 1–16).

79. Egan's account of Shakespeare's environmental sensibility is in no way unusual in its exclusion of the watery realm. For more on this, see my "Shakespeare and the Global Ocean."

80. On the cover of the March 1978 (Vol. 12, no. 60) issue of *Aquaman*, which I read when it came out, the eponymous hero tells his enemy, the Scavenger, "Your machines may rot the seas, Scavenger—But I swear you won't live to hurt another one of my people!"

81. Bate, *Romantic Ecology*.

82. Yaeger, "Editor's Column," p. 537.

83. Quoted in Yaeger, ibid., p. 536.

84. Yaeger, ibid., p. 537.

85. Yaeger, ibid., p. 538.

86. Brown, *A Sense of Things*.

87. Pauly, *Five Easy Pieces*. Kolbert discusses the topic in "The Scales Fall."

88. The *Challenger* expedition, by far the most ambitious attempt to gather information about the global ocean undertaken until then, spectacularly augmented human knowledge about the ocean, yet its significance for advancing the knowledge of marine biota and ocean circulation and its role in creating the discipline of ecology have not been acknowledged by ecocritics. The expedition and the marine sciences it advanced constitute a kind of historical unconscious for ecocriticism.

89. Hamilton-Paterson, *The Great Deep*, p. 179.

90. Hamilton-Paterson, *The Great Deep*, p. 179. See also Schlee, *Edge of an Unfamiliar World*.

91. Haeckel, *General Morphology of Organisms*, p. 354. The Danish botanist Eugenius Warming is considered the founder of modern ecology for systemically laying the foundations of the discipline in the 1890s.

92. Freud famously compares the work of psychoanalysis with the draining of the Zuyder Zee: "Where *id* was, there let ego be."

2. Consider the Crab

1. One of Rachel Carson's enduring legacies is her emphasis on the importance of promoting "wonder" in childhood. For Carson, feeling precedes knowing, and a full engagement with the environment begins in the senses (see *Sense of Wonder*).

2. Editor-in-chief of the journal *Bioinvasions* and director of the Williams-Mystic Program at Mystic Seaport, Jim pioneered the study of invasive marine animals. I am grateful to him for telling me about *Hemigrapsus* in conversations over several years.

3. Joe Wojtas, "Marine Life: Foreign Import Has Clawed Its Way Up," *New York Times*, April 4, 2010, http://www.nytimes.com.

4. See Pauly, "Anecdotes and the Shifting Baseline Syndrome."

5. Carlton is widely considered the pioneer of the study of marine bioinvasions in ballast water and has on several occasions addressed the US Congress on the topic.

6. Ruiz and Carlton, *Invasive Species*.

7. Hidalgo, Baron, and Orensanz, "A Prediction Come True."

8. Long the leading authority on marine flora, Earle is widely known as "Her Deepness" and "the Sturgeon General"; she is now Explorer-in-Residence at *National Geographic*.

9. NOAA is a division of the Department of Commerce; as such it is overseen by the commerce secretary. Earle's warning has been borne out by crisis after crisis, the most recent of which is the oil spill in the Gulf of Mexico caused by the joint mismanagement of multinationals BP, Transocean, and Halliburton, and lax oversight by a government beholden to global corporate interests.

10. Bate, *Song of the Earth*, p. 77.

11. The essay can be found in Wallace, *Consider the Lobster and Other Essays*.

12. Crosby, *Ecological Imperialism*.

13. Ibid., p. 155.

14. In a recent biography of Shakespeare, Bate answers his own rhetorical question by speculating about the playwright's intimate familiarity with English flora: "How many students and playgoers today could identify specimens of fumitory, darnel, or cuckooflower? Shakespeare, brought up in the country, had a field education, in all probability before he even went to school." For Bate it is self-evident that Shakespeare's knowledge of plants and herbs derives from his Warwickshire upbringing, "in the country," which provided him not just with an easy familiarity with English flowers but with something much more significant: a "field education" (*Soul of the Age*, p. 58).

15. The anthropogenic transformation of the marine environment that resulted from

the fishing bonanza in the Northwest Atlantic has been thoroughly studied in recent years. Essential book-length treatments include Kurlansky, *Cod*, and *Last Fish Tale*; see also Dobbs, *The Great Gulf*.

16. Cronon, *Changes in the Land*, pp. 22–23.
17. Roberts, *Unnatural History*, p. 43.
18. Quoted in Safina, "Fishing to the Bottom," p. 1.
19. Roberts, *Unnatural History*, p. 23.
20. Quoted in Bolster, "Opportunities in Marine Environmental History," p. 33.
21. Bolster, ibid., p. 44.
22. Quoted in Cronon, *Changes in the Land*, p. 4.
23. *Shakespeare's Sonnets*, edited by Stephen Booth, p. 56.
24. Sanders, *Cultural Geography of Early Modern Drama*, p. 30.
25. Sullivan, *Drama of Landscape*, p. 2.
26. As I discussed in the previous chapter, the legal scholars Hugo Grotius and John Selden articulated opposing views on whether oceanic space should be "open" (*liberum*) to shipping of all nations or "closed" (*clausem*), subject to national-political control.
27. See Keith Thomas, *Man and the Natural World*, for a discussion of early modern land use. Quoting Walter Blith's *The English Improver Improved* (1653), Thomas notes, "To the agricultural propagandists of the sixteenth and seventeenth centuries, untilled heaths, mountains and fens had been a standing reproach. They wanted the bracken, gorse, and broom removed; and they cherished the ground which had been painfully 'stubbed or won from wood, bushes, broom or furze'" (254). William Harrison also mentions "furzes" in *The Description of England*: "Of foxes we have some, but no great store, and also badgers in our sandy and light grounds, where woods, furzes, broom, and plenty of shrubs are to shroud them" (325).
28. See Hulme, "Cast Away," p. 187.
29. In *Specters of the Atlantic* Baucom reads Ariel's song as "an anthem of postmodernity," while Mentz's *At the Bottom of Shakespeare's Ocean* portrays it as a symptom of the epistemic shift between supernatural and scientific thinking on the eve of the scientific revolution (1–9). G. Wilson Knight saw it as one of the supreme statements of Shakespeare's faith in music as the organization of the chaos of the natural world, as represented by storms and the sea (*"Tempest,"* 247–56).
30. I take up the topic of disorientation in *The Tempest* again in chapter 7 of this book.
31. The *OED* cites the first use of the word *fathom*, derived from an Old English word for the length of a man's outstretched arms, in the abstract sense of understanding, as belonging to Shakespeare: "Another of his fathom they have none" (*Othello*, 1.1.153).
32. Mentz, *At the Bottom*, pp. 9–10.
33. Watson, *Back to Nature*, pp. 5–6.
34. Corbin, *Lure of the Sea*, p. 2.
35. Simon Estok has defined *ecophobia* as "imagining badness in nature and marketing that imagination," which he locates in "representations of nature as an opponent that

hurts, hinders, threatens, or kills us—regardless of the philosophical value or disvalue of the ecosystemic functions of the dynamics being represented" ("Theorizing in a Space of Ambivalent Openness," pp. 203–26).

36. Valdivieso, "He Hourly Humanizes," 269.

37. I use the term *woodland* instead of *forest* because the latter has a specific legal meaning, particularly in the early modern period. See Harrison, *Forests*, pp. 61–106. On the etymological connections between *wilds* and *wood* see Macfarlane, *The Wild Places*, p. 92.

38. See Harrison, *Forests*, pp. 1–106.

39. Vaughan and Vaughan, *Shakespeare's Caliban*, p. ix.

40. Lupton, "Creature Caliban," pp. 1–23.

41. Vaughan and Vaughan, *Shakespeare's Caliban*.

42. Caliban does not deny the accusation of attempted rape, which associates him with the violence of "venery."

43. Gurr, *Playgoing in Shakespeare's London*, p. 61.

44. In "Oysters—the Tudor Version of Popcorn," a Reuters article published on Friday, January 29, 2010, Stefano Ambrogi proclaimed, "Elizabethan theater-goers chomped on an exotic array of foods while enjoying the latest plays of the day, new evidence found at the sites of Shakespearean playhouses in London suggests" (http://uk.reuters.com/article/2010/01/29/us-britain-shakespeare-snacks-idUKTRE60S3NL20100129). In her *Discovery News* article of February 12, 2010, Rossella Lorenzi called oysters and crabs "the popcorn of Elizabethan-theater-goers," citing the work of the London Museum archaeologist Julian Bowsher: "Bowsher explained that remains found underneath the gallery seating suggested that the wealthier classes munched on crabs and sturgeon, as well as imported treats like peaches and dried figs. Meanwhile, oyster shells were found scattered all over the yard area, where commoners stood" ("Oysters and Crabs, the Popcorn of Shakespearean Theatergoers, http://news.discovery.com/history/oysters-and-crabs-the-popcorn-of-shakespearean-theatergoers.html).

3. Shakespeare's Benthic Imagination

1. Blumenberg, *Shipwreck with Spectator*, p. 7.
2. Edwards, *Sea-Mark*, p. 2.
3. Mentz, *At the Bottom*, p. 18.
4. Patton, *Sea Can Wash Away*, p. 50.
5. Auden, *Enchafèd Flood*; Harrison, *Forests*. By the nineteenth century it would become a sailor's adage that God's dominion stopped at Cape Horn.
6. Macfarlane, *Wild Places*, p. 30.
7. Harrison's *Forests* anticipates many ecocritical insights.
8. Rozwadowski, *Fathoming the Ocean*, p. 7.
9. The relationship between sound and the measurement of depth, we might say, is not only technological (e.g., sonar depth-sounders) but also philological (measure = poetic meter).

10. Locke, *Essay Concerning Human Understanding*, p. 58.
11. Falconer, *Shakespeare and the Sea*, p. 86.
12. I am grateful to Jim Berg for noting the connection between Clarence's dream and his subsequent death by drowning.
13. Watson, *Back to Nature*, pp. 77–107.
14. It is worth noting that the blue whale is the largest animal ever to live on this planet, dinosaurs included.
15. For a clear explanation of the importance of soundings, see Falconer, *Shakespeare and the Sea*, pp. 86–88.
16. Raban, *Oxford Book of the Sea*, p. 7.
17. In the famous chapter in *Moby-Dick* titled "Cetology" Melville claims, "It is some systematized exhibition of the whale in his broad genera, that I would now fain put before you. Yet this is no easy task. The classification of the constituents of a chaos, nothing less is here essayed" (p. 115). Hamlet's clever use of the whale as an emblem of what can and cannot be known becomes, in Melville's magnum opus, the central philosophical preoccupation of the chapters on natural history.
18. Deacon, *Scientists and the Sea*, p. 11.
19. Ibid., p. 39.
20. Quoted in ibid., p. 40.
21. Conley, *Self-Made Map*, p. 22.
22. Gillies, *Shakespeare and the Geography of Difference*, pp. 74–75.
23. Gillies, *Shakespeare and the Geography*, p. 49.
24. Abram, *Spell of the Sensuous*.

4. Tidal Bodies

1. Hardie, *Virgil's Aeneid*, p. 6.
2. Peterson, *Time, Tide, and Tempest*.
3. I am grateful to Steve Mentz for his discussion of coenesthesis in a lecture of June 14, 2010, at the Folger Shakespeare Library. The lecture, sponsored by the library, was on the occasion of the opening of his special exhibition, *Lost at Sea*.
4. Cartwright, *Tides*.
5. Quoted in Cartwright, *Tides*, p. 30.
6. Cartwright, *Tides*, p. 25.
7. Ibid., p. 1.
8. Ibid., p. 5.
9. Ibid., p. 1.
10. Quoted in ibid., p. 13.
11. Falconer, who served an officer in the Royal Navy before becoming a scholar, offers a particularly helpful explanation of tidal dynamics: "The term 'tide' applies to the periodic rise and fall of the level of the sea, the heaping up and subsiding of the water. It is a vertical, up and down movement and is not to be confused with the 'stream' which is a horizontal movement, the inflow and outflow caused by the rise and fall. The rising tide

is called the flood tide, and it is accompanied by the flood stream. The falling tide is called the ebb tide and with it goes the ebb stream" (*Shakespeare and the Sea*, p. 73).

12. *Riverside Chaucer*, p. 30.

13. For an excellent discussion of the history of medieval *portulan* charts (*portolani*, in Italian) and the coastal nature of medieval European navigation, see Brown, *Story of Maps*, especially chapters 4 and 5, pp. 81–149.

14. Currents are not identical to tides (although some currents are caused by them). The fact that Chaucer distinguishes between the two speaks worlds about his proto-scientific awareness of marine phenomena.

15. Ackroyd, *Thames*, p. 93.

16. It still is, even for supertankers that cruise at speeds of over 20 knots (roughly 23 miles per hour), for the sake of minimizing the cost of fuel.

17. The first definition of *flood* in the *OED*, from which I quote Smith, is "the flowing in of the tide."

18. "I'll be a park, and thou shalt be my deer. / Feed where thou wilt, on mountain or on dale; / Graze on my lips, and if those hills be dry, / Stray lower, where the pleasant fountains lie" (*Venus and Adonis*, lines 231–34).

19. This is somewhat paradoxical because the Mediterranean itself, like the Baltic, has very little discernible tide. The English poet's knowledge of the sea was clearly local.

20. While the Folio has "lines" instead of "lunes," it seems quite clear that the latter is the correct word choice, for the imagery of "ebbs" and "flows" makes no sense otherwise.

21. Wells, "To Find a Face," p. 98.

22. Ibid., p. 101.

23. Maus, "Taking Tropes Seriously," p. 66.

24. Fineman, *Subjectivity Effect*, p. 211.

25. Pirates are mentioned in nearly all of Shakespeare's plays with saltwater settings—*II Henry VI*, *The Merchant of Venice*, *Hamlet*, *Twelfth Night*, *Antony and Cleopatra*, *Pericles*—as well as in plays that are set in landlocked realms, such as *Measure for Measure*; they seem an inevitable feature of Shakespeare's maritime landscape.

26. The lines evoke the celebrated legend of King Knut vainly attempting to halt the flood tide.

27. Maus, "Taking Tropes Seriously," p. 74.

28. Ibid.

29. One is perversely reminded of the environmentalist's adage "The solution to pollution is dilution," a formulation that exacerbates the myth of inexhaustibility.

30. "Bottomless" refers to the sounding of depths by mariners. See chapter 3 of this work.

31. Fineman, *Subjectivity Effect*, p. 186.

32. Michel de Certeau observes that "in modern Athens, the vehicles of mass transportation are called *metaphorai*. To go to work or come home, one takes a 'metaphor'—a bus or a train" (*Practice of Everyday Life*, p. 115).

33. Puttenham, *Arte of English poesie*, part 1.

34. Maus, "Taking Tropes Seriously," p. 68.

35. The phenomenon known as "a tidal bore," a standing (stationary) wave generally produced by a rising tide in a rapidly flowing river, occurs in several English rivers, including the Severn (into which Shakespeare's Avon flows).

36. Fineman, *Subjectivity Effect*, p. 211.

5. Royal Fish

1. Orcas (*Orcinus orca*) are the largest members of the dolphin family, of the *odonticeti*, or toothed whales.

2. Damien Cave, "Intentions of Whale in Killing Are Debated," *New York Times*, February 26, 2010, A12.

3. Mowat's work galvanized the founders of Greenpeace and its more aggressive stepchild, Sea Shepherd Foundation. *A Whale for the Killing* was originally published in 1972.

4. Perhaps the daunting presence of *Moby-Dick*, that vortex of cetological inquiry, explains why literature scholars working beyond the purview of nineteenth-century American letters have almost entirely neglected the literary significance of whales.

5. "References to creatures of the deep and to various fish are of a general kind," Falconer asserts. "It is only of the crab, dolphin, oyster and whale that some fuller knowledge is shown, and even that is not of an unfamiliar sort." He points out that "the sportiveness of the dolphin, and how the antics of the porpoise herald a storm, are all noted," while "more is made of the whale, its spouting and way of driving small fish before it and devouring them" (*Shakespeare and the Sea*, pp. 138–39).

6. The latter definition is at play in *I Henry IV* in a description of man-to-man combat: "He did confound the best part of an hour / In changing hardiment with great Glendower" (1.3.100). "Scope" also alludes to the length of rope used in anchoring or mooring a vessel. The greater the scope, the better the anchor holds.

7. "As surfet is the father of much fast, / So every Scope by the immoderate use turns to Restraint" (*Measure for Measure*, 1.2.131); "Be angry when you will, it shall have scope" (*Julius Caesar*, 4.3.108). The second meaning is the one the poet employs in Sonnet 29: "Desiring this man's art, and that man's skope" (*OED*).

8. Quoted in Fulton, *Sovereignty of the Seas*, p. 362. Melville comments on this tradition in chapters 89–91 of *Moby-Dick*, pp. 307–12.

9. Government in the United Kingdom maintains strict guidelines for the management of stranded whales and sturgeon, both of which species are classified as royal fish, a legal status that "was resurrected in the nineteenth century, when the land properties of the Sovereign were transferred to the management of the Commissioners of Woods, Forests and Land Revenues (now the Crown Estate Commissioners) by the Crown Lands Acts 1810 and 1829" (UK Coastal Zone Law Notes, Section 2).

10. *Moby-Dick*, p. 59. Melville explores this ontological association still further, deepening and complicating the idea that whales and people have much in common.

11. Conley explicates the semiotics of a symbolic and semiotic association between dolphins, geography, and royalty in *The Self-Made Map*, chapter 6.

12. Raban, *England under Edward I and Edward II*, p. 136.
13. Saccio, *Shakespeare's English Kings*, p. 47.
14. Ibid.
15. Boehrer, *Shakespeare among the Animals*, p. 81.
16. Fudge's account of the hierarchic constitution of humanity can also be seen as contributing to the recuperation of the intellectual currency of the *scala naturae* in early modern literary scholarship.
17. See Bakhtin, *Rabelais and His World*, especially chapters 5 and 6.
18. Wolfe, "Animal Rites," p. 39.
19. Boehrer, *Shakespeare among the Animals*, p. 70. See also Nardizzi, "Felling Falstaff."
20. The superb traveling exhibition *Whales, Tohora* (created by the Museum of New Zealand Te Papa Tongarewa), which I saw at the Carnegie-Mellon Museum of Natural History on February 26, 2010, and again at the Boston Museum of Science on September 4, 2010, demonstrates the centrality of the humpback whale in Maori culture (particularly in etiological myths).
21. Jacques Cousteau articulated this tension in his book *The Whale: Mighty Monarch of the Sea*, in which the great explorer describes the orca as "the strongest of them all."
22. Job 41: 1–3, 7, 31, 33–34. All bible references throughout will be listed by book, chapter, and verse, and are from *The Bible: Authorized King James Version with Apocrypha*, edited by Robert Carroll and Stephen Prickett (Oxford: Oxford University Press, 1998).
23. Psalm 104:26. The emphasis is in the original.
24. Fagan, *Fish on Friday*, p. 4.
25. This passage is also quoted in Fagan, *Fish on Friday*, p. 4. There is some debate among classicists about the identity of Oppian (of Cilicia or Syria?), whose writings are sometimes attributed to Ovid.
26. The fact that the Greeks had many myths about dolphins rescuing humans, of which Arion's story is only the most famous, suggests their widespread awareness of dolphins' sociability and intelligence.
27. The landmark acts of environmental protection passed in the 1970s, in particular the Marine Mammal Protection Act and Endangered Species Act, have often been referred to as the "Flipper laws."
28. Corbin's work has been translated into English by Jocelyn Phelps as *The Lure of the Sea*; the quote in the main text is from page 6 of the translation. Shakespeare's Lear refers to "the sea-monster" as an emblem of the unnatural.
29. Phipson, *Animal Lore*, p. 87.
30. Fagan argues in *Fish on Friday* that the finding and peopling of North America by Europeans in the fifteenth century resulted from years of expanding the market for fish to accommodate Christian fast days.
31. "Fry" can refer to juvenile members of various species of fish (mackerel, sea bass) or to small mature fish (pilchard, sardines, sprat).
32. Trienens, "Symbolic Cloud in *Hamlet*," p. 211.
33. This is not an unusual instance of the playwright's awareness of the social and

economic controversies caused when landowners seeking to profit by raising sheep for their value in the wool market, dispossessed members of the rural peasantry en masse. See Burt and Archer, eds., *Enclosure Acts*.

34. The enclosures, of course, famously have an earlier metaphoric history in the form of Thomas More's man-eating sheep, as described in book I of the *Utopia*. Raphael Hythlodaeus cites the cause of crime as poverty caused by the greed of the wealthy, whose widespread enclosure of land for the purpose of increased wool production for continental markets dispossessed enormous numbers of the peasantry.

35. Hanley, *Natural History in America*, chapter II, p. 157. See also Schiebinger, *Nature's Body*, pp. 40–74.

36. *Natural History in America*, p. 158. Hanley was a prominent environmentalist in the 1960s and 1970s and editor of Massachusetts Audubon Society publications. I am grateful to Wayne Losano for introducing me to his work.

37. Aristotle, *History of Animals*, p. 8. See also Ellis, *Men and Whales*, p. 34.

38. Numerous seventeenth-century accounts of whales emphasize their status as wonders: *Strange News from the Deep: Being a Full Account of a Large Prodigious Whale* . . . (1677); *God's Marvellous Wonders in England: Diverse Strange and Wonderful Relations* . . . (1691). These and numerous others can be found in *Early English Books Online*.

39. The intellectual historian Brian Ogilvie describes Magnus (1490–1558) as the "titular archbishop of Uppsala," whose descriptions of the far North were something of a sensation at the council of Trent (*Science of Describing*, p. 36).

40. For instance, in chapter 9, on what might seem a fanciful topic, "On the Struggle of the Whale Against the Grampus," a heavily anthropomorphic description of predation by "killer whales" (*Orcinus orca*) on baleen whales—now known to occur—is given.

41. Magnus, *Description of the Northern Peoples*, p. 1099.

42. Ibid., pp. 1099–1100.

43. I am grateful to Professor Jane Chaplin of the Classics Department at Middlebury College for her lively and clear translations and for explaining their significance.

44. "Oppianus, divinus omnino poeta . . . seribit, contracoelitum foedera impios Thraces delphinem audere insequi, & tridente adid parato configure." (Camerarius, *Symbola et Emblemata*, p. 12).

45. "Cete (Kete) ex aquatilibus proprie dicuntur, quae perfectum animal ex femine, non ex ouo, gignunt, ut Delphini, Balaenae, Phocae. Et haec pleraque omnia praegrandi sunt corpore: quod Sanguine alitur, ossibusque fulcitur, similiter ut terrestrium respirantium, & cum multo calore nativo abundent, cordis refrigerandi gratia pulmones etiam haec omnia habent. Minimum in hoc genere Phoca uidetur: inde Phocaena, Delphinus. maxima uero, Balaena, Physeter, Pristis. . . . Piscis proprie dicti omnes, brancias habent, & ovipari sunt" (Gesner, *Icones Animalium*, p. 160).

46. Browne, *Pseudodoxia Epidemica*, p. 251.

47. As Melville reminds us in the parergonal "Extracts" with which he opens his cetological novel (*Moby-Dick*, p. 10).

48. Ellis, *Men and Whales*, pp. 33–40.

49. Quoted in Ellis, *Men and Whales*, p. 36.

50. In a striking instance of just how widespread whale strandings are, the Vermont state fossil is of a Beluga whale dug up by railroad navies in 1836 while building the first railroad line in the Champlain Valley. The animal was stranded in the Champlain Sea in the late Pleistocene; the sea retreated; the skeleton fossilized, only to be discovered much later.

51. Schama, *Embarrassment of Riches*, p. 133.

52. Ellis, *Men and Whales*, p. 38.

53. Schama, *Embarrassment of Riches*, p. 133.

54. On the literal and metaphorical significance of fathoming, see chapter 3 of this study.

55. Schama, *Embarrassment of Riches*, p. 132.

56. Retrieved from *Early English Books Online* (EEBO).

57. *Mighty Sea-Monster*, pp. 5–6.

58. *Mighty Sea-Monster*, p. 9.

59. Ogilvie, *Science of Describing*, p. 12.

60. Ogilvie, *Science of Describing*, p. 8.

61. In August 2009 a thirty-three-foot Minke whale stranded itself in a minor tributary of the Severn. (A father and son on jet skis attempted to rescue it but failed.) Similar strandings must have been relatively common in the Tudor-Stuart era, when marine biomass (the total number of living organisms in the ecosystem) was immensely higher than it is now (and the English were not yet engaged in commercial whaling).

62. Phipson, *Animal Lore of Shakespeare's Time*, p. 94.

63. See Freidheim, ed., *Toward a Sustainable Whaling Regime*.

64. The sensationalism of the Discovery Channel television show, which follows Paul Watson and his Sea Shepherd Foundation, can obscure the longer history of the antiwhaling movement (which spawned Greenpeace), galvanized by Farley Mowat's *Sea of Slaughter* and *A Whale for the Killing*. Watson pays homage to the author by naming his vessel the *M/V Farley Mowat*.

65. Psalms 107:26.

66. Raffi has long been the best-selling writer of children's songs in North America, selling on average more than half a million recordings a year. The wildly popular "Baby Beluga" is a classic of the genre.

67. Schama, *Embarrassment of Riches*, p. 144.

6. Shakespeare among the Fishmongers

1. See, for example, Garrett Hardin's "The Tragedy of the Commons"; Burt and Archer, *Enclosure Acts*; Boose, "*Taming of the Shrew*, Good Husbandry, and Enclosure."

2. Fagan, *Fish on Friday*; Sicking and Abreu-Ferreira, eds., *Beyond the Catch*; Poulsen, *Dutch Herring*; Roberts, *Unnatural History*. See also the History of Marine Animals Populations (HMAP) Project, http://www.hmapcoml.org, and the Census of Marine Life.

3. Notwithstanding Jan Kott's decades-old claims to the contrary in *Shakespeare Our Contemporary* (1974).

4. Falconer, in *Shakespeare and the Sea*, strongly implies that the playwright must have been a mariner during the so-called lost years, and he is not alone in doing so.

5. A marketing canard if ever there was one: no FDA organic standard exists for fish.

6. I am grateful to David Steinhardt's keen eye and fine sense of humor for this observation.

7. Ellis, *Empty Ocean*.

8. Other methods of preservation employed drying, smoking, and chemicals such as saltpeter. See Fagan, *Fish on Friday*, especially chapter 4 (pp. 47–58).

9. Ray, *Philosophical Letters*, p. 156. For access to this material I am grateful to the Thomas Fisher Rare Book Library at the University of Toronto.

10. Ibid., p. 261.

11. Anadromous fish (including herring and salmon) spend most of their lives in salt water and only move to freshwater to spawn and die; they are ideal commercial species because they stay relatively close to coastlines and are easily caught by various means (most commonly drift nets and weirs). As Callum Roberts points out, "Herringlike fish occur in huge schools and feed on tiny planktonic organisms drifting in the open sea. Among fish in this family, the herring itself was by far the most important in economic terms. It was the most abundant of all the fishes around northern European shores, each year coming within reach of coastal fishers when the great schools pressed inshore to breed" (*Unnatural History*, p. 115).

12. The North Sea herring fishery has for centuries been the world's most significant. The dominant fishing peoples were those with North Sea coasts—the Dutch, the English, the Scottish, the Norwegians, the Danes, and the French. See Poulsen, *Dutch Herring*, p. 40, and Fagan, *Fish on Friday*, pp. 91–106.

13. "Commerce in fish and the development of towns seem to have gone hand in hand: fish markets are among the earliest identifiable focal points of medieval towns," writes Roberts (*Unnatural History*, p. 20). By the early modern period, transport systems for moving fish from coasts to inland markets were well established in France, Spain, and England.

14. Fagan, *Fish on Friday*, pp. 27–127.

15. The nearly identical Latin names of herring and pilchard, *Clupea harengus harengus* and *Clupea harengus pilchardus*, emphasize their similarity. Other species commonly preserved by salting were hake, cod, and ling. Fagan, *Fish on Friday*, pp. 47–71.

16. Fagan, *Fish on Friday*, p. 197.

17. By the fifteenth century the herring fishery was in competition with cod, the flesh of which is much less fatty, and hence more easily preserved. See Fagan, *Fish on Friday*, chapter 5, pp. 59–72.

18. Poulsen, *Dutch Herring*, pp. 59–60.

19. Fagan calls it "perhaps the hardest of all seafood to preserve" (*Fish on Friday*, p. 52).

20. Fagan, *Fish on Friday*, p. 49.

21. The cultural association between herring and corruption, even debauchery, was likely amplified by the fact that the Elizabethan writer "Robert Greene's death after a banquet of 'pickle herring and Rhenish wine' was notorious" (Mentz, *At the Bottom of Shakespeare's Ocean*, p. 8).

22. Tudor-Stuart era cityscapes, such as those of Claes Visscher and Wenceslaus Hollar, spectacularly evoke the maritime nature of the Thames and its centrality to London in the year of Shakespeare's death.

23. Mentz, *At the Bottom*, p. 61.

24. For example, in the first scene of *The Merchant of Venice*, Gratiano opines that "silence is only commendable / In a neat's tongue dried and a maid not vendible" (1.1.117–18). Here "vendible" means marriageable, which explicitly depicts marriage as a market.

25. James Davidson (*Courtesans and Fishcakes*) describes something similar in classical Athenian culture, a cultural association between the fish desired by the *opsophagos*, or fish-eater, and the bodies of prostitutes (male and female). I am grateful to Professor Mary Ann Eaverly for introducing me to this fascinating book.

26. Hamlet tells him, "You're a fishmonger" (*Hamlet*, 2.2.175).

27. *As You Like It*, 3.2.89; *Romeo and Juliet*, 2.3.32–34.

28. Herring was generally eaten pickled (cured in brine) and available in several grades. Innovations in the preservation of herring developed as markets diversified. See Fagan, *Fish on Friday*, especially chapters 3 and 4 (pp. 27–58).

29. In this respect early modern English culture differed little from that of classical Athens. "Within the exalted ranks of piscifauna," observes Davidson, "distinct hierarchies were recognized, if not always with universal agreement. The preserved fish or *tarichos*, for instance, was generally looked down on and the phrase 'cheaper than salt-fish' is used by Aristophanes to mean 'ten a penny.'" (*Courtesans and Fishcakes*, p. 7).

30. See Greenblatt, *Renaissance Self-Fashioning*.

31. Quoted in Mentz, *At the Bottom*, p. 2.

32. Nashe, quoted in Mentz, *At the Bottom*, p. 226.

33. Mentz, *At the Bottom*, p. 9.

34. Poulsen, *Dutch Herring*, pp. 59–60.

35. Ibid., p. 32.

36. In "Nashe's Red Herring: Epistemologies of the Commodity in *Lenten Stuff* (1599)," Turner convincingly demonstrates the literary conventions that Nashe employs, arguing that the text parodies chorographic writing in a ludic meditation on the logic of the commodity (p. 530.)

37. Turner, "Nashe's Red Herring," p. 539.

38. Ibid., p. 538.

39. "The Limits of the Human" was the title of a seminar at the Shakespeare Association of America in 2009.

40. Fudge, *Brutal Reasoning* and *Perceiving Animals*; Boehrer, *Shakespeare among the Animals*.

41. Berry, "Conservation Is Good Work," in *Sex, Economy, Freedom and Community*, p. 34.

42. Here I rely on Jean-Christophe Agnew's discussion of the historical transformation of market relations and theater in early modern England, in *Worlds Apart*.

43. Raber, "Vermin and Parasites."

44. Turner, "Nashe's Red Herring," p. 9.

45. Butler goes on: "In both the Latin and the Greek matter (*materia* and *hyle*) is neither a simple, brute positivity or referent nor a blank surface or slate awaiting an external signification, but is always in some sense temporalized. This is true for Marx as well, when matter is understood as a principle of transformation, presuming and inducing a future" (*Bodies that Matter*, p. 33).

46. Thersites describes Menelaus as "a herring without a roe" in *Troilus and Cressida* (5.1.54–55).

47. Raber, "Vermin and Parasites," p. 49.

48. Kurlansky, *Cod*; Ellis, *Empty Ocean*, pp. 58–72.

49. The most famous of these fishing grounds, the Grand Banks, are a group of shallow regions where the cold waters of the Labrador Current, flowing south, meet the warm waters of the Gulf Stream. The resultant mixing, known as "upwelling," produces enormous blooms of plankton which, in turn, support marine fauna all across the food web (from krill to blue whales).

50. The fact that the Dutch word proved hegemonic is significant as an indicator of market history: Dutch whalers who depended on stockfish for protein on their long voyages to Spitzbergen began purchasing and exporting the product from Norway in the sixteenth century. See Fagan, *Fish on Friday*, chapter 4.

51. Ackroyd, *Thames*, p. 126.

52. Butler, *Bodies that Matter*, p. 33.

53. This etymology is explicit in Middle English: when Chaucer's Pardoner exclaims, "O belly, O womb, O stinking cod," he condemns appetites of several kinds and the bodily organs associated with them; indeed, he seems to condemn vitality itself—the life-force celebrated later by Rabelais and Bakhtin—as it is located in the "lower bodily stratum" (See Bakhtin, *Rabelais and His World*, especially pp. 315–27).

54. The *OED* defines "cod end" as follows: "The narrow closed part or bag at the lower end of a trawl-net or other fishing net."

55. Most forms of preserved cod were boiled or soaked in fresh water to soften and desalinate the meat. Most recipes require substantial efforts to soften the flesh to make it palatable. See Kurlansky, *Cod*, pp. 61, 142–43, 156–57, 190, 218, 248, 258, 265.

56. In our own day Bobby Bacala, a character in the popular HBO series *The Sopranos*, exemplifies this cultural metaphorics. He is a Baccalieri, but because he is not very worthwhile, he is considered Bacala, salt cod. If Tony Soprano himself is regally Shakespearean, Bacala is a fool worthy of the opus. I am grateful to David Steinhardt for bringing my attention to this example.

57. There is some disagreement about the exact nature of poor-john. Kurlansky describes it as "summer-cured dried cod from the Grand Banks" (*Cod*, p. 55). The editors of *The Norton Shakespeare* gloss both Shakespeare's references to poor-john as "dried salted hake," which is both too precise and not entirely accurate, as the phrase could refer

to cod or any other *gadoid*. In the examples given by the *OED*, some sources describe it as cod, others as hake. This author suspects it did *not* refer to hake, which was so relished by Spaniards that more of it was shipped there.

58. Nashe, *Lenten Stuffe*, p. 180. "Not without mustard" indeed. *The Mariners Mirrour* notes that in the waters off Yarmouth, fresh herring was often traded for salt cod: "The commodities and traffique that the se coastes yield is wooll, Cloth: and in some places, Wheate, Barley, Malte, Beere, herrings and Sprattes: In exchaunge whereof much Salt fish, and Linnen Clothe is broughte thither" (p. 11).

59. Too much has been written about Caliban's origins, American, Mediterranean, classical, and hybrid, to cite here, but the most compendious overview of the subject is in Vaughan and Vaughan, *Critical Essays on Shakespeare's The Tempest*.

60. See Kurlansky, *Cod*; Fagan, *Fish on Friday*.

61. Rimbault, "Shakespeare's Strange Fish," p. 41.

62. Ibid, p. 42.

63. Quoted in Fagan, *Fish on Friday*, p. 12. Ling (etymologically related to "long," from their shape) refers to several species of fish found in the eastern Atlantic, Irish Sea, and North Sea. Atlantic ling (*Molva molva*) is a *gadoid* similar to cusk and hake and was fished in Tudor times. The modern Pacific coast "ling cod" (*Ofiodon elongatus*), however, is unrelated to the *gadoids*.

64. Fagan writes, "The Dutch became adept at salting them in brine, packed tightly in barrels. For centuries they dominated the European trade, developing many varieties of cured herring, including the rich-flavored matjes—young, fat virgin herring cured in salt, sugar, and saltpeter" (*Fish on Friday*, p. 49).

65. Mullaney, *Place of the Stage*.

66. The well-known mislabeling of "the Globe Theater" and "the bull-baiting Theater" in Hollar's "Long Prospect of London" circumstantially suggests their interchangeability.

67. Fagan, *Fish on Friday*, p. 145.

68. Edgar's line, "Nero is an angler in the lake of darkness," may be an obscure reference to this commonplace, as the association of female sexuality with the demonic is explicit in *King Lear* (See Brayton, "Angling in the Lake of Darkness").

69. Herring were overfished in coastal European waters by the fifteenth century; thus, Dutch and English fishermen moved farther afield in search of herring with each decade of the sixteenth, going as far as Iceland and the Azores. See Fagan, *Fish on Fridays*, chapter 4.

70. Examples include Conrad Gesner's *Icones Animalium*, the emblem literature of Camerarius, and Paolo Giovio's *De Piscibus Marinus*. I am grateful to the Folger Shakespeare Library for providing access to these materials.

71. Drawn by Pieter Brueghel the Elder and published by the prominent humanist and printer Hieronymus Cock, this famous illustration was reproduced often enough in the half-century after its composition that it is likely Shakespeare saw it at some point in his life. The particular image reproduced in figure 10 is by Pieter van der Heyden.

72. This phrase from Sonnet 64 seems peculiarly apposite here.

73. Melville, *Moby-Dick*, p. 105.
74. Turner, "Nashe's Red Herring," p. 7.

7. Prospero's Maps

1. As my epigraph suggests, the fluidity of the biophysical environment is atmospheric as well as oceanic (Maury, *Physical Geography of the Seas*, p. 23).
2. Vaughan and Vaughan, introduction to *The Tempest*, p. 48.
3. Goldberg, *Tempest in the Caribbean*, p. 221.
4. Knapp, *Empire Nowhere*, p. 44.
5. The work of Virginia Mason Vaughan and Alden Vaughan, in *Shakespeare's Caliban*, attests to the richness of Caliban's mixed cultural origins.
6. Lupton, "Creature Caliban," p. 2.
7. Thus, the Vaughans point out, "Caliban has been a particularly sensitive barometer of intellectual and social change" (Vaughan and Vaughan, introduction to *The Tempest*, xiv).
8. The language of navigation has long been a topic in *Tempest* scholarship. Thus, for instance, both references in the play to the plummet, Alonso's (3.3.101) and Prospero's (5.1.56), connect political authority with navigational technology. The plummet, and later the lead line, was a crucial device for establishing soundings, or water depths, in coastal waters. Cartographers recorded such data furnished by navigators.
9. Gillies, *Geography of Difference*, p. 3.
10. Greenblatt's notion of a "cultural poetics" is helpful here, for it allows us to understand early modern cartography not so much as a "source" for Shakespeare's play as much as a semiotic context, a characteristic way of producing meaning.
11. Gillies, *Geography of Difference*, p. 5.
12. Conley, *Self-Made Map*, introduction.
13. Vaughan and Vaughan, in their 1999 Arden introduction to *The Tempest*, point out, "At the Blackfriars, Shakespeare had access to instrumentalists and boy singers who could create a magical island out of sheer sound" (p. 19).
14. Kermode, introduction to *The Tempest*, p. 187.
15. Ibid., p. 196.
16. Auden, *Enchafèd Flood*, appendix, p. 64.
17. As Stephen Orgel notes in his introduction the Oxford edition of the play, "*The Tempest* as a whole has certain obvious qualities in common with the masque as Johnson was developing it." Moreover, "two other prime instances of Prospero's art, the opening storm and the harpies' banquet, may also be seen as antimasques to the magician's entertainment, and the figure of Iris is an appropriate exorcist for both" (Introduction to *The Tempest*, pp. 45, 47).
18. Elizabeth Fowler, in "Ship Adrift," observes that "the image calls up an ancient tradition," for "the topos is that of the ship of state." She notes further that "the Latin verb for steering a ship (*gubernare*) also designates political governance" (pp. 37, 38).
19. In *Shakespeare and the Sea*, Falconer provides a description of the nautical maneu-

vers in 1.1 that has become a standard for modern editors. Falconer's work was preceded by W. B. Whall's glossary *Shakespeare's Sea Terms Explained*, which expressed admiration for the precision of nautical description in *The Tempest*.

20. See, for instance, the most recent introductions to the Oxford, Arden, Norton, and Riverside editions.

21. Orgel suggests, "Even a Sunday sailor will feel the justice of the Mariner's expostulations.... In fact, the themes of insubordination and insurrection are as important in this scene as they are to be in Prospero's account of his history in the scene that follows, and none of the courtiers comes off morally unscathed" (Introduction to *The Tempest*, pp. 14–15).

22. Christy Anderson notes that "wind and water are the mobile and fluid forces of nature, and appear in various guises throughout the play: the sea that surrounds the island, the winds controlled by Prospero and Ariel" ("Wild Waters," p. 41).

23. Garber, "Eye of the Storm," p. 49.

24. Just as "the move from conflict to harmony is central to the action of the masque," "Prospero the illusionist, moving his drama towards reconciliation and new life, presents in the betrothal masque his own version of Gonzalo's utopia, a vision of orderly nature and bountiful fruition" (Orgel, introduction to *The Tempest*, p. 47). Not all readers agree that the play moves from discord to harmony. Auden claimed, "*The Tempest* is full of music of all kinds, yet it is not one of the plays in which, in a symbolic sense, harmony and concord finally triumph over dissonant disorder" (*Enchafèd Flood*, appendix, p. 66). Harry Berger Jr. has also explicitly disagreed with the claim that the harmony of "the renunciation theme" prevails in the play ("Swisser-Swatter," 10).

25. Gillies argues that "Shakespeare is demonstrably conversant with quite a variety of geographic discourses and . . . cartographic genres" ("Figure of the New World," p. 5); even his sharp eye has missed this crucial detail about the winds.

26. Vaughan and Vaughan, ed., *The Tempest*, by William Shakespeare, p. 144 (gloss).

27. Brown, "This Thing of Darkness," pp. 58–59.

28. Procházka, "Subjectivity and Dramatic Discourse," p. 205.

29. Terence Hawkes highlights the spatializing function of language with reference to the first exchange between Prospero and Caliban when he notes that Prospero, the colonist, "imposes the 'shape' of his own culture, embodied in his speech, on the new world, and makes that world recognizable, habitable, 'natural,' able to speak his language" ("Swisser-Swatter," p., 24).

30. Prospero's antagonistic rhetorical strategy is far from innocent, as Paul Brown argues, for "Prospero interpellates the various listeners—calls to them, as it were, and invites them to recognize themselves as subjects of his discourse, as beneficiaries of his civil largesse. Thus for Miranda he is a strong father who educates and protects her; for Ariel he is a rescuer and taskmaster; for Caliban he is a coloniser whose refused offer of civilization forces him to strict discipline; for the shipwrecked he is a surrogate providence who corrects errant aristocrats and punishes plebeian revolt" ("This Thing of Darkness," p. 59). In this way, Brown continues, "Prospero's narrative demands of its subjects that they should accede to his version of the past" (59).

31. Christian Jacob, quoted in Conley, *Self-Made Map*, p. 8. The link between colonialism and dramaturgy becomes deeper when we consider Terence Hawkes's claim that "the dramatist is metaphorically a colonist. His art penetrates new areas of experience, his language expands the boundaries of our culture, and makes the new territory over in its own image. His 'raids on the inarticulate' open up new worlds for the imagination" (*Shakespeare in the Present*, p. 212).

32. Quoted in Orgel, ed., *The Tempest*, appendix B, p. 210; emphasis added.

33. Examples include Brown, "This Thing of Darkness" (1985); Sturgess, "A Quaint Device" (1987); Greenblatt, *Learning to Curse* (1990); Hulme, *Colonial Encounters* (1992); and Platt, "Reason Diminished" (1997).

34. Beyond the fact they both plays reference wind with a similar, striking image, "*King Lear* and *The Tempest* display important similarities," as James P. Driscoll notes, also observing that "Shakespeare's last romance is in many respects a direct reversal of his greatest tragedy" ("Shakespearean Metastance," p. 85).

35. It would be a mistake to draw too strong a distinction between the cartographic representation of wind and the depiction of wind in painting, for "the early history of maps is largely inseparable from developments in the world of art. Map-making and landscape painting were often the work of the same artists . . . Until the Renaissance no terminological distinction was made between painting and the map" (King, *Mapping Reality*, p. 23).

36. Shakespeare may have used Golding's translation as well as the Latin of Ovid in writing these lines. See Orgel, ed., *The Tempest*, 5.1.33–50 passim.

37. As George Herbert would claim of the Judeo-Christian deity, "Storms are the triumph of his art" (Quoted in Orgel, introduction to *The Tempest*, p. 47).

38. *Portolan* charts developed concomitantly in twelfth-century Italy and Catalonia; both cultures lay claim to developing the "harbor-finding art" (see Brown, *Story of Maps*, p. 113–49) from a list of safe havens to a sophisticated graphic system of representation. I use the Italian term in part because it is an Italian imaginary—not a Catalan one—that informs *The Tempest*.

39. Brown, *Story of Maps*, 113. Brown points out that portoloni were "originally designed to accompany the early coast pilots (peripli)" (p. 113).

40. Directional terms remain embedded in the language, particularly in regional idioms. In New England, "Down East" refers to the Maine coast, for the simple reason that, as the prevailing winds from June to November in that region are southwesterlies, sailing east means sailing downwind.

41. Brown, *Story of Maps*, pp. 131–32.

42. Bricker and Tooley, *Landmarks*, p. 25.

43. Vespucci was subsequently removed from Waldseemüller's cartographic parerga in an attempt to downplay the role of the Italian navigator in putting the "Americas" on the world map as a New World. But the association of Amerigo with America stuck in the minds of Europeans. There was no retracting the image furnished by Waldseemüller's highly popular map of 1507, so from then on, the New World would bear his name.

44. See my "Maritime Lens" in the December 2010 issue of *Coriolis: Interdisciplinary Journal of Maritime Studies*.

45. Antonio refers to the cheeky, elemental Boatswain as a "wide-chopped rascal," a possible visual clue to the subtext of cartographic illustrations (1.1.55).

46. Hulme, *Colonial Encounters*, p. 94.

47. As the impact of Hurricane Katrina dramatically demonstrated in 2005, tropical cyclones continue to fascinate both because they are extremely difficult to predict and because their devastating effects highlight the political fault lines within the social orders of the regions they affect, as well as failures of leadership.

48. Thus, Conley suggests, "the unknown, graphically inscribed as *terrae incognitae* on the western and southern horizons of early maps, was traditionally included as an important element of the maps' overall depictions. It was to be conquered, or at least to become known insofar as the gain of knowledge would assure the discoverer's founding illusion of immortality.... Because the unknown was located by being named, it became a form of a relation rather than an unfathomable menace or delusion (*Self-Made Map*, p. 8).

49. As De Certeau reminds us in the passage quoted earlier. See also Gillies, *Shakespeare and the Geography of Difference*.

50. Mullaney, *Place of the Stage*, p. 6.

51. De Certeau, *Practice of Everyday Life*, p. 121.

Coda

1. Genesis 1:2. All bible references throughout will be listed by book, chapter, and verse in this form and are from *The Bible: Authorized King James Version with Apocrypha*, edited by Robert Carroll and Stephen Prickett (Oxford: Oxford University Press, 1998).

2. Patton, *Sea Can Wash Away*, pp. 2–3.

3. The exact publication date for *A Christian Turned Turk* is uncertain. The scene referred to is scene 2 (Quoted in Jowitt, *Culture of Piracy*, p. 3).

4. *Culture of Piracy*, pp. 2–5.

5. See the opening chapter of *Moby-Dick*, "Loomings."

6. Simon Estok uses the term *ecophobia* to denote the cultural tendency to relate antagonistically to nature. See Estok, "Ecocriticism and Ecophobia," especially pp. 1–17.

7. Raban's introduction to *The Oxford Book of the Sea* curiously neglects the early modern period. Although the text argues that "the sea is one of the most 'universal symbols in literature,'" the book fails to include a single passage from Shakespeare (p. 3).

8. Scholars continue to debate the degree to which Shakespeare was influenced by fresh accounts of sea voyages at various times in his career. See Strittmatter and Kositsky, "Shakespeare and the Voyagers Revisited."

9. Abram, *Spell of the Sensuous*.

BIBLIOGRAPHY

Abram, David. *The Spell of the Sensuous: Perception and Language in a More-Than-Human World.* New York: Vintage Books, 1997.
Ackroyd, Peter. *Thames: The Biography.* London: Chatto and Windus, 2007.
Agnew, Jean-Christophe. *Worlds Apart: The Market and Theater in Anglo-American Thought, 1550–1750.* Cambridge, UK: Cambridge University Press, 1987.
Albers, Jan. *Hands on the Land: A History of the Vermont Landscape.* Cambridge, MA: MIT Press, 2000.
Albion, Robert G. *Forests and Seapower, 1652–1862.* Cambridge, MA: Harvard University Press, 1926.
Alpers, Paul. *What Is Pastoral?* Chicago: University of Chicago Press, 1996.
Alpers, Svetlana. *The Art of Describing: Dutch Art in the Seventeenth Century.* Chicago: University of Chicago Press, 1983.
Anderson, Christy. "Wild Waters: Hydraulics and the Forces of Nature." In Hulme and Sherman, *Tempest and Its Travels*, 41–48.
Aristotle. *History of Animals*, books 7–10. Edited and translated by D. M. Balme. Cambridge, MA: Harvard University Press, 1991.
Armbruster, Karla, and Kathleen R. Wallace, eds. *Beyond Nature Writing: Expanding the Boundaries of Ecocriticism.* Charlottesville: University of Virginia Press, 2001.
Auden, W. H. *The Enchafèd Flood, or The Romantic Iconography of the Sea.* 1950. Reprint, New York: Faber and Faber, 1985.
———. *The Sea and the Mirror.* Princeton: Princeton University Press, 2003.
Bakhtin, Mikhail. *Rabelais and His World.* Translated by Helene Iswolsky. Bloomington, IN: Indiana University Press, 1984.
Balasopoulos, Antonis. "'Suffer a Sea Change': Spatial Crisis, Maritime Modernity, and the Politics of Utopia." *Cultural Critique* 63 (Spring 2006): 123–56.
Barber, C. L. *Shakespeare's Festive Comedy: A Study of Dramatic Form and Its Relation to Social Custom.* Princeton: Princeton University Press, 1959.
Bartolovich, Crystal. "Shakespeare's Globe?" In Howard and Shershow, *Marxist Shakespeares*, 178–205.
Bate, Jonathan. *Romantic Ecology: Wordsworth and the Environmental Tradition.* New York: Routledge, 1991.

Bibliography

———. *The Song of the Earth*. Cambridge, MA: Harvard University Press, 2000.

———. *Soul of the Age: The Life, Mind and World of William Shakespeare*. New York: Penguin, 2008.

Baucom, Ian. *Specters of the Atlantic: Finance Capital, Slavery, and the Philosophy of History*. Durham, NC: Duke University Press, 1999.

Bavington, Dean. *Managed Annihilation: An Unnatural History of the Newfoundland Cod Collapse*. Vancouver: University of British Columbia Press, 2010.

Belsey, Catherine. *The Subject of Tragedy: Identity and Difference in Renaissance Drama*. London: Routledge, 1985.

Berger, Harry, Jr. "Miraculous Harp: A Reading of Shakespeare's *The Tempest*." In Bloom, *Modern Critical Interpretations: The Tempest*, 9–42.

———. *Second World and Green World: Studies in Renaissance Fiction-Making*. Selected and arranged, with an introduction by John Patrick Lynch. Berkeley: University of California Press, 1988.

Berners, Julianna. *A treatyse of fysshynge with an angle*. London: Elliot Stock, 1880. Facsimile.

Berry, Wendell. *Sex, Economy, Freedom, and Community*. New York: Pantheon, 1993.

Bierce, Ambrose. *The Enlarged Devil's Dictionary*. New York: Penguin, 2001.

Billings, Timothy. "Squashing the Shard-borne Beetle Crux: A Hard Case and a Few Pat Readings." *Shakespeare Quarterly* 56, no. 4 (2005): 434–47.

Blackstock, Michael. "Blue Ecology: A Cross-Cultural Approach to Reconciling Forest-Related Conflicts." *BC Journal of Ecosystems and Management* 6, no. 2 (2005): 38–54.

Bloom, Harold, ed. *Modern Critical Interpretations: William Shakespeare's The Tempest*. Philadelphia: Chelsea House, 1988.

Blue Ocean Institute. http://www.blueocean.org.

Blumenberg, Hans. *Shipwreck with Spectator: Paradigm of a Metaphor for Existence*. Translated by Steven Rendall. Cambridge, MA: MIT Press, 1997.

Boehrer, Bruce. *Shakespeare among the Animals*. Philadelphia: University of Pennsylvania Press, 2004.

Bolster, W. Jeffrey. *Black Jacks: African American Seamen in the Age of Sail*. Cambridge, MA: Harvard University Press, 1997.

———. "Opportunities in Marine Environmental History." *Environmental History* 11 (July 2006): 1–31.

Boose, Linda. "*The Taming of the Shrew*, Good Husbandry, and Enclosure." In McDonald, *Shakespeare Reread*, 193–225.

Bower, K. Jack. *A Maritime History of the United States: The Role of America's Seas and Waterways*. Columbia, SC: University of South Carolina Press, 1988.

Bowerbank, Silvia. *Speaking for Nature: Women and Ecologies of Early Modern England*. Baltimore: Johns Hopkins University Press, 2004.

Branch, Michael, and Scott Slovic. "Surveying the Emergence of Ecocriticism." In *The ISLE Reader: Ecocriticism, 1993–2003*, edited by Branch and Slovic, xv. Athens: University of Georgia Press, 2003.

Bibliography

Brayton, Dan. "Angling in the Lake of Darkness: Possession, Dispossession, and the Politics of 'Discoverie' in *King Lear*." *ELH* 70, no. 2 (2003): 399–426.

———. "Rethinking Literature and Culture through a Maritime Lens: The Coriolis Effect, Oceanic Gyres, and the Black Atlantic." *Coriolis* 1, no. 2 (December 2010): 1–3.

———. Review of *Alternative Shakespeares 3*, edited by Diana Henderson. *Shakespeare Quarterly* 60, no. 2 (Summer 2009): 241–49.

———. "Shakespeare and the Global Ocean." In Bruckner and Brayton, *Ecocritical Shakespeare*, 173–90.

———. "Sounding the Deep: *Shakespeare and the Sea* Revisited." *Forum for Modern Language Studies* 46, no. 2 (2010): 189–206.

Bricker, Charles, and R. V. Tooley. *Landmarks of Mapmaking*. New York: Thomas Y. Crowell Company, 1976.

Broadus, James M., and Raphael V. Vartanov, eds. *The Oceans and Environmental Security: Shared U.S. and Russian Perspectives*. Washington, DC: Island Press, 1994.

Brotton, Jerry. "'This Tunis, Sir, Was Carthage': Contesting Colonialism in Shakespeare's *The Tempest*." In *Post-Colonial Shakespeares*, edited by Ania Loomba and Martin Orkin, 23–42. London: Routledge, 1998.

Brown, Bill. *A Sense of Things: The Object Matter of American Literature*. Chicago: University of Chicago Press, 2003.

Brown, Lloyd A. *The Story of Maps*. New York: Dover, 1949.

Brown, Paul. "This Thing of Darkness I Acknowledge Mine: *The Tempest* and the Discourse of Colonialism." In Dollimore and Sinfield, *Political Shakespeare*, 48–71.

Browne, Thomas. *Pseudodoxia Epidemica*. Vol. 2 of *The Works of Thomas Browne*. Edited by Geoffrey Keynes. Chicago: University of Chicago Press, 1964.

Bruckner, Lynne Dickson, and Dan Brayton, eds. *Ecocritical Shakespeare*. Farnham, UK: Ashgate, 2011.

Bryson, Bill. *Shakespeare: The Illustrated Edition*. London: Harpercollins, 2009.

Bryson, Michael. *Visions of the Land: Science, Literature, and the Environment from the Era of Exploration to the Age of Ecology*. Charlottesville: University of Virginia Press, 2002.

Buell, Lawrence. *The Environmental Imagination: Thoreau, Nature-Writing, and the Formation of American Culture*. Cambridge, MA: Belknap Press of Harvard University Press, 2002.

———. *Writing for an Endangered World: Literature, Culture, and Environment in the U.S. and Beyond*. Cambridge, MA: Belknap Press of Harvard University Press, 2001.

Burt, Richard, and John Michael Archer, eds. *Enclosure Acts: Sexuality, Culture, and Property in Early Modern England*. Ithaca: Cornell University Press, 1994.

Bushnell, Rebecca. *Green Desire: Imagining Early Modern English Gardens*. Ithaca: Cornell University Press, 2003.

Butler, Judith. *Bodies that Matter: On the Discursive Limits of "Sex."* New York: Routledge, 1993.

Camerarius, Joachim. *Symbola et Emblemata*. Nuremberg: 1590–1604. Facsimile, Graz, Austria: Akademische Druck Verlagsanstalt, 1988.

Bibliography

Carroll, Robert, and Stephen Prickett, eds. *The Bible: Authorized King James Version*. Oxford: Oxford University Press, 1998.
Carson, Rachel. *The Sea around Us*. New York: Oxford University Press, 1951.
———. *The Sense of Wonder*. New York: HarperCollins, 1998.
———. *Silent Spring*. Boston: Houghton Mifflin, 2002.
Cartwright, David Edgar. *Tides: A Scientific History*. Cambridge, UK: Cambridge University Press, 2001.
Census of Marine Life. http://www.coml.org.
Certeau, Michel de. *The Practice of Everyday Life*. Translated by Stephen Rendell. Berkeley: University of California Press, 1993.
Chaucer, Geoffrey. *The Riverside Chaucer*. 3rd ed. Edited by Larry D. Benson. Boston: Houghton Mifflin, 1987.
Clover, Charles. *The End of the Line: How Overfishing Is Changing the World and What We Eat*. Berkeley: University of California Press, 2006.
Cohen, Walter. "The Undiscovered Country: Shakespeare and Mercantile Geography." In Howard and Shershow, *Marxist Shakespeares*, 128–58.
Conforti, J. A. *Saints and Strangers: New England in British North America*. Baltimore: Johns Hopkins University Press, 2006.
Conley, Tom. *The Self-Made Map: Cartographic Writing in Early Modern France*. Minneapolis: University of Minnesota Press, 1996.
Connery, Christopher. "Ideologies of Land and Sea: Alfred Thayer Mahan, Carl Schmitt, and the Shaping of Global Myth Elements." *Boundary 2* 28, no. 2 (2001): 173–201.
———. "There Was No More Sea: The Supersession of the Ocean, from the Bible to Cyberspace." *Journal of Historical Geography* 32 (2006): 495–511.
Conrad, Joseph. *The Mirror of the Sea*. Ithaca: Cornell University Press, 2009.
Corbin, Alain. *Territoire du vide: L'Occident et le desir du rivage, 1750–1840*. Paris: Aubier, 1988. Translated by Jocelyn Phelps as *The Lure of the Sea: The Discovery of the Seaside in the Western World, 1750–1840* (Berkeley: University of California Press, 1994).
Cousteau, Jacques. *The Whale: Mighty Monarch of the Sea*. Translated by J. F. Bernard. New York: Doubleday, 1972.
Cramer, Deborah. *Great Waters: An Atlantic Passage*. New York: W. W. Norton, 2001.
Creighton, Margaret, and Lisa Norling, eds. *Iron Men, Wooden Women: Gender and Seafaring in the Atlantic World, 1700–1920*. Baltimore: Johns Hopkins University Press, 1995.
Cronon, William. *Changes in the Land: Indians, Colonists, and the Ecology of New England*. 2nd ed. New York: Farrar, Straus, and Giroux, 2003.
Crosby, Alfred. *Ecological Imperialism: The Biological Expansion of Europe, 900–1900*. 1986. Reprint, Cambridge, UK: Cambridge University Press, 2006.
Cunliffe, Barry. *Europe between the Oceans: Themes and Variations, 9000 BC–AD 1000*. New Haven: Yale University Press, 2008.
———. *Facing the Ocean: The Atlantic and Its Peoples, 8000 BC–AD 1500*. Oxford: Oxford University Press, 2001.

Bibliography

Cutting, Charles L. *Fish Saving: A History of Fish Processing from Ancient to Modern Times.* London: Leonard Hill Books, 1955.
Cutts, John P. "Music in *The Tempest.*" *Music and Letters* 39 (1958): 347–58.
Daborne, Robert. *A Christian Turned Turk.* London: 1612.
Davidson, James. *Courtesans and Fishcakes: The Consuming Passions of Classical Athens.* New York: St. Martin's Press, 1997.
Da Vinci, Leonardo. *The Notebooks of Leonardo Da Vinci.* Edited by Irma A. Richter. New York: Oxford University Press, 1991.
Deacon, Margaret. *Scientists and the Sea, 1650–1900.* Aldershot: Ashgate, 1997.
Dening, Greg. "Deep Times, Deep Spaces: Civilizing the Sea." In Klein and Mackenthun, *Sea Changes,* 13–36.
———. *Mister Bligh's Bad Language: Passion, Power, and Theatre on the Bounty.* Cambridge, UK: Cambridge University Press, 1992.
Dobbs, David. *The Great Gulf: Fishermen, Scientists, and the Struggle to Revive the World's Greatest Fishery.* Washington, DC: Island Press, 2000.
Dollimore, Jonathan, and Alan Sinfield, eds. *Political Shakespeare: Essays in Cultural Materialism.* Manchester, UK: Manchester University Press, 1985.
Drakakis, John, ed. *Alternative Shakespeares.* London: Routledge, 1988.
Driscoll, James P. "The Shakespearean 'Metastance.'" In Bloom, *Modern Critical Interpretations: The Tempest,* 85–99.
Du Jourdin, Michel Mollat, and Monique de la Roncière. *Sea Charts of the Early Explorers: 13th to 17th Century.* Translated by L. le R. Dethan. New York: Thames and Hudson, 1984.
E. S. *Britaines Busse, or A Computation as well of the Charge of a Busse or Herring-Fishing Ship. As also of the gaine and profit thereby.* London: 1615.
Earle, Sylvia. *Sea Change: A Message of the Oceans.* New York: GP Putnam's Sons, 1995.
———. *The World Is Blue!* Washington, DC: National Geographic, 2009.
Ebbesmeyer, Curtis, and Eric Scigliano. *Flotsametrics and the Floating World: How One Man's Obsession with Runaway Sneakers and Rubber Ducks Revolutionized Ocean Science.* New York: HarperCollins, 2009.
Edwards, Philip. *Sea-Mark: The Metaphorical Voyage, Spenser to Milton.* Liverpool: Liverpool University Press, 1997.
Egan, Gabriel. *Green Shakespeare: From Ecopolitics to Ecocriticism.* London: Routledge, 2006.
Elder, John. *Pilgrimage to Vallombrosa: From Vermont to Italy in the Footsteps of George Perkins Marsh.* Charlottesville: University of Virginia Press, 2006.
———. *Reading the Mountains of Home.* Cambridge, MA: Harvard University Press, 1998.
Elder, John, and Glenn Adelson. "Robert Frost's Ecosystem of Meanings in 'Spring Pools.'" *Interdisciplinary Studies in Literature and Environment* 13 (Summer 2006): 1–17.
Elder, John, and Robert Finch, eds. *The Norton Book of Nature Writing.* 2nd ed. New York: W. W. Norton, 2002.

Bibliography

Elder, John R. *The Royal Fishery Companies of the Seventeenth Century*. Glasgow: James Maclehose and Sons, 1912.

Ellis, Richard. *The Empty Ocean: Plundering the World's Marine Life*. Washington, DC: Island Press, 2003.

———. *Men and Whales*. New York: Knopf, 1991.

———. *Singing Whales and Flying Squid: The Discovery of Marine Life*. Guilford, CT: Lyons Press, 2005.

———. *Tuna: Love, Death, and Mercury*. New York: Random House, 2008.

Estok, Simon C. "Doing Ecocriticism with Shakespeare." In *Early Modern Ecostudies: From the Florentine Codex to Shakespeare*, edited by Thomas Hallock, Ivo Kamps, and Karen L. Raber, 77–92. New York: Palgrave Macmillan, 2008.

———. *Ecocriticism and Shakespeare: Reading Ecophobia*. New York: Palgrave Macmillan, 2011.

———. "Environmental Implications of the Writing and Policing of the Early Modern Body: Dismemberment and Monstrosity in Shakespearean Drama." *Shakespeare Review* 33 (2001): 107–41.

———. Letter. PMLA 114, no. 5 (October 1999): 1095–96.

———. "Teaching the Environment of *The Winter's Tale*: Ecocritical Theory and Pedagogy for Shakespeare." In *Shakespeare Matters: History, Teaching, Performance*, edited by Lloyd Davis, 177–90. Newark, DE: University of Delaware Press, 2003.

———. "Theorizing in a Space of Ambivalent Openness: Ecocriticism and Ecophobia." *ISLE* 16, no. 2 (Spring 2009): 203–25.

———. "Theory from the Fringes: Animals, Ecocriticism, Shakespeare." *Mosaic* 40, no. 1 (March 2007): 61–78.

Fagan, Brian. *Fish on Friday: Feasting, Fasting, and the Discovery of the New World*. New York: Basic Books, 2007.

Falconer, Alexander. *Shakespeare and the Sea*. London: Constable, 1964.

Fernández-Armesto, Felipe. *Pathfinders: A Global History of Exploration*. New York: W. W. Norton, 2006.

Fineman, Joel. *The Subjectivity Effect in Western Literature: Essays toward the Release of Shakespeare's 'Will.'* Cambridge, MA: MIT Press, 1991.

Foulke, Robert. *The Sea Voyage Narrative*. London: Palgrave Macmillan, 2001.

Fowler, Elizabeth. "The Ship Adrift." In Hulme and Sherman, *The Tempest and Its Travels*, 37–40.

Freud, Sigmund. *New Introductory Lectures on Psycho-Analysis*. New York: W. W. Norton, 1964.

Friedheim, Robert L., ed. *Toward a Sustainable Whaling Regime*. Seattle: University of Washington Press, 2001.

Fudge, Erika. *Brutal Reasoning: Animals, Rationality, and Humanity in Early Modern England*. Ithaca: Cornell University Press, 2006.

———. *Perceiving Animals: Humans and Beasts in Early Modern English Culture*. Macmillan, 2000.

Bibliography

Fulton, Thomas Wemyss. *The Sovereignty of the Seas.* Oxford: Blackwell, 1911.
Gajowski, Evelyn, ed. *Presentism, Gender, and Sexuality in Shakespeare.* New York: Palgrave, 2006.
Garber, Marjorie. "The Eye of the Storm: Structure and Myth in *The Tempest*." In Bloom, *Modern Critical Interpretations: The Tempest*, 43–63.
Garrard, Greg. *Ecocriticism.* London: Routledge, 2004.
Gesner, Conrad. *Icones Animalium Quadrupedum Viviparorum et Oviparorum.* Rome: 1610.
Giamatti, A. Bartlett. *The Earthly Paradise and the Renaissance Epic.* New York: W. W. Norton, 1989.
Gillies, John. "The Figure of the New World in *The Tempest*." In Hulme and Sherman, *Tempest and Its Travels*, 180–201.
———. *Shakespeare and the Geography of Difference.* Cambridge, UK: Cambridge University Press, 1994.
Glotfelty, Cheryl, and Harold Fromm, eds. *The Ecocriticism Reader: Landmarks in Literary Ecology.* Athens, GA: University of Georgia Press, 1996.
Goldberg, Jonathan. *The Tempest in the Caribbean.* Minneapolis: University of Minnesota Press, 2004.
Gordon, Andrew, and Bernhard Klein. *Literature, Mapping, and the Politics of Space in Early Modern Britain.* Cambridge, UK: Cambridge University Press, 2001.
Grady, Hugh, and Terrence Hawkes. *Presentist Shakespeares.* London: Routledge, 2006.
Greenblatt, Stephen. *Learning to Curse: Essays in Early Modern Culture.* New York: Routledge, 1990.
———. *Marvelous Possessions: The Wonder of the New World.* Chicago: University of Chicago Press, 1991.
———. *Renaissance Self-Fashioning.* Chicago: University of Chicago Press, 1984.
———. *Shakespearean Negotiations.* Berkeley: University of California Press, 1988.
Grzegorzewska, Malgorzata. "*Theatrum Orbis Terrarum* and the Court Stage." In *Shakespeare and His Contemporaries*, edited by Jerzy Limon and Jay L. Halio, 219–42. Cranbury, NJ: Associated University Presses, 1993.
Gurr, Andrew. *Playgoing in Shakespeare's London.* 2nd ed. Cambridge, UK: Cambridge University Press, 1996.
Haeckel, Ernst. *General Morphology of Organisms; General Outlines of the Science of Organic Forms based on Mechanical Principles through the Theory of Descent as reformed by Charles Darwin.* Berlin: 1866.
Halpern, Richard. *The Poetics of Primitive Accumulation: English Renaissance Culture and the Genealogy of Capital.* Ithaca: Cornell University Press, 1991.
Hamilton-Paterson, James. *The Great Deep: The Sea and Its Thresholds.* New York: Random House, 1992.
Hanley, Wayne. *Natural History in America: From Mark Catesby to Rachel Carson.* New York: Demeter Press, 1977.
Hardie, Philip. *Virgil's Aeneid: Cosmos and Imperium.* Oxford: Clarendon Press, 1986.

Bibliography

Hardin, Garrett. "The Tragedy of the Commons." *Science*, n.s., 162, no. 3859 (December 13, 1968): 1243–48. Essay can also be found online at http://www.garretthardinsociety.org.
Harrison, Robert Pogue. *Forests: The Shadow of Civilization*. Chicago: University of Chicago Press, 1992.
Harrison, William. *The Description of England: The Classic Contemporary Account of Tudor Life*. 1587. Edited by Georges Edelen. Washington: Folger Shakespeare Library, 1997.
Harvey, P. D. A. *Maps in Tudor England*. Chicago: University of Chicago Press, 1993.
Hattendorf, John, ed. *Ubi Sumus? The State of Naval and Maritime History*. Newport, RI: Naval War College Press, 1994.
Hawkes, Terence. *Shakespeare in the Present*. London: Routledge, 2002.
———. *Shakespeare's Talking Animals*. London: Edward Arnold, 1973.
———. "Swisser-Swatter: Making a Man of English Letters." In Drakakis, *Alternative Shakespeares*, 26–46.
Heise, Ursula K. *Sense of Place and Sense of Planet: The Environmental Imagination of the Global*. Oxford: Oxford University Press, 2008.
Helgerson, Richard. *Forms of Nationhood: The Elizabethan Writing of England*. Chicago: University of Chicago Press, 1992.
Henderson, Diana. *Collaborations with the Past: Reshaping Shakespeare across Time and Media*. Ithaca: Cornell University Press, 2006.
Herring, Scott. *Lines on the Land: Writers, Art, and the National Parks*. Charlottesville: University of Virginia Press, 2004.
Hidalgo, Fernando J., Pedro J. Baron, and Jose Maria Orensanz. "A Prediction Come True: The Green Crab Invades the Patagonian Coast." *Biological Invasions* 7, no. 3 (May 2005): 547–52.
Hill, Christopher. *Liberty against the Law: Some Seventeenth-Century Controversies*. London: Penguin, 1997.
———. *The World Turned Upside Down: Radical Ideas during the English Revolution*. London: Penguin, 1991.
Hiltner, Ken. *Milton and Ecology*. Cambridge, UK: Cambridge University Press, 2004.
———. *Renaissance Ecology: Imagining Eden in Shakespeare's England*. Pittsburgh: Duquesne University Press, 2008.
———. "Renaissance Literature and Our Contemporary Attitude toward Global Warming." *ISLE* 16, no. 3 (Summer 2009): 429–42.
History of Marine Animal Populations. http://www.hmapcoml.org.
Hobbes, Thomas. *Leviathan, or the Matter, Forme and Power of a Commonwealth Ecclesiasticall and Civill*. Edited by Michael Oakeshott. London: Collier, 1971.
Horden, Peregrine, and Nicholas Purcell. *The Corrupting Sea: A Study of Mediterranean History*. Oxford, UK: Blackwell, 2000.
Horwitz, Tony. *Blue Latitudes: Boldly Going Where Captain Cook Has Gone Before*. New York: Henry Holt, 2002.
Howard, Jean E., and Scott Cutler Shershow. *Marxist Shakespeares*. New York: Routledge, 2001.

Bibliography

House, Freeman. *Totem Salmon: Life Lessons from Another Species.* Boston: Beacon Press, 1999.

Huggan, Graham. "Decolonizing the Map: Postcolonialism, Post-Structuralism, and the Cartographic Connection." *Ariel* 20, no. 4 (1989): 115–31.

Hulme, Peter. "Cast Away: The Uttermost Parts of the Earth." In Klein and Mackenthun, 187–202.

———. *Colonial Encounters: Europe and the Native Caribbean, 1492–1797.* New York: Routledge, 1992.

Hulme, Peter, and William H. Sherman, eds. *The Tempest and Its Travels.* Philadelphia: University of Pennsylvania Press, 2000.

Innis, Harold A. *The Cod Fisheries: The History of an International Economy.* Toronto: University of Toronto Press, 1954.

Jackson, Jeremy B. C., Michael X. Kirby, Wolfgang H. Berger, Karen A. Bjorndal, Louis W. Botsford, Bruce J. Bourque, Roger H. Bradbury et al. "Historical Overfishing and the Recent Collapse of Coastal Ecosystems." *Science* 293 (July 27, 2001): 629–38.

Jay, Peter, ed. *"The Sea! The Sea!" An Anthology of Poems.* London: Anvil Press, 2005.

Jowitt, Claire. *The Culture of Piracy, 1580–1630: English Literature and Seaborne Crime.* Farnham, UK: Ashgate Publishing, 2010.

Kamps, Ivo. *Materialist Shakespeare: A History.* London: Verso, 1995.

Kantorowicz, Ernst H. *The King's Two Bodies: A Study in Medieval Political Theology.* 1957. Princeton: Princeton University Press, 1997.

Kermode, Frank. Introduction to *The Tempest.* In Palmer, *Shakespeare, The Tempest,* 176–95.

King, Geoff. *Mapping Reality: An Exploration of Cultural Geographies.* London: Macmillan, 1996.

Klein, Bernhard, ed. *Fictions of the Sea: Critical Perspectives on the Ocean in British Literature and Culture.* Aldershot: Ashgate, 2002.

Klein, Bernhard, and Gesa Mackenthun, eds. *Sea Changes: Historicizing the Ocean.* New York: Routledge, 2004.

Knapp, Jeffrey. *An Empire Nowhere: England, America, and Literature from Utopia to The Tempest.* Berkeley: University of California Press, 1992.

Knight, G. Wilson. *The Shakespearean Tempest.* London: Oxford University Press, 1932.

Kolbert, Elizabeth. "The Scales Fall: Is There Any Hope for Our Overfished Oceans?" *New Yorker,* August 2, 2010, 70–73.

Kott, Jan. *Shakespeare Our Contemporary.* New York: W. W. Norton, 1974.

Kroeber, Karl. *Ecological Literary Criticism: Romantic Imagining and the Biology of Mind.* New York: Columbia University Press, 1994.

Kurlansky, Mark. *Cod: A Biography of the Fish that Changed the World.* New York: Penguin, 1997.

———. *The Last Fish Tale: The Fate of the Atlantic and Survival in Gloucester, America's Oldest Fishing Port and Most Original Town.* New York: Riverhead Books, 2008.

L. M. *A Booke of fishing with Hook and Line, and of all other instruments thereunto belonging.* London: 1599.

Bibliography

Landstrom, Bjorn. *Sailing Ships: In Words and Pictures from Papyrus Boats to Full-Riggers.* Garden City, NY: Doubleday, 1969.

———. *The Ship: An Illustrated History.* New York: Doubleday, 1983.

Langewiesche, William. *The Outlaw Sea: A World of Freedom, Chaos, and Crime.* New York: North Point Press, 2004.

Latour, Bruno. *Politics of Nature: How to Bring the Sciences into Democracy.* Translated by Catherine Porter. Cambridge, MA: Harvard University Press, 2004.

Lavender Law, Kara, Skye Morét-Ferguson, Nikolai A. Maximenko, Giora Proskurowski, Emily E. Peacock, Jan Hafner, and Christopher M. Reddy. "Plastic Accumulation in the North Atlantic Subtropical Gyre." *Science* 3 (September 2010): 1185-88. doi: 10.1126/science.1192321.

Leopold, Aldo. *A Sand County Almanac.* Oxford: Oxford University Press, 1966.

Locke, John. *An Essay Concerning Human Understanding.* Oxford: Oxford University Press, 1979.

Louv, Richard. *Last Child in the Woods: Saving Our Children from Nature-Deficit Disorder.* Chapel Hill, NC: Algonquin Books, 2005.

Love, Glen A. "Ecocriticism and Science: Toward Consilience?" *New Literary History* 30, no. 3 (1999): 561–76.

———. *Practical Ecocriticism: Literature, Biology, and the Environment.* Charlottesville: University of Virginia Press, 1999.

Lupton, Julia Reinhard. "Creature Caliban." *Shakespeare Quarterly* 51, no. 1 (Spring 2000): 1–23.

Lyon, Thomas, ed. *This Incomperable Lande: The Book of American Nature Writing.* Boston: Houghton Mifflin, 1989.

Macfarlane, Robert. *The Wild Places.* New York: Penguin, 2008.

Machiavelli, Niccolo. *The Prince.* New York: Bantam Classics, 1984.

Magnus, Olaus. *Historia de Gentibus Septentionalibus.* Rome: 1555. Facsimile edition, *Description of the Northern Peoples*, edited by Peter Foote and translated by Peter Fisher and Humphrey Higgens. London: The Hakluyt Society, 1998.

Manwood, John. *A Treatise and Discourse of the Lawes of the Forrest.* London: Thomas Wight and Bonham Norton, 1598.

Marin, Louis. *Utopics: Spatial Play.* Translated by Robert Vollrath. Atlantic Highlands, NJ: Humanities Press, 1984.

Markham, Gervase. *Cheape and Good Husbandry For the well-Ordering of all Beasts and Fowles, and for the generall Cure of their Diseases.* London: 1631.

Marsh, George Perkins. *So Great a Vision: The Conservation Writings of George Perkins Marsh.* Edited by Stephen C. Trombulak. Hanover, NH: University Press of New England, 2001.

Marx, Karl, *Capital: A Critical Analysis of Capitalist Production.* Vols. 1–3. Edited by Frederick Engels. London: Lawrence and Wishart, 1954.

Marx, Leo. *The Machine in the Garden: Technology and the Pastoral Ideal.* New York: Oxford University Press, 1964.

Bibliography

Mascall, Leonard. *A booke of fishing with hooke & line, and of all other instruments thereunto belonging.* London, 1590.

Massey, Doreen. *For Space.* London, UK: Sage, 2005.

Maury, Matthew Fontaine. *The Physical Geography of the Seas and Its Meteorology.* 1856. Cambridge, MA: Belknap Press of Harvard University Press, 1963.

Maus, Katharine Eisaman. *Inwardness and Theater in the English Renaissance.* Chicago: University of Chicago Press, 1995.

———. "Proof and Consequences: Inwardness and Its Exposure in the English Renaissance." *Representations* 34 (Spring 1991): 29–53.

———. "Taking Tropes Seriously: Language and Violence in Shakespeare's *Rape of Lucrece*." *Shakespeare Quarterly* 37, no. 1 (Spring 1986): 66–82.

Mazel, David. "Ecocriticism as Praxis." In *Teaching North American Environmental Literature*, edited by Laird Christensen, Mark C. Long, and Fred Waage, 37–43. New York: MLA, 2008.

McColley, Diane K. *Poetry and Ecology in the Age of Milton.* Aldershot: Ashgate, 2007.

McDonald, Russ, ed. *Shakespeare Reread: The Texts in New Contexts.* Ithaca: Cornell University Press, 1994.

McEachern, Claire. *The Poetics of English Nationhood.* Cambridge, UK: Cambridge University Press, 1996.

McKibben, William. *The End of Nature.* 2nd ed. New York: Random House, 2006.

McLuskie, Kathleen. "'The Future in an Instant.'" In *Presentism, Gender, and Sexuality in Shakespeare*, edited by Evelyn Gajowski, 239–51. New York: Palgrave Macmillan, 2006.

McRae, Andrew. *God Speed the Plough: The Representation of Agrarian England, 1500–1660.* Cambridge, UK: Cambridge University Press, 1996.

———. "'On the Famous Voyage': Ben Jonson and Civic Space." *Early Modern Literary Studies* 3 (1998): 8.1–31.

Meeker, Joseph. *The Comedy of Survival: Literary Ecology and a Play Ethic.* 3rd ed. Tucson: University of Arizona Press, 1997.

Meine, Curt. *Aldo Leopold: His Life and Work.* Madison, WI: University of Wisconsin Press, 1988.

Melville, Herman. *Moby-Dick, or The Whale.* Edited by Hershel Parker and Harrison Hayford. New York: W. W. Norton, 2002.

Mentz, Steven. *At the Bottom of Shakespeare's Ocean.* New York: Continuum, 2009.

———. "Toward a Blue Cultural Studies: The Sea, Maritime Culture, and Early Modern English Literature." *Literature Compass* 6, no. 5 (September 2009): 997–1013.

Merchant, Carolyn. *The Death of Nature: Women, Ecology, and the Scientific Revolution.* 2nd ed. New York: HarperCollins, 2000.

Milton, John. *The Riverside Milton.* Edited by Roy Flanagan. Boston: Houghton Mifflin, 1998.

Moore, Charles. "Trashed: Across the Pacific Ocean, Plastics, Plastics Everywhere." *Natural History Magazine* 112, no. 9 (November 2003): 1–11.

Bibliography

Moore, Stuart A., and Hubert Stuart Moore. *The History and Law of Fisheries.* London: Stevens and Haynes, 1903.

Morton, Timothy. *Ecology without Nature: Rethinking Environmental Aesthetics.* Cambridge, MA: Harvard University Press, 2007.

Mowat, Farley. *Sea of Slaughter.* Toronto: Stackpole Books 1996.

———. *A Whale for the Killing.* Toronto: Stackpole Books, 2005.

Muldoon, James. "Who Owns the Sea?" In Klein, *Fictions of the Sea,* 13–27.

Mullaney, Steven. *The Place of the Stage: License, Play, and Power in the English Renaissance.* Chicago: University of Chicago Press, 1988.

Nardizzi, Vin. "Felling Falstaff in Windsor Park." In Bruckner and Brayton, *Ecocritical Shakespeare,* 123–38.

Nashe, Thomas. *Nashes Lenten Stuffe.* In Vol. 3 of *The Works of Thomas Nashe,* edited by Ronald B. McKerrow, 141–226. Oxford: Blackwell, 1958.

Nicolson, Adam. *Seamanship: A Voyage along the Wild Coasts of the British Isles.* New York: HarperCollins, 2004.

———. *Seize the Fire: Heroism, Duty, and the Battle of Trafalgar.* New York: HarperCollins, 2005.

O'Dair, Sharon. "Is It Shakespearean Ecocriticism if It Isn't Presentist?" In Bruckner and Brayton, *Ecocritical Shakespeare,* 71–87.

———. "The State of the Green: A Review Essay on Shakespearean Ecocriticism." *Shakespeare* 4, no. 4 (December 2008): 475–93.

Ogilvie, Brian. *The Science of Describing: Natural History in Renaissance Europe.* Chicago: University of Chicago Press, 2006.

Oppianus. *Oppian's Halieuticks in Five Books of the nature of fishes and fishing of the ancients in five books.* Translated by William Diaper and John Jones. ESTCT139002. Farmington Hills, Michigan: Thomson Gale, 2003.

Orgel, Stephen. Introduction to *The Tempest,* by William Shakespeare, 1–87. Oxford: Oxford University Press, 1987.

Palmer, D. J., ed. *Shakespeare, The Tempest: A Casebook.* New York: Palgrave Macmillan, 1991.

Parker, Patricia. *Shakespeare from the Margins: Language, Culture, Context.* Chicago: University of Chicago Press, 1996.

Parry, J. H. *The Discovery of the Sea.* New York: Dial Press, 1974.

Paster, Gail Kern. *The Body Embarrassed: Drama and the Disciplines of Shame in Early Modern England.* Ithaca: Cornell University Press, 1993.

Patton, Kimberly C. *The Sea Can Wash Away All Evils: Modern Marine Pollution and the Ancient Cathartic Ocean.* New York: Columbia University Press, 2007.

Pauly, Daniel. "Anecdotes and the Shifting Baseline Syndrome of Fisheries." *Tree* 10, no. 10 (October 1995): 430.

———. "Fishing Down Marine Foodwebs." *Science* 279, no. 5352 (February 6, 1998): 860–63.

———. *Five Easy Pieces: How Fishing Impacts Marine Ecosystems.* Washington, DC: Island Press, 2010.

Bibliography

Pauly, Daniel, Jackie Alder, Elena Bennett, Villy Christensen, Peter Tyedmers, and Reg Watson. "The Future for Fisheries." *Science* 302, no. 5649 (2003): 1359–61.

Peck, John. *Maritime Fiction*. London: Palgrave, 2001.

Peters, Edward. "*Quid nobis cum pelago?* The New Thalassology and the Economic History of Europe." *Journal of Interdisciplinary History* 34, no. 1 (Summer 2003): 49–61.

Peterson, Douglas L. *Time, Tide, and Tempest: A Study of Shakespeare's Romances*. San Marino, CA: Huntington Library, 1973.

Petkovic, Tomislav, and Kristian Hengster-Movric. "Patricius' Phenomenonological Theory of Tides and Its Modern Relativistic Interpretation." *Synthesis Philosophica* 21, pt. 2 (2006): 135–36.

Philbrick, Nathaniel. *In the Heart of the Sea: The Tragedy of the Whaleship Essex*. New York: Penguin, 2000.

Philbrick, Thomas. *James Fenimore Cooper and the Development of American Sea Fiction*. Cambridge, MA: Harvard University Press, 1961.

Phillips, Dana. *The Truth of Ecology: Nature, Culture, and Literature in America*. Oxford: Oxford University Press, 2003.

Phipson, Emma. *The Animal Lore of Shakespeare's Time Including Quadrupeds, Birds, Reptiles, Fish and Insects*. London: Kegan Paul, Trench & Co., 1883.

Platt, Peter G. "Reason Diminished: Wonder in *The Winter's Tale*." In *Reason Diminished: Shakespeare and the Marvelous*, pp. 153–68. Lincoln: University of Nebraska Press, 1997.

Porter, Roy. *Flesh in the Age of Reason*. London: Penguin, 2004.

Poulsen, Bo. *Dutch Herring: An Environmental History, c. 1600–1860*. Amsterdam: Aksant, 2008.

Procházka, Martin. "Subjectivity and Dramatic Discourse in *The Tempest*." In *Shakespeare and His Contemporaries*, edited by Jerzy Limon and Jay L. Halio, 205–18. Cranbury, NJ: Associated University Presses, 1993.

Puttenham, George. *The arte of English poesie: Contriued into three . . .* London: A. Constable, 1906.

Raban, Jonathan, ed. *The Oxford Book of the Sea*. Oxford: Oxford University Press, 2001.

Raban, Sandra. *England under Edward I and Edward II, 1259–1327*. Oxford, UK: Blackwell, 2000.

Raber, Karen. "Recent Ecostudies in Tudor and Stuart Literature." *English Literary Renaissance* 37 no. 1 (Winter 2007): 151–71.

———. "Vermin and Parasites: Shakespeare's Animal Architectures." In Bruckner and Brayton, *Ecocritical Shakespeare*, 13–32.

Rackin, Phyllis. *Stages of History: Shakespeare's English Chronicles*. Ithaca: Cornell University Press, 1990.

Ray, John. *Philosophical Letters Between the late, Learned Mr. Ray and several of his Ingenious Correspondents, Native and Foreigners*. London: William and John Innys, 1718.

Rediker, Marcus. *Between the Devil and the Deep Blue Sea: Merchant Seamen, Pirates, and*

Bibliography

the Anglo-American Maritime World, 1700–1750. Cambridge, UK: Cambridge University Press, 1987.
———. *Villains of All Nations: Atlantic Pirates in the Golden Age.* Boston: Beacon Press, 2004.
Rimbault, Edward F. "Shakespeare's Strange Fish." *Notes and Queries,* 2nd ser., 7 (January 15, 1859): 41–43.
Roberts, Callum. *The Unnatural History of the Sea.* Washington, DC: Island Press.
Robinson, A. H. W. *Marine Cartography in Britain: A History of the Sea Chart to 1855.* Leicester, UK: Leicester University Press, 1962.
Roman, Joe. *Whale.* London: Reaktion Books, 2006.
Rosenberg, Andrew A., W. Jeffrey Bolster, Karen E. Alexander, William B. Leavenworth, Andrew B. Cooper, and Matthew G. McKenzie. "The History of Ocean Resources: Modeling Cod Biomass Using Historical Records." *Frontiers in Ecology* 3, no. 2 (2005): 78–84.
Rozwadowski, Helen. *Fathoming the Ocean: The Discovery and Exploration of the Deep Sea.* Cambridge, MA: Belknap Press of Harvard University Press, 2005.
Ruiz, Gregory M., and James T. Carlton, eds. *Invasive Species: Vectors and Management Strategies.* Washington, DC: Island Press, 2003.
Saccio, Peter. *Shakespeare's English Kings: History, Chronicle, and Drama.* 1977. New York: Oxford University Press, 2000.
Safina, Carl. "Fishing to the Bottom—and Back? Ocean Fishing Can Remain Viable—If We Act Now." *Insights on Law and Society* 6, no. 3 (Spring 2006): 1–4.
———. *Song for the Blue Ocean: Encounters along the World's Coasts and beneath the Seas.* New York: Henry Holt, 1998.
Sanders, Julie. *The Cultural Geography of Early Modern Drama, 1620–1650.* Cambridge, UK: Cambridge University Press, 2011.
Sanders, Scott Russell. *The Country of Language.* Minneapolis: Milkweed Editions, 1999.
Santner, Eric L. *On Creaturely Life: Rilke, Benjamin, Sebald.* Chicago: University of Chicago Press, 2006.
Schama, Simon. *The Embarrassment of Riches: An Interpretation of Dutch Culture in the Golden Age.* New York: Knopf, 1987.
———. *Landscape and Memory.* New York: Knopf, 1995.
Schiebinger, Londa. *Nature's Body: Gender in the Making of Modern Science.* Boston: Beacon Press, 1993.
Schlee, Susan. *The Edge of an Unfamiliar World: A History of Oceanography.* New York: Dutton, 1973.
Sea Education Association. http://www.sea.edu.
Shakespeare, William. *The First Folio of Shakespeare: The Norton Facsimile.* 2nd ed. New York: W. W. Norton, 1996.
———. *King Lear* (conflated text). In Greenblatt et al., *The Norton Shakespeare.* New York: W. W. Norton, 1997.
———. *The Norton Shakespeare,* edited by Stephen Greenblatt, Walter Cohen, Jean E. Howard, and Katherine Eisaman Maus. New York: W. W. Norton, 1997.

Bibliography

———. *The Norton Shakespeare*. 2nd ed. Edited by Stephen Greenblatt, Walter Cohen, Jean E. Howard, and Katherine Eisaman Maus. New York: W. W. Norton, 2008.

———. *The Riverside Shakespeare*. 2nd ed. Edited by Gwynne Blakemore Evans and J. J. Tobin. Boston: Houghton Mifflin, 1997.

———. *Shakespeare's Sonnets*. Edited by Stephen Booth. New Haven: Yale University Press, 1977.

———. *The Tempest*. Edited by Virginia Mason Vaughan and Alden T. Vaughan. London: Arden, 1999.

———. *The Tempest*. Edited by Stephen Orgel. Oxford: Oxford University Press, 1998.

———. *The Tempest*. In Greenblatt et al., *The Norton Shakespeare*. New York: W. W. Norton, 1997.

Sicking, Louis, and Darlene Abreu-Ferreira, eds. *Beyond the Catch: Fisheries of the North Atlantic, the North Sea, and the Baltic, 900–1850*. Leiden: Brill, 2008.

Smith, Bruce R. *The Key of Green: Passion and Perception in Renaissance Culture*. Chicago: University of Chicago Press, 2009.

Soja, Edward M. *Postmodern Geographies: The Reassertion of Space in Critical Social Theory*. London: Vero, 1989.

Solley, George C., and Eric Steinbaugh. *Moods of the Sea: Masterworks of Sea Poetry*. Annapolis, MD: Naval Institute Press, 1981.

Steinberg, Philip E. *The Social Construction of the Ocean*. Cambridge, UK: Cambridge University Press, 2001.

Stow, John. *A Survey of London*. Vol. 1. Oxford: Clarendon Press, 1908.

Strittmatter, Roger, and Lynne Kositsky. "Shakespeare and the Voyagers Revisited." *Review of English Studies* 58, no. 236 (April 17, 2007): 447–72.

Sturgess, Keith. "'A Quaint Device': *The Tempest* at the Blackfriars." In Hulme and Sherman, *Tempest and Its Travels*, 107–29.

Sullivan, Garrett A., Jr. *The Drama of Landscape: Land, Property, and Social Relations on the English Stage*. Stanford, CA: Stanford University Press, 1998.

Tanner, Tony, ed. *The Oxford Book of Sea Stories*. New York: Oxford University Press, 1994.

Taverner, John. *Certaine Experiments Concerning Fish and Fruite*. Manchester: Sherratt and Hughes, 1928.

Taylor, Joseph E., III. *Making Salmon: An Environmental History of the Northwest Fishing Crisis*. Seattle, WA: University of Washington Press, 1999.

Theis, Jeffrey S. *Writing the Forest in Early Modern England: A Sylvan Pastoral Nation*. Pittsburgh: Duquesne University Press, 2009.

Thirsk, Joan. *The Agrarian History of England and Wales*. Vol. 4, *1500–1640*. 4th ed. Edited by Joan Thirsk. Cambridge, UK: Cambridge University Press, 1967.

———. *Food in Early Modern England: Phases, Fads, Fashions, 1500–1760*. London: Hambledon Continuum, 2007.

———. "The 'ill kill'd' Deer: Poaching and Social Order in *The Merry Wives of Windsor*." *Texas Studies in Literature and Language* 43 (2001): 46–73.

Bibliography

———."Tudor Enclosures." In *The Rural Economy of England*, edited by Joan Thirsk, 65–83. London: Hambledon Press, 1984.

Thomas, Keith. *Man and the Natural World: Changing Attitudes in England, 1500–1800.* Oxford: Oxford University Press, 1983.

Thoreau, Henry David. *Walden and Civil Disobedience.* New York: Penguin, 1983.

Trienens, Roger J. "The Symbolic Cloud in *Hamlet*." *Shakespeare Quarterly* 5 (Spring 1954): 211–13.

A true report and exact description of a mighty sea-monster or whale, cast vpon Langar-shore ouer against Harwich in Essex, this present moneth of Februarie 1617. With a briefe touch of some other strange precedent and present occurents. Pamphlet. London: H. Holland, 1617. STC 20892a. Retrieved from Early English Books Online (EEBO).

Tuan, Yi-Fu. *Space and Place: The Perspective of Experience.* Minneapolis: University of Minnesota Press, 1977.

———. *Topophilia: A Study of Environmental Perception, Attitudes, and Values.* Minneapolis: University of Minnesota Press, 1974.

Turner, Henry. "Nashe's Red Herring: Epistemologies of the Commodity in *Lenten Stuffe* (1599)." *ELH* 68, no. 3 (2001): 529–61.

Valdivieso, Sofia M. "'He Hourly Humanizes': Transformations and Appropriations of Shakespeare's Caliban." *Sederi* 7 (1996): 269–72.

Vaughan, Alden T., and Virginia Mason Vaughan, eds. *Critical Essays on Shakespeare's The Tempest.* New York: G. K. Hall, 1998.

———. Introduction to *The Tempest*, by William Shakespeare, 1–138. Edited by Virginia Mason Vaughan and Alden T. Vaughan. London: Arden, 1999.

———. *Shakespeare's Caliban: A Cultural History.* Cambridge, UK: Cambridge University Press, 1993.

Walch, Günter. "'What's Past Is Prologue': Metatheatrical Memory and Transculturation in *The Tempest*." In *Travel and Drama in Shakespeare's Time*, edited by Jean-Pierre Maquerlot and Michèle Willems, 223–38. Cambridge, UK: Cambridge University Press, 1996.

Wallace, David Foster. *Consider the Lobster and Other Essays.* New York: Little, Brown, 2005.

Wallerstein, Immanuel. *The Modern World-System: Capitalist Agriculture and the Origins of the European World-Economy in the Sixteenth Century.* New York: Academic Press, 1976.

Warren, Roger. "Rough Magic and Heavenly Music: *The Tempest*." In Vaughan and Vaughan, *Critical Essays on the Tempest*, 152–89.

Watson, Robert N. *Back to Nature: The Green and the Real in the Late Renaissance.* Philadelphia: University of Pennsylvania Press, 2006.

———. "The Ecology of Self in *Midsummer Night's Dream*." In *Ecocritical Shakespeare*, edited by Lynne Dickson and Dan Brayton, 33–56. Burlington, VT: Ashgate, 2011.

Wedgwood, C. V. *The King's Peace, 1637–1641.* London: Collins Fontana, 1970.

Wells, Marion. "'To Find a Face Where All Distress Is Stell'd': *Enargeia, Ekphrasis,* and

Mourning in *The Rape of Lucrece* and *The Aeneid*." *Comparative Literature* 54, no. 2 (Spring 2002): 97–126.
Wessels, Tom. *Reading the Forested Landscape: A Natural History of New England*. Woodstock, VT: Countryman Press, 1997.
West, Rinda. *Out of the Shadow: Ecopsychology, Story, and Encounters with the Land*. Charlottesville: University of Virginia Press, 2007.
Westling, Louise Hutchings. *The Green Breast of the New World: Landscape, Gender, and American Fiction*. Athens: University of Georgia Press, 1996.
Whall, W. B. *Shakespeare's Sea Terms Explained*. London: Simpkin, Marshall, Hamilton, Kent, 1910.
White, Lynn, Jr. "The Historical Roots of Our Ecologic Crisis." *Science* 155, no. 3767 (March 1967): 1203–7.
Whitfield, Peter. *The Image of the World*. San Francisco: Pomegranate Books, 1994.
———. *New Found Lands: Maps in the History of Exploration*. New York: Routledge, 1998.
Williams, Michael. *Deforesting the Earth: From Prehistory to Global Crisis*. Chicago: University of Chicago Press, 2003.
Williams, Raymond. *The Country and the City*. New York: Oxford University Press, 1973.
Wilson, E. O. *Consilience: The Unity of Knowledge*. London: Abacus, 1999.
Wilson, Mary Floyd, and Garrett A. Sullivan Jr. *Environment and Embodiment*. New York: Palgrave MacMillan, 2008.
Wolf, Clark. "Environmental Ethics and Marine Ecosystems: From a 'Land Ethic' to a 'Sea Ethic.'" In *Values at Sea: Ethics for the Marine Environment*, edited by Dorinda Dallmeyer, 19–32. Athens: University of Georgia Press, 2003.
Wolfe, Cary. *Animal Rites: American Culture, the Discourse of Species, and Posthumanist Theory*. Chicago: University of Chicago Press, 2003.
———. "Human, All Too Human: 'Animal Studies' and the Humanities." *PMLA* 124, no. 2 (March 2009): 564–75.
———. "Old Orders for New: Ecology, Animal Rights, and the Poverty of Humanism." *Diacritics* 28, no. 2 (Summer 1998): 21–40.
Woodard, Colin. *Ocean's End*. New York: Perseus Books, 2000.
Wordsworth, William, and Samuel Taylor Coleridge. *Lyrical Ballads*. 2nd ed. Edited by W. J. B. Owen. Oxford: Oxford University Press, 1969.
Yaeger, Patricia. "Editor's Column: Sea Trash, Dark Pools, and the Tragedy of the Commons." *PMLA* 125, no. 3 (2010): 523–45.

INDEX

Abram, David, 37, 200
Adelson, Glenn, 204n19
Agnew, Jean-Christophe, 221n42
Albers, Jan, 206n21
alewives, 157
algae, 10, 204n32, 207n50
All's Well That Ends Well (Shakespeare), 118–19, 120
Ambrogi, Stefano, 212n44
Anderson, Christy, 224n22
Animal Lore of Shakespeare's Time Including Quadrupeds Birds Reptiles and Fishes, The (Phipson), 117
Antony and Cleopatra (Shakespeare): ocean in, 8; pirates in, 214n25; "Sink Rome," 106; on slime, 41; tidal metaphor in, 96–97, 105
"Apostrophe to the Ocean" (Byron), 29–31
Aquaman (comic), 39, 209n80
Arcimboldo, Giuseppe, 162–64, *163*
Arion, 116, 216n26
Aristotle: *History of Animals*, 122, 126–27; on hylomorphism, 149, 150, 151; on oceans, 80; portrayed as cuttlefish, 165; on whales, 122, 126–27
Arnold, Matthew, 28–29
Ashley, Anthony, 2
Asian shore crabs, 43–44
At the Bottom of Shakespeare's Ocean (Mentz), 13
Auden, W. H., 12, 23, 172

"Baby Beluga" (Cavoukian), 134–35
Bacon, Francis, 122
Bakhtin, Mikhail, 113, 221n53
Balasopoulos, Antonis, 23, 26–27
Bartolovich, Crystal, 203n15
Bate, Jonathan, 39, 210n14
Baucom, Ian, 211n29
Beached Whale (Gouwen), *130*
Beached Whale near Beverwijk (Saenredam), 130–31, *131*
Bede, Venerable, 89–90
Belsey, Catherine, 177
beluga whales, 134–35, 218n50
benthic realm. *See* seafloor
benthos, 67
Beowulf, 117
Berger, Harry, Jr., 224n24
Berry, Wendell, 150
Bible: Genesis, 24, 115, 196; Job, 115–16; Psalms, 25, 116, 134–35; Revelation, 24; on the sea, 24–25; on whales, 115–16
Bierce, Ambrose, 86, 196
Big Fish Eat Little Fish (Pieter Brueghel the Elder), 160–62, *161*
Billingsgate Fishmarket (London), 159–60
Birth of Venus, The (Botticelli), 94, 180
Blackfriars Theatre, 160, 194, 223n13
Blackstock, Michael, 205n49
Blith, Walter, 211n27
Blue Ocean Institute, 206n18
Blumenberg, Hans, 62, 73

Index

Boehrer, Bruce, 113, 114, 149
Bolster, W. Jeffrey, 35, 36, 48, 208n59
Book of Husbandry (Fitzherbert), 47
Boreas, 183, 185
Botticelli, Sandro, 94, 180
Bowsher, Julian, 212n44
Brancheau, Dawn, 107, 134
British Isles: crown rights to stranded whales, 110, 215n9; enclosure of land in, 121, 217n34; late Renaissance transformation of status of sea in, 117; in rethinking relationship of human world to global ocean, 27; tides in, 89. *See also* England
Brown, Bill, 40
Brown, Paul, 176–77, 224n31
Browne, Thomas, 126
Brueghel, Pieter, the Elder, 160–62, *161*
Buell, Lawrence, 17
Butler, Judith, 151, 154, 221n45
Byron, Lord (George Gordon), 29–31, 39, 40

Callis, Robert, 110
Camerarius, Joachim, 123–25, *124*, *125*, *126*, *127*, *128*
Canterbury Tales (Chaucer), 90, 221n53
Carlton, James, 44, 210n2, 210n5
Carson, Rachel, 31, 34–35, 36, 43, 210n1
cartography: cultural preoccupation with measuring in, 75; More's *Utopia* engages with cartographic impulse, 172; mythopoetic dimensions of Renaissance maps, 195; navigational technologies in Shakespeare's writings, 81–84; *portolani*, 90, 181–82, 185, 191–92, 225n38; in *The Tempest*, 169, 170, 179, 191–95; theater and, 177, 193–94, 195; winds in early modern, 175–76, 177, 180, 181–91, 225n35. *See also mappae mundi*
Cartwright, David, 88, 89
Cavoukian, Raffi, 134–35, 218n66
Census of Marine Life, 205n39
cetaceans. *See* dolphins; whales

Challenger expedition, 41, 209n88
Changes in the Land (Cronon), 21, 206n22
Charles I (king of England), 48
Chaucer, Geoffrey, 90, 91, 214n14, 221n53
Childe Harold's Pilgrimage (Byron), 29
chlorophilia, 37
Christian Turned Turk, A (Daborne), 197
Clarke, Arthur C., 15
climate change, 5, 9, 16
Clover, Charles, 33
Clupea, 139
coastlines: coastal development, 204n32; representation of, 50
cod, 153–57; crash of North Atlantic stocks, 33, 208n65; herring compared with, 219n17; in North Atlantic fishery, 47, 118; preparation of preserved, 221n55; as ubiquitous in early modern England, 37
codpieces, 155–56
Cohen, Walter, 12
Coleridge, Samuel Taylor, 5, 25
Columbus, Christopher, 187
Comedy of Errors, The (Shakespeare): crisis of identity in, 143–44; human life likened to sea voyage in, 64–65; tidal metaphor in, 93–94
Conley, Tom, 81, 226n48
Corbin, Alain, 51, 55–56, 117
cosmology, 86, 106
Cousteau, Jacques, 216n21
Cove, The (documentary), 108, 134
crabs: eaten in Elizabethan theaters, 60, 212n44; in English diet, 136; invasive species, 43–44; in *The Tempest*, 58–61
Cramer, Deborah, 7, 8, 32, 35, 196, 197
Cronon, William, 21, 206n22
Crosby, Alfred, 2, 46–47
Cunliffe, Barry, 36, 208n66
Cusanus (Nicholas of Cues), 80
Cutts, John P., 172

Daborne, Robert, 197
Dante, 67

246

Index

Darwin, Charles, 31, 41, 150
Dauphin, 112
Davidson, James, 220n25, 220n29
Deacon, Margaret, 80
dead zones, 10
De Certeau, Michel, 195, 214n32
Deepwater Horizon oil spill, 15
"Des Cannibales" ("Of Cannibals") (Montaigne), 168, 171
Description of England, The (Harrison), 126
Description of the Northern Peoples (Olaus Magnus), 122–23
Digges, Thomas, 110
dolphins: Aristotle on, 122; in Camerarius emblems, 124–25, 124, 125; cetacean family, 115; commercial exploitation of, 118; communicating with, 134; Flipper, 115, 117, 206n10, 216n27; and French Dauphin, 112; in Greek culture, 116–17, 216n26; linking with human traits, 121; orcas (killer whales), 107, 115, 134, 215n1, 216n21, 217n40; porpoises, 118, 125; Shakespeare's knowledge of, 215n5
"Dover Beach" (Arnold), 28–29
Driscoll, James P., 225n34
Dryden, John, 171
Dürer-Stabius map, 187, *190*

Earle, Sylvia, 45, 210n8, 210n9
Eastern Garbage Patch, 9–10
Ebbesmeyer, Curtis, 10
ecocriticism: critique of, 15–42; fetishization of the land in, 18; as "green," 38–39, 198; and interdisciplinarity, 17, 22; ocean neglected in, 6–8, 11, 18–19, 36–37, 198; posthumanist, 9; significance of ocean in Shakespeare ignored by, 4; studies of human-animal relationships open new vistas for, 113; as subfield and metafield, 16, 205n2; terminology of, 17; terrestrial bias in, 18–21; toward a terraqueous, 196–201; traditional boundaries of, 11, 16, 36; Yaeger on "ecocriticism$," 23

Ecocriticism Reader, The (Glotfelty), 19
Ecological Literary Criticism (Kroeber), 21
ecology: Haeckel coins term, 42; Warming in development of, 210n91
ecophobia, 56, 211n35
Eden, 38, 39
Edge of the Sea, The (Carson), 35
Edward I (king of England), 111
Edwards, Philip, 62
Egan, Gabriel, 37, 38–39
Elder, John, 204n19
Ellis, Richard, 127
emblem literature, 122–25
Endangered Species Act, 216n27
England: dangers of tides in, 91; emergence as major maritime power, 106; emergence of empirical science in, 55; fish in diet of, 37, 136; new textual and actual practices regarding global ocean, 27; in North Sea herring fishery, 140, 219n12; reclamation of waste in Tudor and Stuart, 38; representations of beached whales in, 131–32; Severn River, 133, 158, 218n61; stockfish in, 156. *See also* London
Essay of Dr. John Wallis, exhibiting his Hypothesis about the Flux and Reflux of the Sea, An, 88
Estok, Simon, 211n35, 226n6
Euripides, 26
European green crab, 44
Eurus, 183

fact, cult of the, 133
Fagan, Brian, 116, 140, 216n30, 222n64
Falconer, Alexander, 11, 12, 69–70, 108–9, 199, 213n11, 215n5, 219n4, 223n19
Falstaff, Sir John: dies at turning of the tide, 91; portrayed as beached whale, 119, 120, 133; unregulated appetite of, 119
fathoming, 68–84; in Gouwen's *Beached Whale*, 129; Shakespeare coins term in abstract sense, 68–69, 211n31; in *The Tempest*, 53, 54

247

Index

fertilizer runoff, 204n32
Finé, Oronce, 184
Fineman, Joel, 98, 101–3
fish: in Arcimboldo's *The Water*, 162–64, *163*; in English diet, 37, 136; fish-eating, 160–62; as floating signifier for materiality, 150; global market in, 136–65; haddock, 47, 153; hake, 37, 47, 153; halibut, 48; human kinship with, 196–97; as metaphors for human qualities, 150–53; overfishing, 9, 32–33, 47–48, 222n69; religious proscription of eating meat on Fridays and market for, 118, 140, 216n30; Shakespeare's figurative fishmongering, 144–45; stockfish, 153–54, 155–57, 221n50; as symbol of Christianity, 136; universal plasticity evoked by, 164–65; we are of the fish we eat, 147, 150, 160, 162, 164. *See also* cod; herring; North Atlantic fisheries; pilchard
fish markets, 140, 159, 163
Fishmonger's Hall (London), 159–60
fish ponds, 159
Fitzherbert, John, 47
Flipper, 115, 117, 206n10, 216n27
food: as metaphorical and literal in Shakespeare's works, 137; as metaphorically and symbolically charged, 151. *See also* fish
Fool's Cap mappa mundi, 82–85, *84*
form: hylomorphism, 149, 150, 151, 154; versus matter, 151–52
Fowler, Elizabeth, 223n18
Freud, Sigmund, 210n92
Fridays, fish eaten on, 118, 140, 216n30
Frost, Robert, 204n19
Fudge, Erica, 113, 114, 149, 216n16

gadoids, 153
garbage patches, 9–10, 205n37
Garber, Marjorie, 175
Garrard, Greg, 206n10
Genesis, 24, 115, 196

Geographia (Ptolemy), 185–86, *186*, 187, 195
geography: poetic, 170, 175; Shakespeare's knowledge of new sixteenth-century, 81–82; in Shakespeare's plays, 169–70. *See also* cartography
Gesner, Conrad, 125–26, 158, 222n70
Gilbert, William, 88
Gillies, John, 81–82, 169–70, 224n25
Glendower, Owen, 111, 215n6
global ocean: defined, 1; European bourgeoisie's impact on, 136; European discovery of, 2–4, 53; human impact on, 7, 9–11, 32, 45, 50, 54; incorporation into European imaginary, 54; as marginal, 67; origin of term, 203n1; technical developments link humanity with, 81. *See also* oceans
Globe Theatre, 1, 159, 194
Glotfelty, Cheryl, 19
Goldberg, Jonathan, 168
Goltzius, Hendrik, 128–30
Gouwen, Willem van de, 128, *130*
Grand Banks, 33, 54, 157, 208n58, 221n49
Great Southern Ocean, 2
Greece, ancient: on dolphins, 116–17, 216n26; on the sea, 25–26
"green," 38–39, 198
Greenblatt, Stephen, 6, 223n10
Greene, Robert, 147, 220n21
Green Shakespeare: From Ecopolitics to Ecocriticism (Egan), 37, 38–39
Grotius, Hugo, 27–28, 211n26
groundfish, 153
Gulf oil spill of 2011, 15, 210n9

haddock, 47, 153
Haeckel, Ernst, 41, *42*
hake, 37, 47, 153
Hale, Sir Matthew, 110
halibut, 48
Halieutica (Oppian of Cilicia), 116–17
Hamlet (Shakespeare): "aloof" in, 78–79; on appearances hiding corruptibility, 165;

Index

on eating fish that fed on the worm that ate the king, 164; figurative fishmongering in, 145; Hamlet's "sea of troubles," 78; "inky cloak" in, 165; inscrutable or unfathomable character in, 75–77; language of parasites and vermin in, 152; language of soundings in, 78; maritime imagery in, 66; navigational hazards in, 91; on Neptune's empire, 4; pirates in, 214n25; Polonius likened to crab in, 61
Hanley, Wayne, 122, 217n36
Hardie, Philip, 86, 106
Harrison, G. B., 199
Harrison, Robert Pogue, 57, 67
Harrison, William, 126, 211n27
Hawkes, Terence, 224n29, 225n31
Heise, Ursula K., 6, 204n20
"Hemp-seed, The" (Taylor), 154
Henry IV, Part I (Shakespeare): allure of the unfathomable in, 74–75; Falstaff's unregulated appetite in, 119; on Glendower, 111; Hotspur seeks control over biophysical environment in, 166; Prince of Wales pun in, 110–11, 133; on "scope," 215n6; on "shotten herring," 152; on stockfish, 155–56; tidal metaphor in, 105; Wales and English royal family in, 111–12
Henry IV, Part II (Shakespeare): Falstaff's unregulated appetite in, 119; Prince Hal compared with whales in, 109–10; Wales and English royal family in, 111
Henry V (Shakespeare): Falstaff dies at turning of the tide in, 91; French Dauphin in, 112; "Heave him away upon your winged thoughts Athwart the sea," 62; tidal metaphor in, 95–96; "wild and wasteful ocean" in, 9, 66
Henry VI, Part I (Shakespeare), 93
Henry VI, Part II (Shakespeare), 214n25
Herbert, George, 225n37
herring, 138–42; cod compete with, 153; consumption on fast days, 118; corruption associated with, 142, 164, 220n21; crash of North Sea stocks, 33; Dutch fishery, 148, 158, 222n64; in I *Henry IV*, 152; as ideal commercial species, 219n11; mortality emblematized by, 164; in Nashe's *Lenten Stuffe*, 147–49, 151, 156–57; North Sea fishery, 33, 140, 219n12; open-air theaters and trade in, 159–60; overfished in European waters, 222n69; preservation of, 141–42, 153, 220n28; red, 141, 147, 148, 151; in *Romeo and Juliet*, 145–47, 152; salted and smoked, 139, 140, 141, 142–43, 146, 148, 159; similarity to pilchard, 138, 219n15; Thomas's failure to mention, 37; trade for salt cod, 222n58; in *Twelfth Night*, 138–39, 142–43, 151–52; white, 141, 148
Hesiod, 25
historicism, 6, 11, 77, 199, 205n2
History of Animals (Aristotle), 122, 126–27
Hobbes, Thomas, 107, 108
Homer, 25–26
Homer, Winslow, 48
Hulme, Peter, 53, 191
human-animal relations, 113–14, 149
human body, physical universe related to, 86, 93
humanism, 8, 23, 38, 55, 113–14
"Hungry Ocean" conference, 205n47
hurricanes, 167, 168, 191, 226n47
Huxley, Thomas Henry, 31–34
hybridity, 56, 58, 157
Hydrographiae Descriptio (Wright), 82, 83
hylomorphism, 149, 150, 151, 154
Hythlodaeus, Raphael, 217n34

Icones Animalium (Gesner), 125–26, 222n70
Idiot, The (Nicholas of Cues), 80
Iliad, The (Homer), 26
imago mundi, 4, 82, 83, 85, 187
Inexhaustible Sea, The (Minot), 35
interdisciplinarity, 17, 22, 199
international law, 27–28
International Whaling Commission, 134

Index

invasive species, 43–61; crabs, 43–44; from Europe to North America, 46–47
Iphigenia in Tauris (Euripides), 26
irrealism, 12

Jackson, Jeremy B. C., 35, 204n31
Jacob, Christian, 178
Job, Book of, 115–16
Jonah, Book of, 115
Josselyn, John, 47
Jowitt, Claire, 27, 197
Julius Caesar (Shakespeare): human life likened to sea voyage in, 64; *ocean* in, 8; "scope" in, 215n7; tidal metaphor in, 91–92, 105

Keats, John, 1, 12, 26
Kermode, Frank, 172
killer whales (orcas), 107, 115, 134, 215n1, 216n21, 217n40
King John (Shakespeare): on dangers of tides, 91; *ocean* in, 9; tidal metaphor in, 95
King Lear (Shakespeare): on adultery as unlicensed fishing, 222n68; "cheeks" given to winds in, 180; herring in, 141; language of soundings in, 70; Lear seeks control over biophysical environment in, 166; maritime imagery in, 66; *sea* in, 9; self as a stranger in, 165; *The Tempest* compared with, 225n34
Klein, Bernhard, 26
Knapp, Jeffrey, 168–69
Knight, G. Wilson, 12, 211n29
Knights, L. C., 11
Kolbert, Elizabeth, 32, 208n56
Kott, Jan, 219n3
"Kraken, The" (Tennyson), 207n
Kroeber, Karl, 21, 22, 207n23
Kurlansky, Mark, 47, 221n57

land: Gonzalo's plea for dry land in *The Tempest*, 51–52; Huxley contrasts sea-floor with, 33; nature constructed in terms of, 23; terrestrial bias in ecocriticism, 18–21; terrestrial imagery associated with "green," 38–39
landscapes: constructed nature of, 21; social phenomena associated with, 50–51
Langewiesche, William, 28
Latour, Bruno, 5, 10
lead lines, 69–70, 71, 80, 223n8
Lent, fish eaten during, 118, 140, 216n30
Lenten Stuffe (Nashe), 147–49, 151, 154, 156–57
Leonardo da Vinci, 181, 192
Leopold, Aldo, 19, 39
Leviathan (Hobbes), 107, 108
Life and Works (Mainwaring), 69
ling, 158, 222n63
Linnaeus, 121–22
Locke, John, 69
London: as center of English shipping, 1–2; fish as everyday item in, 136; fish markets in, 159; Fishmonger's Hall and Billingsgate Fishmarket, 159–60; importance of Thames to, 143, 220n22; as maritime city, 48; Southwark, 159; tides on the Thames, 90, 91, 103
Lorenzi, Rossella, 212n44
Lost at Sea exhibition, 205n47
Louv, Richard, 7
Love, Glen, 22
Lupton, Julia Reinhard, 169
"Lycidas" (Milton), 34

Macbeth (Shakespeare): Macbeth seeks control over biophysical environment in, 166; maritime images in, 65–66; navigational hazards in, 91; oceanic vastness in, 73; *ocean* in, 9
Macfarlane, Robert, 66
Machiavelli, Niccolo, 108
Mackenthun, Gesa, 26
Magnus, Olaus, 122–23, 217n39
Mainwaring, Sir Henry, 69

Index

mammals, marine. *See* marine mammals
Man and the Natural World (Thomas), 36–37
Map of the Northern Regions (Olaus Magnus), 122
mappae mundi: as cartographic imaginary, 175; Fool's Cap mappa mundi, 82–85, *84*; the unknown as conventional site on, 192, 194; winds depicted in, 185–90
maps. *See* cartography
Mare Liberum (Grotius), 27–28
marine ecosystems: collapse of, 9; overfishing, 32–33; Shakespeare and anthropogenic impacts on, 66. *See also* crabs; fish; marine mammals
Marine Mammal Protection Act, 216n27
marine mammals: resemblance to humans, 118; seals and sea lions, 37, 122, 126, 163. *See also* dolphins; whales
Mariners Mirrour, The (Waghenaer), 2, 3, 69, 222n58
Markham, Gervase, 159
Marx, Karl, 221n45
Masefield, John, 25
Mason, John, 34
Matham, Jakob, 128
matter: fish associated with, 154; versus form, 151–52; hylomorphism, 149, 150, 151, 154; as temporalized, 221n45
Maury, Matthew Fontaine, 41, 166
Maus, Katharine Eisaman, 98
McKibben, Bill, 9, 10
Measure for Measure (Shakespeare): pirates in, 214n25; "scope" in, 215n7; on stockfishes, 155
Mediterranean Sea: cartographic conventions of, 182; in *The Tempest*, 167, 168, 170; tides in, 95, 101, 214n19; winds of, 180, 183; in *The Winter's Tale*, 66–67
Meeker, Joseph, 22
Meine, Curt, 20
Melville, Herman: *Moby-Dick*, 110, 162, 198, 213n17, 215n4, 215n10; on the ocean as a chaos, 27; on "the watery part of the world," 21
Mentz, Steven, 2, 13, 54–55, 63, 144, 205n47, 213n3, 220n21
Merchant of Venice (Shakespeare): "All my fortunes are at sea," 13; figurative fishmongering in, 220n24; navigational hazards in, 91; pirates in, 214n25
Merry Wives of Windsor, The (Shakespeare), 119, 120, 133
Metamorphoses (Ovid), 180–81
metaphor, 102, 214n32
Milton, John, 34
Minot, Francis, 35
Mistral, 180, 183
Moby-Dick (Melville), 110, 162, 197, 213n17, 215n4, 215n10
Montaigne, Michel de, 168, 169, 171
Moore, Charles, 10
More, Thomas, 171–72, 192, 217n34
Morton, Timothy, 18
Mowat, Farley, 108, 215n3, 218n64
Mullaney, Steven, 159, 194

Nashe, Thomas, 147–49, 151, 154, 156–57
natural history: emblem literature and, 123, 125; Nashe's *Lenten Stuffe* and, 148–49; in representation of stranded whales, 127; Shakespeare's knowledge of, 11, 126, 133; on shared ontology of whales and humans, 114, 118, 126; taxonomic systems developed by, 122; transforms notion of the sea, 133
nature: characters in *The Tempest* associated with, 175–76; constructed in terms of terrestrial life, 23; as contentious issue in early modern culture, 55; end of, 10; as green, 38, 39; as key term of ecocriticism, 17; oceanic environment's role in cultural imaginary of, 198; relationship of humans to, 85; sea seen as transitional space between natural and supernatural, 55, 63, 64; whales as mediating humanity and, 115

251

Index

navigation: lead lines, 69–70, 71, 80, 223n8; navigational hazards in Shakespeare, 91; navigational technologies in Shakespeare, 81–84; rhumb lines, 2–3, 182, 187, 194; sounding, 68–84; *The Tempest* as about navigational arts, 192–93; by wind, 2–3, 182–83. *See also* cartography

Near Eastern religions, ancient, 24–25

Netherlands: depictions of beached whales in, 127–31; herring fishery of, 148, 158, 222n64

New Philosophy of our Sub-Lunar World, A (Gilbert), 88

Newton, Sir Isaac, 88

Nicholas of Cues (Cusanus), 80

Nicolson, Adam, 24

North Atlantic fisheries: cod in, 47, 118, 153, 157; in global fishing boom, 139; Grand Banks, 33, 54, 157, 208n58, 221n49; overfishing in, 33, 47, 48; voyages of discovery motivated by, 140

North Sea: beached whales on Dutch coast, 127; destruction of fish stocks in, 32; Dogger Bank, 208n58; as herring market, 140, 141; trawling in, 33

Notus, 183

oceanic studies, 204n17

oceans: in ancient Near Eastern religions, 24–25; Bierce's definition of, 86, 196; early modern response to, 55–56; ecocritical neglect of, 6–8, 11, 18–19, 36–37, 198; finitude of, 11; historicity of, 22–23, 28–32, 63–64; humanity's kinship with, 5, 6, 143, 145, 197–98; human life likened to sea voyage in Shakespeare, 62–67; human life's ontological connection with, 7–8, 87, 92; as inexhaustible, 32–34, 40, 214n29; measuring depth of, 80–81; *ocean* and *sea* in Shakespeare's works, 8–9; pH of seawater changing, 9; religio-cultural status of, 11; Renaissance view of, 117; seventeenth-century movement towards science of, 80; as space of invisibility and unknowing, 67; as a stage, 2; strangeness of, 58, 64; as sublime, 29, 30; as timeless, 29–32, 34–36, 40, 43, 49, 63–64; tragedy of the commons, 136; as transitional space between natural and supernatural, 55, 63, 64; as uncertain epistemological ground, 55, 67, 76, 77, 85; as universal commons, 27–28, 211n26; vastness of, 28, 73, 166; as a void, 23, 26–27, 55, 133; as waste space, 28; as wild, 63, 66, 166. *See also* global ocean; marine ecosystems; Mediterranean Sea; North Atlantic fisheries; North Sea; seafloor

O'Dair, Sharon, 17

Odysseus, 25

"Of Cannibals" ("Des Cannibales") (Montaigne), 168, 171

Ogilvie, Brian, 133

oil spills, 15, 210n9

Okeanos, 25–26

Oliver, Mary, 16

open-air theaters, 1, 60, 136, 159–60, 212n44

Opera de Temporibus (Bede), 89–90

Oppian of Cilicia, 116–17, 122, 124, 216n25

orcas (killer whales), 107, 115, 134, 215n1, 216n21, 217n40

Orgel, Stephen, 223n17, 224n21, 224n24

Othello (Shakespeare): human life likened to sea voyage in, 67; inscrutable or unfathomable character in, 75; language of fathoming in, 68–69; *sea* in, 9

overfishing, 9, 32–33, 47–48, 222n69

Ovid, 180–81

parasites, 152–53

Parry, J. H., 2

pastoral images, 34, 198

Patton, Kimberly, 7, 8, 11, 24, 26, 63, 196

Pauly, Daniel, 35, 40

peak fish, 208n65

Pericles (Shakespeare): death and the depths associated in, 74; encoded comparison of humans and whales in, 120–21; on

Index

fish-eating fish, 160–62; fishes' figurative work in, 137; navigational hazards in, 91; pirates in, 214n25; on porpoises, 125
Peterson, Douglas L., 87
Phillips, Dana, 17–18
Phipson, Emma, 117, 133
Physical Geography of the Seas and Its Meteorology, The (Maury), 41
pilchard, 138–42; preservation of, 142, 153; Shakespeare's familiarity with, 158; similarity to herring, 138, 219n15
pirates, 99–100, 214n25
plastic garbage, 9–10
Pliny, 48, 80, 122
poetry: cosmology as preoccupation in, 86; divergence of scientific and poetic discourses, 86; measurement likened to, 68, 212n9; Shakespeare on *poesis*, 68, 86, 106
pollution: Eastern Garbage Patch, 9–10; in *The Rape of Lucrece*, 101; "the solution is dilution," 214n29; spiritual and literal, 63
Pontus, 25–26
poor-John, 156–57, 221n57
porpoises, 118, 125
"Portait d'une Femme" (Pound), 39–40
portolani, 90, 181–82, 185, 191–92, 225n38
posthumanism, 8, 9
Poulsen, Bo, 140
Pound, Ezra, 39–40
presentism, 5–6, 11, 77, 199
Prince, The (Machiavelli), 108
Prince of Wales, 110–12
Procházka, Martin, 177
Psalm 104, 116
Psalm 107, 25, 134–35
Pseudodoxia Epidemica (Browne), 126
Ptolemy, 185–86, *186*, 187, 192, 195
purification, 26
Puttenham, George, 102

Raban, Jonathan, 12, 78–79, 200, 226n7
Raban, Sandra, 111
Raber, Karen, 113, 151, 152

Rape of Lucrece, The (Shakespeare): as epyllion, 105–6; language of soundings in, 77; *ocean* in, 8; on seafloor, 70; tidal metaphor in, 97–104, 105–6; *Titus Andronicus* compared with, 104, 105
Ray, John, 139–40
Revelation, Book of, 24
rhumb lines, 2–3, 182, 187, 194
Richard II (Shakespeare): language of soundings in, 70–71, 77; tidal metaphor in, 95
Richard III (Shakespeare): nightmare vision of seafloor in, 71–73, 74; on "slimy bottom of the deep," 41, 72
Rimbault, Edward F., 158
"Rime of the Ancient Mariner" (Coleridge), 25
Roberts, Callum, 35, 48, 219n11, 219n13
romances: Daborne's *A Christian Turned Turk* compared with, 196–97; the sea in, 64; tidal metaphors in late, 87. *See also by title*
Romanticism, 11, 16, 28–29, 36, 38
Romeo and Juliet (Shakespeare): figurative fishmongering in, 145–47, 148, 154; fish in, 137, 145–47, 151, 152; language of parasites and vermin in, 152; on poor-John, 157
Rozwadowski, Helen, 67–68
Rueckert, William, 204n25

Saccio, Peter, 111
Saenredam, Jan, 130–31, *131*
Safina, Carl, 206n18
salmon, 136, 138
salvage, 57, 58, 61, 63, 110, 143
sampling, benthic, 70
Sand County Almanac, A (Leopold), 19
Sanders, Julie, 2, 50
"Save the Whales" movement, 134–35
Scarborough, 140
Schama, Simon, 127, 129, 135
science: divergence of scientific and poetic

Index

science (*continued*)
discourses, 86; in seventeenth-century English culture, 55; tides explained in, 87–88. *See also* natural history
Scirocco, 180, 183
"scope," 109, 215n6, 215n7
Sea around Us, The (Carson), 35
Sea Change: A Message of the Oceans (Earle), 45
Sea Education Association, 10
"Sea-Fever" (Masefield), 25
seafloor: in Ariel's song in *The Tempest*, 53, 54, 55; in Byron's "Apostrophe," 30; Huxley contrasts farm land with, 33; Shakespeare's imagining of, 67–84; Shakespeare's poetics of, 68; slime and, 41, 42; trawlers' effects on, 32–33
seals and sea lions, 37, 122, 126, 163
Seaman's Grammar, A (Smith), 94
seas. *See* oceans
Sea Shepherd Foundation, 108, 134, 215n3, 218n64
Selden, John, 27–28, 211n26
Severn River, 133, 158, 218n61
Shakespeare, William: beached whales in, 132–34; career-long preoccupation with marine phenomena, 12–13, 199–200; on chaotic deep, 63; as cultural text, 4; empirical observation by, 12; environmental disasters in, 6; familiarity with flora of, 47, 210n14; figurative fishmongering in, 144–45; food as metaphorical and literal in, 137; as "green," 37–39, 209n72; on humanity's kinship with the sea, 145, 197–98; human life likened to sea voyage in, 62–67, 73; imagining the seafloor in, 67–84; knowledge of natural history, 11, 126, 133; marine environment in, 4–5; maritime dimension of conflicts in, 12; metaphorics of fish of, 137, 149–50, 154; as model for terraqueous ecocriticism, 199; on natural world as constructed, 55; new geography of sixteenth century known to, 81–82; nuanced model of biophysical environment of, 11–12; *ocean* and *sea* in, 8–9; piscatory imagery in, 136–37; proto-human ecology in, 8; sea voyages in, 63; slime's fascination for, 41; tidal metaphors in, 86–106; whales in, 118–21, 126. *See also* works by title
"Shakespeare and the Maritime Scene" seminar, 205n47
Sherret, Francis, 158
shipwrecks: as metaphor for the vicissitudes of human existence, 62, 73; paintings of, 203n7; and *Richard II*, 71; in Shakespeare's plays, 63, 64
Shokalsky, Yuly Mikhailovich, 203n1
slime, 40–42
Smith, Bruce R., 209n75
Smith, John, 94, 158
social hierarchy, storm in opening scene of *The Tempest* challenges, 173–74
Sonnet 64 (Shakespeare): "hungry ocean" in, 8, 49, 50, 96, 162, 222n72; mutability of coastal landscape as theme of, 49–51
Sopranos, The (television program), 221n56
sounding (navigation), 68–84; in *Hamlet*, 78; in *King Lear*, 70; in *The Rape of Lucrece*, 77; in *Richard II*, 70–71, 77; in *The Tempest*, 75. *See also* fathoming
sounding (whales), 79
Spenser, Edmund, 67
sperm whales, 126, 127, 128, 129
Steinberg, Philip E., 207n41
stews, urban, 159
stockfish, 153–54, 155–57, 221n50
Strachey, William, 179–80
Sullivan, Garrett, 50–51
sustainability, 6
Symbola et Emblemata (Camerarius), 123–25, 124, 125
Systema Naturae (Linnaeus), 121–22

Taverner, John, 159
Taylor, John, 153–54

254

Index

Tempest, The (Shakespeare), 166–95; as about human control over biophysical environment in terms of quasi-colonial occupation, 52; as about navigational arts, 192–93; airs in, 173, 174, 176, 185; "And deeper than did ever plummet sound / I'll drown my book," 75; as antimasque, 173, 175, 176, 223n17, 224n24; Ariel's song, 53–54, 57, 172, 175, 211n29; "brave new world," 63; breath in, 172–73, 177, 190, 191, 194; Caliban as monster, 57, 157–58, 168; Caliban's indeterminacy and hybridity, 56–58, 169; Caliban's ontological proximity to the island, 169; cartography in, 169, 170, 191–95; coastal space transformed from abomination to site of fascination in, 56; on crabs, 43, 58–61; dislocation and disorientation in, 167–72, 191; fishes' figurative work in, 137; Gonzalo's plea for dry land, 51–52; human life likened to sea voyage in, 67; hurricanes in, 167, 168, 191; ideology of territorial mastery in, 51; the island as magical, 171; the island as strategic space, 193; *King Lear* compared with, 225n34; locating setting of, 51, 167–69, 170–71, 194–95; Malvolio and Caliban compared, 82; maritime environment as setting of, 51; musicality of, 172; navigational hazards in, 91; navigational language in, 223n8; New World imagery permeates, 167, 168; the ocean as redemptive in, 13; opening scene's storm, 173–74, 176, 179–80, 181, 190, 224n21; Ovid's *Metamorphoses* as source for, 180–81; on poor-John, 157; power conflicts in, 177; Prospero as thaumaturg, 169, 177–78, 193; Prospero's control over the winds and waves, 54, 166, 176–77, 178; Prospero's geographical hegemony, 178–79, 224n31; roaring in, 173–74; "rotten carcase of a butt" that carries Prospero and Miranda to safety, 73; "sea-change" in, 46, 53, 54–55; sea, land, and human survival in, 51–61; seen as prologue for technological modernity, 45; spatial order of, 194; staging of Renaissance codes in, 192–93; on stockfish, 156; Strachey's "True Reportery" as source for, 179–80; on "strange fish," 57, 157–58; terra incognita in, 191, 192; tidal metaphor in, 96; as utopian, 169, 171, 172; winds in, 172–80, 184–85, 190, 191

Tennyson, Alfred, Lord, 131, 207n28
terra incognita, 169, 170, 171, 182, 185, 191, 192, 226n48
terrestrial bias, 18–21
Territoire du Vide (Corbin), 117
Tertullian, 136
Thames, 48, 90, 91, 103, 143, 220n22
theater: Blackfriars Theatre, 160, 194, 223n13; and cartography, 177, 193–94, 195; Globe Theatre, 1, 159, 194; open-air theaters, 1, 60, 136, 159–60, 212n44
Theogony (Hesiod), 25
Thomas, Keith, 36–37, 211n27
Thoreau, Henry David, 34, 48–49, 200
Three Beached Whales (Wierix), 129
tidal metaphors, 86–106; arbitrariness associated with tides, 105; dangers of tides, 89–90; embarking at turning of the tide, 91; etymology of *tide*, 89; female bodies associated with tides, 94–95; human emotions compared with tides, 86–87; knowledge of tides in navigation, 88–89; loss, calamity, and mourning associated with tides, 95; scientific explanation of tides, 87–88; tidal dynamics, 213n11; "time and tide," 89
Titus Andronicus (Shakespeare): maritime imagery in, 66; *The Rape of Lucrece* compared with, 104, 105; seafloor as symbol of despair in, 73–74; tidal metaphor in, 104–5
trade winds, 190–91

255

Index

tragedies: nautical metaphors in, 65. *See also by title*
"trash fish," 33
trawlers, 32–33
Trienens, Roger, 119
Troilus and Cressida (Shakespeare): Hector compared with ramping whale in, 119–20; tidal metaphor in, 92, 97
True report and exact description of a mighty sea-monster or whale, A (1617), 131–32
"True Reportery" (Strachey), 179–80
tsunamis, 204n32
Turner, Henry, 148–49, 151, 154, 220n36
Twelfth Night (Shakespeare): crisis of identity in, 138–39, 142–43, 144, 165; Feste as corrupter of words, 138, 146; Feste on "We Three" in, 83–84; figurative fishmongering in, 144, 145, 147, 148, 150, 154; fish in, 137, 138–39, 142–43, 144, 151; on human kinship with the sea, 143; inscrutable or unfathomable character in, 75; and matter-form distinction, 151–52; navigational hazards in, 91; "new map" in, 81–82; pirates in, 214n25; sea as disruptive force in, 144
Two Gentlemen of Verona (Shakespeare): human life likened to sea voyage in, 67; tidal metaphor in, 92–93; "wild ocean" in, 8, 66

Under the Sea Wind (Carson), 35
upwelling, 33, 221n49
Utopia (More), 171–72, 217n34
utopian fiction, 168, 169, 171–72

Vaughan, Alden T., 58, 176, 223n7, 223n13
Vaughan, Virginia Mason, 58, 176, 223n7, 223n13
Venus and Adonis (Shakespeare), 94–95
vermin, 152–53, 164–65
Vespucci, Amerigo, 187, 225n43
Vico, Giambattista, 170
voyages, human life likened to sea voyage in Shakespeare, 62–67

Waghenaer, Lukas Jansz, 2, 3, 69
Walden (Thoreau), 200
Waldseemüller, Martin, 186–87, *188–89*, 192, 194
Wales, Prince of, 110–12
Wallace, David Foster, 46
Wallerstein, Immanuel, 3, 27
Wallis, John, 88
Warming, Eugenius, 41
water: aesthetic possibilities of, 198; instability associated with, 23; in purification, 26. *See also* oceans
Water, The (Arcimboldo), 162–64, *163*
Watson, Paul, 218n64
Watson, Robert N., 55, 162–63
Wells, Marion, 98
Whale for the Killing, A (Mowat), 108, 215n3, 218n64
whales, 107–35; Aristotle on, 122; beluga whales, 134–35, 218n50; the Bible on, 115–16; categorization as fish or flesh, 117–18; cetacean family, 115; in early modern natural history and art, 122–35; in emblem literature, 122–25; as emblems of environmental ethics, 134; as emblems of innocence, 135; epistemological uncertainty regarding, 76, 112, 126; films about, 108, 134; in Greek culture, 116–17; in *Hamlet*, 76, 77, 79–80; in Linnaeus's *Systema Naturae*, 121–22; as mediating humanity and nature, 115; medieval demonization of, 117; Melville on, 213n17; monstrous force associated with, 107, 115, 132; moratorium on commercial whaling, 134; orcas (killer whales), 107, 115, 134, 215n1, 216n21, 217n40; overharvesting of, 208n59; playfulness associated with, 107; porpoises, 118, 125; Prince of Wales pun, 110–12; princes associated with, 108–9, 112, 114, 122; psychology of, 108; Renaissance view of, 117–18; "Save the Whales" movement, 134–35; in Shakespeare's works,

256

118–21; songs of, 134; special kinship between humans and, 108–18, 121, 135; sperm whales, 126, 127, 128, 129; stranded (beached), 109–10, 119, 126–33, 215n9; as wonders, 122, 217n38

Whales, Tohora (exhibition), 216n20

Whale Wars (television program), 108, 134

Whall, W. B., 224n19

Wierix, Johan, 127–28, 129, *129*

wind blowers, 180, 185–87, 190, 194, 195

wind roses, 182, *183*

winds: in early modern cartography, 175–76, 177, 180, 181–91, 225n35; hurricanes, 167, 168, 191, 226n47; in Leonardo da Vinci's description of storms, 181; Mediterranean, 180, 183; navigating by, 2–3, 182–83; in painting, 180, 181, 225n35; Renaissance fascination with, 180; in *The Tempest*, 172–80, 184–85, 190, 191

Winter's Tale, The (Shakespeare): on adultery as unlicensed fishing, 159; Mediterranean as barrier and means of connection in, 66–67; venturing on the sea as self-discovery in, 166

Wolf, Clark, 8

Wolfe, Cary, 113–14

women: female bodies associated with tides, 94–95; matter associated with, 151

Wordsworth, William, 30

Worshipful Company of Fishmongers, 160

Wright, Edward, 82, *83*, 192

Yaeger, Patricia, 7, 23, 28–29, 31, 39–40

Yarmouth, 136, 140, 141, 147, 148, 156, 159

Zephyr, 180, 183

Under the Sign of Nature
EXPLORATIONS IN ECOCRITICISM

Rachel Stein
*Shifting the Ground: American Women Writers'
Revisions of Nature, Gender, and Race*

Ian Marshall
Story Line: Exploring the Literature of the Appalachian Trail

Patrick D. Murphy
Farther Afield in the Study of Nature-Oriented Literature

Bernard W. Quetchenbach
*Back from the Far Field: American Nature
Poetry in the Late Twentieth Century*

Karla Armbruster and Kathleen R. Wallace, editors
Beyond Nature Writing: Expanding the Boundaries of Ecocriticism

Stephen Adams
*The Best and Worst Country in the World:
Perspectives on the Early Virginia Landscape*

Mark Allister
Refiguring the Map of Sorrow: Nature Writing and Autobiography

Ralph H. Lutts
The Nature Fakers: Wildlife, Science, and Sentiment (reprint)

Michael A. Bryson
*Visions of the Land: Science, Literature, and the American
Environment from the Era of Exploration to the Age of Ecology*

Robert Bernard Hass
Going by Contraries: Robert Frost's Conflict with Science

Ian Marshall
*Peak Experiences: Walking Meditations on
Literature, Nature, and Need*

Glen A. Love
Practical Ecocriticism: Literature, Biology, and the Environment

Scott Herring
Lines on the Land: Writers, Art, and the National Parks

Heike Schaefer
*Gender, Genre, and Geography:
Mary Austin's Concept and Practice of Regionalism*

Mark Allister, editor
Eco-Man: New Perspectives on Masculinity and Nature

Kate Rigby
Topographies of the Sacred: The Poetics of Place in European Romanticism

Alan Williamson
Westernness: A Meditation

John Elder
*Pilgrimage to Vallombrosa: From Vermont to Italy in
the Footsteps of George Perkins Marsh*

Mary Ellen Bellanca
Daybooks of Discovery: Nature Diaries in Britain, 1770–1870

Rinda West
Out of the Shadow: Ecopsychology, Story, and Encounters with the Land

Bonnie Roos and Alex Hunt, editors
Postcolonial Green: Environmental Politics and World Narratives

Paula Willoquet-Maricondi, editor
Framing the World: Explorations in Ecocriticism and Film

Deborah Bird Rose
Wild Dog Dreaming: Love and Extinction

Axel Goodbody and Kate Rigby, editors
Ecocritical Theory: New European Approaches

Scott Hess
*William Wordsworth and the Ecology of Authorship:
The Roots of Environmentalism in Nineteenth-Century Culture*

Dan Brayton
Shakespeare's Ocean: An Ecocritical Exploration

www.ingramcontent.com/pod-product-compliance
Lightning Source LLC
Chambersburg PA
CBHW021350300426
44114CB00012B/1156